HANDBOOK
OF
INDIAN SOCIAL WORK

About the Editors

Dr Chittaranjan Subudhi is working as an Associate Professor in the Department of Social Work (Delhi School of Social Work), University of Delhi. He started his academic journey as an Assistant Professor, in the Department of Social Work in Central University of Tamil Nadu, Thiruvarur, India. He has a Bachelor Degree in Commerce and a Master Degree in Social Work from the Utkal University of Odisha, India. He has completed his PhD from the Department of Humanities and Social Sciences, National Institute of Technology, Rourkela, India. He has conducted research in various areas like Health and Mental Health, Indigenous Social Work, Family and Child Welfare, Disability Studies, Women Studies and Tribal Issues. He teaches Psychiatric Social Work, Working with Individuals and Communities, Qualitative Research, ICTs in Social Development and Health System Management. He has written many articles including conference papers and published in national and international reputed peer-reviewed journals including Elsevier, Springer, Sage, Taylor & Francis (Routledge), Web of Science, SCOPUS and other UGC-CARE indexed journals.

Dr Bishnu Mohan Dash, MSW, MPhil, PhD, ICSSR Post-Doctoral fellow, presently working as professor in Department of Social Work, Dr Bhim Rao Ambedkar College (University of Delhi) and Former Associate Professor in Rural Development, Indira Gandhi National Open University, New Delhi. He is having more than 18 years of teaching experience. He is the recipient of "Best Teacher Award" from Government of Delhi 2019-20, and the prestigious University of Delhi excellence award for teachers in 2021. As General Secretary of Bharatiya Samaj Karya Parishad, he is engaged in spearheading the movement towards Bhāratīyakaraṇa/Indianization of social work education in India. He is also an editorial board member/advisory member in several national and international journals including *Practice: Social Work in Action* Routledge, Taylor and Francis, London (published by British Association of Social Workers), Associate Editor of *South Asian Journal of Participative Development*, Member Editorial Board of *Bhopal Journal of Social Work*. He has also authored/co-authored/edited 16 books. He has published more than sixty papers in various reputed national and international journals including Sage, Routledge, Emerlad, Springer, etc. and frequently contributes in leading national newspapers. He has presented papers and chaired sessions in various national/international conferences including Canada, Japan, and Sri Lanka and delivered invited lectures in various academic forums. He was also member of the Expert Committee in the Course Revision/Member, School Board, Indira Gandhi National Open University, New Delhi; Orissa State Open University; Mahatma Gandhi Antarrashtriya Hindi Vishwa Vidyalaya; Maharashtra; BPS University, Sonepat and Member, Board of Studies in Social Work, Indore; School of Social Work, Indore; and Academic Advisory Board, School of Social Sciences, Doon University; Member, Expert Committee, NCF, Government of India; Member, Expert Committee, Bharatiya Bhasha Samiti, MoE, GoI; Member, Academic Council, Indira Gandhi National Open University, New Delhi; Member, Board of Studies in Social Work, Jagadguru Rambhadracharya Divyanga University, Chitrakoot; Member, LOCF, UGC; Member, Board of Studies, Tata Institute of Social Sciences; Member, Board of Studies, Sardar Patel University and Member, Board & Studies, Deccan University, Pune. He has completed a number of research projects sponsored by ICSSR and UGC and organized various workshops and seminars. His areas of interest are Rural Development, Child Welfare, and Social Work Education.

HANDBOOK
OF
INDIAN SOCIAL WORK

As per NEP 2020

Edited by

Chittaranjan Subudhi

Bishnu Mohan Dash

CONCEPT PUBLISHING COMPANY PVT. LTD.

NEW DELHI - 110 059

ISBN: 978-93-6344-264-1 (HB)
ISBN: 978-93-6344-453-9 (PB)

First Published 2026

Published and Printed by

Concept Since 1974

Concept Publishing Company Pvt. Ltd.
A/15-16, Commercial Block, Mohan Garden
New Delhi-110059 (India)
T: +91-11-41101460
E: publishing@conceptpub.com, *W*: www.conceptpub.com

Cataloging in Publication--Courtesy: D.K. Agencies (P) Ltd. <docinfo@dkagencies.com>

Handbook of Indian social work : as per NEP 2020 / edited by Chittaranjan Subudhi, Bishnu Mohan Dash.
pages cm
Contributed articles.
Includes bibliographical references and index.
ISBN 9789363442641 (HB)
ISBN 9789363444539 (PB)

1. Social service--India. 2. Social service--Religious aspects--Hinduism. I. Subudhi, Chittaranjan, 1989- editor. II. Dash, Bishnu Mohan, editor.

LCC HV393.H36 2026 | DDC 361.954 23

Foreword

The teachings of *bhāratīya jñāna sampadā* texts offer profound insights into social work practice. Ancient teachings can inform and enhance contemporary approaches to community development. The verse *sarvam khalvidam brahma*, which translates to "All this is indeed *Brahman*", emphasizes the interconnectedness of all beings and the idea that the divine is present in all aspects of existence.

Universal Oneness

The verse *sahasra śīrṣa puruṣaḥ, sahasrākṣa sahasrapāta* illustrates the concept that the divine manifests in countless forms within society. This verse highlights the significance of recognizing the divinity inherent in every individual. The Western philosophy that humans have descended from monkeys, undermines our true nature. Such misconceptions diminish our understanding of humanity and neglect the essential sensitivity that defines human existence. Without this sensitivity, one cannot even be considered truly human. Therefore, the question, "how humanity has evolved?", should be a focal point of research and contemplation in this era of *amṛtakāla* and *bhāratīya* thought.

Universal oneness, which means that the *cetanā* of the Almighty is present in every object, in both living and non-living entities. The same *tattva,* the *caitanya* exists in all the *brahmāṇḍa*; this is the *tattva* of universal oneness. So, we are all the creation of that only *tattva*. So we must behave with the perspectives "one earth, one family, and one future" without any type of disparity and discrimination.

The *śloka bhuñjate te tvagham pāpa, ye pacantyātma-kāraṇāta* signifies the meaning of selflessness. Those who cook or act solely for "self" accumulate negative *karma*, which is detrimental to community spirit. This idea reinforces the value of service and altruism in social work, encouraging every individual to prioritize the welfare of others.

Thy Need is Greater-Living for others

The *mantra sarve bhavantu sukhinaḥ* calls for universal happiness and well-being. This ethos is foundational to community development, reminding social workers of their role in fostering environments where all individuals can thrive. The *śloka* has often been misunderstood as merely wishing happiness (*sukha*) for others; however, it emphasizes a more profound commitment to endure personal suffering for the happiness of others.

"Universal oneness" and "living for others", these two values should be instilled in every person through education. By living for others, a person can experience a sense of bliss. Vivekananda wrote a letter to the Mysore Mahārājā, stating that they only live who live for others; the rest all are dead, more than alive. This is a fantastic message he conveyed in his letter!

Social work is a practice and evidence-based profession that calls for becoming more human and in real sense, divine. It is not just an act of charity but an opportunity for everyone to elevate themselves. The profession emphasizes that education should extend beyond the classroom to include field exposure, study tours, and socially relevant curricula. Schemes like "Unnat Bharat Abhiyan" (UBA), an initiative run by the Ministry of Education aimed at uplifting rural communities through holistic development, need to be replicated by professional social workers.

Social Work: An Attitude more than Duty and Policy

Every person is part and parcel of the society. One cannot live alone. Any individual can not grow, accomplish, or develop alone; without the help of the society. One can reach to a higher level either in the materialistic world or in the spiritual space with dedication and strong commitment towards social work. But at every stage of social work, the question arises: "What am I getting for this work?". Every individual in this world must do good for others as *Īśvara sevā* without expecting anything in return. Social work should be done as an attitude beyond the sense of duty and policy.

This attitude should prevail at the individual or at family levels. But without policy, we cannot accomplish the purpose of social work at the institutional and government levels. Therefore, a firm policy must be established to motivate individuals and institutions to commit themselves to some form of social work. To form the strong policy of social work, there should be a paradigm shift in the vision towards social work. The vision should be *bhāratīya* that is *bhāratīya dṛṣṭi*. This *bhāratīya dṛṣṭi* is to be developed at school level in each and every child. In school education, itself, we must ingrain and instil the *bhāratīya dṛṣṭi*. The *bhāratīya* vision of social work emphasizes universal oneness.To emphasize on social work, the philosophy and values of social work should be instilled in children through education.

"We are not indifferent, we are one", because the same *tattva* exists in all of us. So, we belong to one family. This thought inspires us to live for others. This *dṛṣṭi* is ingrained in our lives from the birth. We must ignite this and make these values vibrant through burning examples, which will develop this attitude significantly in each and every child. Therefore, "your need is greater" is a crucial principle to transform the society through social work. This inspiration is inside in each and every human being to take forward the social work for social transformation.

Minimizing the Needs

Day by day our needs should be minimized to lead successful and meaning life. By minimizing the needs one can reduce the desires. This is the beautiful way of regulating the desires. This regulation of desires is crucial and should be a part of the curriculum.The world is suffering from serious problems like poverty, unemployment, climate change, global warming, terrorism and so on. These problems can be solved by these *bhāratīya* values of universal oneness, thy need is greater (living for others).

Yogaḥ Karmasu Kauśalam

Doing the best without expecting any thing in return is *yogaḥ karmasu kauśalam*.

Whatever we do, we must strive hard to do our best?

If we do our best today, what about tomorrow? This question may arise for some people. If we do our best today, we have to beat the best tomorrow, and the day after tomorrow again beat the best. Thus going on surpassing the best every day, we will reach the pinnacle of excellence. The true vision of social work will lead every individual to this pinnacle of excellence and a sense of bliss.

Managing the Ego

Through social work, one can also learn to regulate their ego. Managing the ego is a significant *sādhanā* in everyone's life. Social work, or *sevā*, will be an effective tool for each individual to manage their ego. The ego cannot be destroyed; we cannot make it zero. Instead, we must draw a bigger line, and then it becomes very small. To draw this more significant line, social work is the most effective tool for everyone to make the life successful and meaningful.

Through many NGOs, many people manage their livelihoods through social work. Engaging in social work can be beneficial, and many are paid, which is not an issue. However, strong dedication and commitment is essential. Each NGO must maintain this work ethics to make its team very hard working, dedicated and committed.

The Western thought, "The Struggle for Existence" and "Survival of the Fittest" applies to the animal world. Even then it has been applied to the civil society. Because of this perspective towards civil society, humans have been viewed as bundles of desires and economic entities, leading the society to disaster, which is evident today.

In this scenario, we need to adopt a *bhāratīya* vision that recognizes each human as divine to bring about a fundamental transformation in social work in this modern era. A person is not a bundle of desires; instead possesses divinity within. This divinity should be expressed in thoughts, words, and deeds. Every individual is unique and born with enormous potential. By utilizing this potential, one has to exhibit his/her uniqueness. This is the purpose of life. Presenting that uniqueness is the soul of social work. This is the essence of *bhāratīya jñāna sampāda*.

In *Gītā*, Bhagvān Śrī Kṛṣṇa in the chapter 3 verse 10 preaches that our life should become *yagyamaya* (यज्ञमय). *To make the life yagyamaya* means the purification of oneself inside and living for others outside; that is, the expression of divinity from within to without. This is the mode of expressing uniqueness in one's life. If we integrate this through the social work curriculum, we can bring about meaningful change in the social work space.

The present *Handbook of Indian Social Work* edited by Dr Chittaranjan Subudhi and Professor Bishnu Mohan Dash is comprised of various chapters related to *bhāratīya jñāna sampadā*. I am sure the book will be essential for social work practitioners, students, academicians, and policymakers. This book will be an eye-opening for Western social work professionals, as it discusses the Indian enriched and scientific social work practices from ancient times.

Shankranand, B.R.
Eminent Thinker and National Organising Secretary,
Bharatiya Shikshan Mandal

Contents

SECTION TWO
Indian Social Work Practice

Contributor's Profile

Professor Bishnu Mohan Dash is a Professor in Department of Social Work, Bhim Rao Ambedkar College, University of Delhi. Professor Bishnu Mohan Dash, MSW, MPhil, PhD, ICSSR Post-Doctoral fellow, working as Professor in Department of Social Work, Dr Bhim Rao Ambedkar College (University of Delhi), Delhi. He was former Associate Professor in Rural Development, Indira Gandhi National Open University, New Delhi. He is the recipient of Best Teacher Award from Government of Delhi 2019-20, and the prestigious University of Delhi Excellence Award for teachers 2021. As General Secretary of Bharatiya Samaj Karya Parishad, he is engaged in spearheading the movement towards Bhāratīyakaraṇa/ Indianization of social work education in India. He is also an editorial board member/advisory member in several national and international journals including *Practice: Social Work in Action*, Routledge, Taylor and Francis, London; Associate Editor of *South Asian Journal of Participative Development*; Member Editorial Board of *Bhopal Journal of Social Work* and *Journal of Development Administration*, Zimbabwe. He has also authored/ co-authored/edited sixteen books. He has published more than sixty papers in various reputed national and international journals including Sage, Routledge Emerlad,

Springer, etc. and frequently contributes in leading national newspapers. He was also member of the Expert Committee in the Course Revision/Member, School Board, Indira Gandhi National Open University, New Delhi; Orissa State Open University; Mahatma Gandhi Antarrashtriya Hindi Vishwa Vidyalaya, Maharashtra; BPS University, Sonepat; and Member, Board of Studies in Social Work, Indore School of Social Work, Indore; Member, Board of Studies, TISS and Academic Advisory Board, School of Social Sciences, Doon University; Member, Expert Committee, NCF, Government of India; Member, Expert Committee, Bharatiya Bhasha Samiti, MoE, GoI; Member, Academic Council, Indira Gandhi National Open University, New Delhi; Member, Board of Studies in Social Work, Jagadguru Rambhadracharya Divyanga University, Chitrakoot, etc. Recently Professor Dash has been nominated as Expert Committee Member of Revision of Social Work Curriculum by UGC. Member, Board of Studies in Tata Institute of Social Sciences, Sardar Patel University and Deccan University. He has completed a number of research projects sponsored by ICSSR and UGC and organized various workshops and seminars. His areas of interest are Rural Development, Child Welfare and Social Work Education.

Email: bishnudash2006@gmail.com

Dr Chittaranjan Subudhi is working as an Associate Professor in the Department of Social Work (Delhi School of Social Work), University of Delhi. He started his academic journey as an Assistant Professor, in the Department of Social Work in Central University of Tamil Nadu, Thiruvarur, India. He has a Bachelor Degree in Commerce and a Master Degree in Social Work from the Utkal University of Odisha, India. He has completed his PhD from the Department of Humanities and Social Sciences, National Institute of Technology, Rourkela, India. He has conducted research in various areas like Health and

Mental Health, Indigenous Social Work, Family and Child Welfare, Disability Studies, Women Studies and Tribal Issues. He teaches Psychiatric Social Work, Working with Individuals and Communities, Qualitative Research, ICTs in Social Development and Health System Management. He has written many articles including conference papers and published in national and international reputed peer-reviewed journals including Elsevier, Springer, Sage, Taylor & Francis (Routledge), Web of Science, SCOPUS and other UGC-CARE indexed journals.

Email: chittaranjan.subudhi@gmail.com/csubudhi@socialwork.du.ac.in

Professor Sunil D. Santha is Professor and Dean (Academic Affairs) at the Tata Institute of Social Sciences (TISS), Mumbai, India. He is affiliated with the Centre for Livelihoods and Social Innovation in the School of Social Work. He commenced his career with strong grassroots-level work towards strengthening local institutions in managing common property resources. He recognizes the strengths of indigenous knowledge systems and cultural practices in sustaining people's eco-social worlds. His rich field experience in small-scale fisheries, agriculture, and rural development has also shaped his expertise in blending the political ecology of development discourses with social innovation and social work practice in a more-than-human world.

Email: sunilds@tiss.ac.in

Professor Prasanta K. Ghosh is Retired Professor, Department of Social Work, Visva-Bharati, Sriniketan. Educated in Social Work and Human Resource Management in 1981 from University of Indore, MP began career as Management Trainee in corporate sector. After three years he joined the Durgapur Projects Ltd. as Personnel Officer (Jr.) for another three years. Thereafter, he was selected by UPSC, to work as Enforcement and Conciliation Officer for the states of Tripura and Mizoram. Within a short span of time he choose to work as Lecturer in Visva-Bharati

from 1988. After completing PhD in Workers' Participation in Management in 1996 he joined TISS, Mumbai as Reader in the Department of Personnel Management & Industrial Relations from 1997 to 1999. Joined back Visva-Bharati in 1999 and continued as a Professor and Head of the Department of Social Work, Visva-Bharati.
Email: prasanta1958@gmail.com

Professor Rakesh Dwivedi currently serves as the Head of the Department of Social Work and as Chief Proctor at the University of Lucknow. With over two decades of academic experience, he previously held the position of Programme Coordinator for the National Service Scheme at the university, earning the prestigious State National Service Scheme Award from the Department of Higher Education, Government of Uttar Pradesh for his contributions. Professor Dwivedi's expertise spans several specialized areas within social work including Social Case Work, Medical Social Work, Health Communication and Counselling, Youth-Friendly Health Services, Social Action, and Community Development. His academic contributions are substantial, with numerous research papers published in reputed journals and authorship of twelve books covering topics such as social work practice, community development initiatives, social action frameworks, counselling methodologies, and effective communication techniques. As Department Head and Chief Proctor, he leads academic development while maintaining campus discipline. His combined administrative leadership and academic scholarship have established him as an influential figure in social welfare education, mentoring generations of social work professionals who drive positive change throughout India.
Email: dr.rakeshdwivedi@gmail.com

Dr Rama Srivastava is working as an Associate Professor, Department of Social Work, Amity University, Noida. Her research interest areas are Children; Education;

Governance; Women; Gender Issues; Labour & HR; Social Policy; CSR; Community Health. Her teaching interest in Children; Elderly; Governance; Family; Gender; Labour Welfare & HR; Social Policy; CSR; Social Policy and Development; Development Paradigms.

Email: rsrivastava2@amity.edu

Dr R. Belinda MA (SW), MPhil (SW), PhD (SW), is Director of Extension Programme & former Head of the Department of Social Work (SFS) at Madras Christian College. With twenty-three years of research experience, she has done researches in the area of Human Resource Management, Psycho-Socio-Economic studies of various weaker and vulnerable sections of society and intervention studies. She was the head of department for sixteen years and served as placement officer of the college for seven years. With more than twenty-five research publications, one book authored and five books edited, she has completed thirteen funded projects for various national and international bodies including a UGC minor research project.

Email: belinda@mcc.edu.in

Dr Kavitha R. started her career as an HR Executive with Mafoi Management & Consultant. With a high passion for teaching started as an Assistant Professor with the Department of Social Work, at PSG College of Arts & Science. She had over sixteen years of experience in academics. She has presented around twenty-six papers at national and international conferences/seminars and attended more than fifteen workshops in nationally reputed institutions. She has published eighteen research articles in various international books and journals. She has been an Advisory Executive Committee Member of the central government scheme JNNURM (Jawaharlal Nehru National Urban Renewal Rural Mission) for Coimbatore district since 2012.

Email: kavitha@psgcas.ac.in

Dr Anvita Verma is presently working as Assistant Professor in Department of Social Work, University of Lucknow. She has an additional responsibility of university as

Assistant Proctor, Assistant Dean Students Welfare and she is also serving as programme officer in the National Service Scheme (NSS). She has seven years of teaching and Research experience on various aspects of Sustainable Development and Environment. She is postgraduate in social work with specialization in health, MPhill in social work with research on Sanitation and Hygiene and PhD on "Interweaving Aspects of Climate Change and Human Beings". She has seven book chapters and thirteen research articles published on various social and environmental issues. She also has working experience with CEE—North (Centre for Environment Education), Consultancy work in UPSAC (Uttar Pradesh AIDS Control Society), and SIRD (State Institute of Rural Development).

Email: Anvita.verma74@gmail.com

Dr Mohini Gautam is an Assistant Professor, Department of Social Work, Guru Ghasidas Vishwavidyalaya, Bilaspur, Chhattisgarh.

Email: mohinilko521@gmail.com

Dr Sandeep Kumar Morishetty has been teaching in the Department of Social Work, Guru Ghasidas Vishwavidyalaya, Bilaspur, Chhattisgarh for the last four years. He did his BA from Sri Venkateshwara Degree College, Suryapet; Osmania University and MSW in Medical and Psychiatric Social Work Specialization from Osmania University Post-Graduate College, Secunderabad, Osmania University, Hyderabad, and Telangana. He holds PhD degree in Social Work from Osmania University, Hyderabad, and qualified UGC-NET JRF in the year 2014. His academic and research interests are community health and development, urbanization and slums, social policy and planning, environmental issues.

Email: morishettysandeepkumar17@gmail.com

Dr Apoora Patel is an educator, trainer and researcher with over a decade of interdisciplinary experience. An alumna of Tata Institute of Social Sciences (TISS), Mumbai, she has been associated with Gujarat National Law University

(GNLU) since 2016. Her work spans social justice, disaster resilience, impact entrepreneurship, access to justice and corporate social responsibility. As Head of the GNLU Centre for Law & Society, she leads national and international initiatives bridging law, social policy, and human rights.
Email: apoorva.tiss@gmail.com

Dr Arif Ali is an Assistant Professor in the Department of Psychiatric Social Work, Institute of Human Behaviour and Allied Sciences (IHBAS), New Delhi, India. He has a Doctoral degree in Psychiatric Social Work from RINPAS, Ranchi. He has presented various papers at both national and international conferences and published ninety research articles in reputed national and international journals.
Email: arifalipsw@gmail.com

Dr Wakar Amin Zargar is an Associate Professor in the Department of Social Work, University of Kashmir, Srinagar, Jammu and Kashmir, India. He has presented various papers at both national and international conferences and published several articles in reputed national and international journals.
Email: wakaramin78@gmail.com

Dr Ramesh Kumar Tripathi is an Assistant Professor in Department of Social Work, University of Lucknow, Lucknow. He has completed his MSW from Dr R.M.L. Awadh University, Ayodhya and PhD from University of Lucknow in 2009.
Email: dr.rk.tripathi19@gmail.com

Dr Manish Dwivedi, MSW, PhD in Social Work from University of Lucknow. Apart from these professional qualifications he has written seven books and published more than six articles and five chapters in different journals and books. Dr Dwivedi contributed with *Encyclopedia of Social Work in India* edited by Late Professor Surendra Singh. His expertise is Teaching of Medical and Psychiatric Social Work. He is deeply associated with some developmental organizations. Now he is Faculty Member of Social Work

Department, Dr Shakuntala Misra National Rehabilitation University, Lucknow.
Email: dr.manishdwivedi10@gmail.com

Dr Saumya Sisodia currently working as an Assistant Professor in the Department of Political Science at Gautam Buddha University, Greater Noida. He completed BA (Political Science; Economics) from the University of Allahabad, MA (Political Science) from IGNOU, BEd from the University of Allahabad, and PhD from Gautam Buddha University, Greater Noida. He qualified UGC-NET in Political Science subject.
Email: saumya_sisodia@yahoo.co.in

Dr Braja S. Mishra is an academic and development practitioner in the areas of Livelihoods, Governance and Policy Studies. About thirty years of pan-India working experience with Government of India, Corporates, Academic Institutions, INGO and as a consultant to government in policy studies, corporate (especially in CSR), NGOs, and INGOs in programme design, evaluation and bringing learning document through qualitative research. He offered mentorship in the prestigious ICICI Fellowship Programme for about two years and coordinated one international and one national level Livelihood Learning Workshops (in 2007 and 2013 respectively) supported by Ford Foundation. He has a blend of experience in teaching, practice, action research and advocacy. His core areas of expertise are Livelihoods, Governance, Labour and Employment, Policy Studies, Partnership Building, Knowledge Building, Training and Development.
Email: braja.mishra@gmail.com

Dr Mukshita Y. Dhrangadharia (PhD, NET, MPhil, MSW) is an accomplished academician and researcher with over eleven years of dedicated experience in the fields of Social Work and Human Resource Management. She served at the Department of Social Work, Sardar Patel University, Vallabh Vidyanagar, where she contributed significantly to teaching, research, and academic development. Currently, she is associated with the Ahmedabad Group of Institutes, Ahmedabad, where she is actively engaged in shaping management programmes at the business institute. With a strong research orientation, Dr Dhrangadharia has several publications and paper presentations at prestigious national and international forums. Passionate about academic excellence and social impact, she continues to mentor future professionals and contribute meaningfully to the evolving landscape of management and social sciences education.

Email: myd.6790@gmail.com

Dr Anamika Christi (PhD, NET, MPhil, MSW, DLP) is an Assistant Professor at Department of Social Work, Sardar Patel University. She has fourteen years rich experience in the field of academic and social work. Expertise in Correctional Social Work & Child Protection and also as project officer for "CHILDLINE India Foundation-1098" at Vadodara Centre; she was also inclusively associated with India's prestigious distance learning university—Indira Gandhi National Open University (IGNOU) as visiting faculty member. Freelance consultant and philanthropist by nature, she has not only participated in international, national and state level seminars, conferences and symposia, but also presented and published insightful and highly investigative research articles in some esteemed research journals of national and international repute.

Email: anamikachristi581@gmail.com

Dr Esha Ghosh did her master's in Social Work from University of Delhi in 2007. She was awarded PhD for her work on the Impact of Industry-led Displacement on Indigenous People in 2014 from Jamia Millia Islamia University, New Delhi. She has worked in various corporate and government organizations at different capacities. Her last engagement was as a visiting faculty at the Amity Institute of Social Sciences, Amity University, Noida.

Email: esha.krishna1@gmail.com

Dr Gaurav Kumar is a UGC NET qualified ICSSR Doctoral Fellow from Wardha Samaj Karya Sansthan, Mahatma Gandhi Antarrashtriya Hindi Vishwavidyalaya, Wardha (Maharashtra). He has achieved gold medal in his bachelor's and master's degree in social work. The title of his PhD research is "Indian Vision of Holistic Rural Development (with Special Reference to Vivekananda Kendra NARDEP and Deendayal Research Institute)". His research interests include Indian Social Work, Community Development, Social Problems, Social Policies and Planning. He has authored at *The Organiser Weekly*, *The Narrative* and published acrticles, book reviews in national and international journals. **Email:** gkjamui01@gmail.com

Dr Anjali Mishra is presently working as Field Work Supervisor in the Department of Social Work, University of Lucknow. She has Undergraduate with B.A. (Hons) in Social Work & MSW from University of Lucknow. She has qualified UGC-NET and Awarded Doctorate Degree in Social Work in 2024 from Department of Social Work, University of Lucknow as well. She has received multiple scholarship and fellowship from the University of Lucknow and ICSSR during her PhD. She has published eight research articles in UGC Care-Listed and peer reviewed journals. While supervising the UG&PG students in fieldwork, she is actively involved in academic and research activities. **Email:** anjali.mishra14oct@gmail.com

Dr Nikita Singh has completed PhD from University of Lucknow, department of philosophy in 2024, qualified UGC-NET and obtained fellowship from Indian council of philosophical research (ICPR). She also holds the degree of BA (Hons.) in philosophy and MA in philosophy respectively from the University of Lucknow. Her research work has contributed extensively to several disciplines such as philosophy of religion, Greek, contemporary and applied philosophy, yoga, etc. She has published

several research articles in leading UGC care-listed and peer-reviewed journals and paper presentations in different national and international seminars.
Email: pariharneha48@gmail.com

K. Bala Subramaniam has been working in the public health and development sector for over 20+ years with national and international organizations. Large-scale Project Management, Monitoring and evaluation, Networking, Community Engagement, and Research are some of his core areas of operation in care and support programs of both the public and private domains. He has a PhD in Social Work (Public Health) and is actively involved in health research, developing training modules and clinical trials. He contributed to the UNION online course on TB-Preventive Therapy as a review committee member and regularly wrote field-based best practices at different conferences.
Email: baluprovo@gmail.com

Safiya, R. is a doctoral scholar at PSG College of Arts & Science and has a master's in Social Work specializing in the field of Human Resource Management and Industrial Relations. She is a Senior Research Fellowship Scholar under the UGC. She has attended various workshops and presented papers at national and international conferences and has also published a few papers. She previously worked as a Communication Officer at the IGCSE block of CS Academy International School and has experience in the field of recruitment and administration activities. She has also completed a course offered by Harvard University in collaboration with Aircel India in 2014.
Email: safiya.ahmed1993@gmail.com

Sheethal, M.J. is a research scholar in women's mental health at PSG College of Arts & Science, Coimbatore, Tamil Nadu. She has completed her postgraduation in Social Work specializing in Medical and Psychiatry. She has attended workshops and presented papers at national and

international conferences and has published a few papers. She had worked at the Railway Child Help Desk and a community-based organization for the queer community.
Email: sheethalvineed@gmail.com

Hareem Fatima Nomani is a Research Scholar, Department of Social Work, University of Lucknow.
Email: nomanihareem@gmail.com

Vaishag Velayudhan is a PhD scholar in the Department of Social Work, University of Delhi. He has received his bachelor's degree in Sociology from the Maharaja Sayajirao University of Baroda in Vadodara, Gujarat and master's degree in Social Work from Christ (Deemed to be University), Bangalore. The title of his PhD research is "Stress & Coping among Caregivers of Childcare Institutions amidst COVID-19: A Qualitative Study of Select Organizations in India". His research interests include Caregiving, Family & Children, Research on Elderly, Social Development and on Themes Relating to Indian Social Work Practice such as Culture, Value Systems and Beliefs.
Email: vaishagvelu@gmail.com

Hemant Patange is a Doctoral Scholar at the School of Social Work, Tata Institute of Social Sciences, Mumbai. Presently, he is researching development, indigenous worldviews and forms of resistance in Aarey Colony, Mumbai. He has around three years of experience working with Adivasi communities in Maharashtra, primarily in areas related to the Forest Rights Act, livelihood, and development. He was a research associate and senior research officer on two projects at TISS, Mumbai, which were focused on the assessment of the implementation of laws related to tribal communities.
Email: mp2022sw007@stud.tiss.ac.in

Fayaz Ahmad Paul is an Assistant Professor in Department of Social Work, Rajagiri College of Social Sciences (Autonomous), Kalamassery, Cochin, Kerala, India. He was a research scholar at LGB Regional Institute of Mental Health, Tezpur, Assam, India. The author has a Master of Philosophy degree in Psychiatric Social Work from the Government Medical College and Hospital (GMCH), Chandigarh. He has presented various papers at both national and international conferences and published twenty-seven research articles in reputed national and international journals. His areas of specialization are in Adult Psychiatry, Addiction Medicine, Academic Stress, Disability, and Mental Health.

Email: paulfayazpaul@gmail.com

Priyanka Saikia is currently a Research Scholar at LGB Regional Institute of Mental Health, Tezpur, Assam, India. She has presented various papers at both national and international conferences and published several articles in reputed national and international journals.

Email: priyankasaikia187@gmail.com

Ghanshyam Chaudhury is a Psychiatric Social Work Professional, currently associated with Department of Psychiatric Social Work, LGB Regional Institute of Mental Health, Tezpur, Assam as a PhD Scholar. He has been working in the field of mental health for the last five years. He has completed his Master's in Social Work from Central University of South Bihar, Gaya, and MPhil, in Psychiatric Social Work from Government Medical College and Hospital, Chandigarh.

Email: ghanshyam.psw@yahoo.com

Maya Kumari is a Social Work Professional, currently pursuing her PhD from Delhi School of Social Work, University of Delhi. She has completed her Bachelor's Degree in Social Work from Patna University and Master's Degree in Social Work from Central University of South Bihar, Gaya.

Email: mayajha810@gmail.com

Suraqua Fahad is a dedicated scholar and social work professional currently pursuing a PhD in Social Work from the University of Delhi, with a research focus on

the lived experiences of leprosy sufferers in India. He has qualified the UGC-NET multiple times and has extensive experience in research, monitoring, and evaluation across reputed organizations such as the Indian Institute of Corporate Affairs, the India Child Protection Fund and the ASK Foundation. With a rich portfolio of over ten peer-reviewed, three UGC-Care Listed, six Scopus Indexed journal articles, seven multiple book chapters, and presentations at national and international seminars, his work spans Public Health, Artificial Intelligence in Social Work, Human Rights, and Social Work Ethics. As an emerging voice in the fields of medical social work and community development, he brings academic rigour and grounded field experience to his writing and advocacy.
Email: fahadsuraqua@gmail.com

Saro Jos is now teaching in a model school in Santinekatan. She has done sociology (Hons.) and MSW from Visva-Bharati University, Santiniketan.
Email: oceansoulofstranger@gmail.com

Nimisha Singh is presently a research scholar in Department of Social Work. She has undergraduate with social work (Hons.) and Master's Degree of Social Work from University of Lucknow. She has qualified UGC-NET twice and awarded fellowship from University of Lucknow. She has published several research articles in UGC care-listed and peer-reviewed journals. Beyond the academic realm, she has played a vital role in various non-governmental organizations (NGOs), focusing on child education, women empowerment and in many more sectors.
Email: parihar01@gmail.com

SECTION ONE
Basic Foundations of Indian Social Work

1

Re-rooting Indic Approaches in Social Work Education and Practice

Bishnu Mohan Dash and *Chittaranjan Subudhi*

In the Indian context, the social work theory, practice and pedagogy is almost completely borrowed from the West. The relevance and utility of imported knowledge of social work has been criticized in many academic forums as it is not compatible with Indian social cultural context. The European hegemony and colonial legacy in social work education in India since its inception has halted the growth and progress of social work profession in India. To fulfil the goal of "Vikasita Bhārata" and to establish "Rāma Rājya", professional social workers have important role to play to ideate and contribute to the vision of Vikasita Bhārata by 2047. In order to properly utilize the skills and efficiencies of our young social workers, we need to decolonize the Euro-American-centric social work curriculum in Indian universities. During the COVID-19 pandemic, it was realized that our professional social workers completely failed in their duties while the social workers engaged in various nationalist organizations played a tremendous role. The theories/models/values and principles taught in the social work curriculum in most of the social work institutions are outdated and are purely Western. They have lost their significance. The Euro-centric scholars in social work in India still maintain the *status quo* and have completely sidelined the Indic wisdom and Indian knowledge systems in the field of social work (Dash & Prasad, 2024). In this turbulent situation of the social work profession, where in recent times social work discipline is listed as an interdisciplinary course by University Grants Commission (UGC), there is a need to revive the Indic social, moral, and spiritual values and integrate it into the fold of social work profession, so that social work as a professional course is recognized in Indian context. Since time immemorial, Indian knowledge systems in social work was quite useful for the integrated and holistic development of society. Indic social work provides various methodologies and models to engage with and address the concerns of society, from individual to family, community to nation and the whole world. Indian civilization was the first to present the philosophy of international peace by presenting the concept of a global family or *vasudhaiva kuṭumbakam*. The contribution of ancient Indian academicians has been recognized by their modern counterparts across nationalities, particularly in contemporary interdisciplinary researches where social work needs to borrow ideas from Indian philosophy through cross-pollination for negotiating functional deadlocks related to human behaviour.

In the Indian concept, social work is a passion rather than a profession. Nowadays, social work practitioners focus on self-development and institutionalizing profit-making because of the dominance of contemporary social work practice and models that best fit the Eurocentric culture. For them, the economy is more important than emotional development. The term "sustainable development" has been misinterpreted in social work practicum. In the name of sustainable development, they induce modernization, Western cultures, and lifestyles instead of restoring the native practices. Those practices (so-called social evils) hindering their progress can be modified or removed. According to Jacob, the Western concept of social work has focused on the peculiar problems and particular conditions of those countries. So, it is not the best fit for the Indian context: all countries' socio-economic conditions and cultural patterns are different. Therefore, one type of medicine cannot cure the same kind of diseases across the globe.

Recognizing the limitations of existing literature and curriculum in these subjects has prompted countries worldwide to reconsider and adopt indigenous elements. Several discussions and conferences, including those held in Asian countries, have stressed the importance of developing indigenous approaches and study materials. For example, in India, seeking help from a psychologist was considered taboo and stigmatized. However, in foreign countries, individuals prioritize themselves and their well-being and readily seek professional help from clinics.

The edited volume *Handbook of Indian Social Work* is divided into three sections. Section One discusses the basic foundations of Indian social work, Section Two discusses the Indian social work practice, and Section Three discusses Indian spiritualism, philosophy, and social work. The book is comprised of twenty-two chapters from eminent scholars, academicians, and practitioners across India.

Section One has six chapters, including the introductory chapter written by the editors. In the Introductory chapter, the editors discuss the Indic approaches in social work education and practice and its sustainable importance in the country's development. Chapter 2 explores the teachings of the *Bhagavad Gītā* as expounded by Sri Aurobindo in his work, *Essays on the Gītā* with social work. Chapter 3 emphasizes on applying social case work principles in India, focusing on adapting them to the Indian context while maintaining cultural relevance. It stresses the importance of cultural sensitivity, inclusivity, and incorporating traditional knowledge systems in social work practice. Additionally, recommendations are provided to enhance the effectiveness and appropriateness of social work interventions in India. Chapter 4 highlights the importance of a sustainable environment, as described in our religious scriptures, and the efficient role of social workers in promoting a sustainable environment. Chapter 5 by Vaishag Velayudhan reconnects the meaning of social work values in the *Bhagavad Gītā* and understands how they play a significant role in social work practice in India. The chapter also aims to know how the *Bhagavad Gītā* contributes to understanding the professional self in the context of social work practice. Chapter 6 by Sandeep Kumar Morishetty traces the social welfare in ancient India through a professional social work perspective.

Section Two deals with Indian social work practice that comprises eleven chapters from the eminent academicians and the practitioners. Chapter 7 explores the importance and usages of the humanistic approach in Indian social work practice. Her chapter focused on humanitarianism in India, integral humanism and radical humanism. Chapter 8 reflects role of street theatre in social work practice. She mentioned the social work practitioners deploy folk theatre to propagate vital information and ideas to rural and urban societies. Chapter 9 by Apoorva Patel explores the imperative of decolonizing social work pedagogy within the Indian context, advocating for an integrative and Indianized approach to curriculum development. The chapter highlights the need to disrupt colonial legacies and centre indigenous perspectives by critically examining Eurocentric frameworks prevalent in social work education (SWE). Chapter 10 highlights the significant challenge for the Adivasi communities who rely on the forest for their livelihoods and cultural practices. The chapter argues that social work education and practice can play a crucial role in working towards sustainable development in eco-fragile regions like Aarey forests. Chapter 11 delves into the role of indigenous healing and traditional healers in mental health care, highlighting their significance while acknowledging that these healers may lack a deep understanding of mental illnesses, potentially hindering the recovery of those afflicted. Chapter 12 explores indigenous approaches to social work practice in India, highlighting their integration of traditional Indian philosophies, cultural values, and community-based practices, aiming to provide culturally sensitive services to address unique community needs and challenges. The objective of Chapter 13 is to find out *yoga* and postures for mental health benefits, *yoga*'s rehabilitative efforts for people suffering from stress, anxiety, and other mental illnesses and to know the improvement in the quality of life after *yoga* treatment. Chapter 14 by Manish Dwivedi highlights the structure of Hindu society: its contradictions and dynamics. Chapter 15 provides a comprehensive overview of the philosophical underpinnings of Indianized approaches to public health, elucidating key concepts and principles derived from Indian philosophical traditions; and second to explore the implications of cultural integration for addressing health disparities, promoting community well-being, and fostering social change. This chapter seeks to contribute to a deeper understanding of Indianized approaches' and its role in advancing health equity and social justice in India and beyond. Chapter 16 by Saro Jos and Prasanta Kumar Ghosh explains Tagore and community development as an indigenous approach to social work practice. Chapter 17 is developed based on the ideas of the welfare state in Kauṭilya's *Arthaśāstra*, which the students and practitioners of social work must know and put into practice.

Section Three broadly focuses on Indian spiritualism, philosophy, and social work and comprises five chapters. Chapter 18 explores the interaction of Indian social work approaches, primarily counselling and casework, supported by the holiest scriptures of the time, the *Bhagavad Gītā*. This chapter also aims to close the gap between traditional and modern applications by recognizing the *Bhagavad Gītā*'s offerings within the framework of contemporary social work.

Chapter 19 discusses the social reformers' contribution to preventive health on social work perception and its urgent transformation to the current and future of India with social work. Chapter 20 explores the relevance of the Buddha's Four Noble Truths, encapsulating the essence of his teachings on the nature of suffering and its cessation, and holds profound implications for the field of social casework. Chapter 21 focuses on the significant social work ideas of Swami Vivekananda, highlighting their role in improving society. It also analyses their relevance in present times of ethical crises, especially in establishing good governance for nation-building. The last chapter, 22, aims to explore indigenous rural development models that place community participation at the forefront, blending traditional wisdom, spirituality, and modern methodologies to achieve sustainable outcomes.

The book aims to enhance Indian social work knowledge among professionals, academicians, and practitioners. To enable indigenous skills among professional social workers, they must equip themselves with the skills and confidence to critically appraise the theoretical knowledge and evidence-based interventions conducted within the indigenous methods. Indian social workers should be trained in the Indian model of social work and have in-depth knowledge to provide high-quality, evidence-based interventions. This edited volume is the best source of knowledge about different dimensions of Indian and indigenous social work practice. This book will add evidence-based social work practice to the indigenous model.

Conclusion

The editors believe that the social work profession with indigenous roots will make a heroic effort to provide a quality social work education in the country. This book attempts to capture indigenous resilience and model that best fits for India's social and community development. The book will be helpful for social work academicians, practitioners, policymakers, students, and other social science disciplines to get in-depth and enriched knowledge about the Indian social work models and practice.

2

Social Work as *Karma-yoga*

Some Reflections on Sri Aurobindo's Writings

Esha Ghosh

Introduction

Social work is not just an academic discipline but a practice-based profession that aims to promote social cohesion and change, develop, and empower people (IFSW, 2014). In doing so, the social worker is expected to demonstrate a non-judgemental attitude free of personal bias and preference, prioritizing the right of the individuals or communities to decide for themselves over the social worker's own ideas and ambitions. The social worker is also expected to prevent subjective emotional involvement and maintain professional relationships (Engelbrecht, 1999).

A look at the different studies regarding stress among social workers reveals that such ideals of social work are better said than practised. For instance, Urdang (2010) points out the boundary problems social work students face regarding their concerns on emotional involvement or closeness with the client and ways to deal with this problem. She gives the example of a student who complains of alterations in his mood depending on the mood of his client, who had schizophrenia or a case worker who over-identifies with the client as the latter belonged to the same ethnic background of the case worker. Further, in a study by Travis, Lizanno, and Barak (2016), role ambiguity, role conflict and work-family conflict are found to be important reasons for work withdrawal and exit-seeking behaviour among frontline social workers and supervisors at child welfare organizations in USA. Similarly, the National Association of Social Workers (2022) of the USA discusses about Compassion Fatigue among social workers which is a culmination of secondary traumatic stress and burnout resulting from indirect exposure to trauma. According to the association, 70 per cent of the social workers in USA experience such fatigue characterized by physical and emotional distress to some degree.

Social workers in India, like counterparts in Western and other countries, experience stress. Nevertheless, Stanley, Gnanapragasam, and Arumugam (2018) found low compassion fatigue and high compassion satisfaction among women social workers in Tiruchirappalli district, though age and work experience are more negatively correlated with distress and anxiety. In another study by Stanley and Gnanapragasam (2022) "moderate" stress level is observed among majority of the social work students with higher stress levels among students of the first year.

Questioning the position of a social worker, Vareed (2023) mentions that the very identity, authority and position of social worker places her/him in an asymmetrical power relation with the client, where one is the provider of services and the others who seek those services. This is especially true in countries like India where the society is arranged on a social hierarchy based on caste, gender, income and so on. The possession of these privileges by the social worker may affect his/her behaviour towards their clients and vice versa, thereby sabotaging the very ideals of social work. Vareed highlights the importance of critical self-reflection of the social worker's privileges and advantages to initiate a genuine and empathetic relationship with persons at a disadvantaged position. Similarly, Urdang (2010) and Laming (2009) emphasize the importance of self-awareness and reflection through the use of tools like critical incidents, reflective diaries, and supervision. Self-awareness is defined as a deep knowledge of oneself.

However, Sri Aurobindo points out the fallacy of a simple cognitive self-analysis as the mind depends on the limited scope of its experience in matter and life to draw conclusions. Consequently, not only we do not get accurate and complete information but misinterpretation is highly probable as our understanding is based on our standpoint and fundamental assumptions (Sri Aurobindo, 1997). Moreover, there is every possibility of inconsistent behaviour despite enough self-reflection. One may cite the quote *jānāmi dharmaḥ na ca pravṛttaḥ* by Duryodhana from the *Mahābhārata*, which means,

> "It is not that I did not knew what was *dharma*.... I cannot follow *dharma* because it is not in my nature (*svabhāva*) and I cannot abandon *adharma* because I cannot desist from not doing it."

Sri Aurobindo writes about the dual nature of human personality having two different tendencies—one which seeks the better and higher things and the other which is turned towards lower impulses like anger, greed, personal ambitions, etc. Human behaviour depends on the dominant tendency (Sri Aurobindo, 1997) and not necessarily on simple mental understandings. Swami Vivekananda uses the term *saṁskāra* for such inherent tendencies. He defines *saṁskāra* as impressions or imprints of our action, thought, movements, etc., on our mind which determines our behaviour at the conscious as well as the unconscious level (Swami Vivekananda, 1895). The Buddhist Piṭaka texts also mention the terms *saṅkhāra* or *saṁskāra*, which stands for accumulated impressions of current and past lives that mold our personality and determine our action (Scholarly Community Encyclopaedia, 2024). Sri Aurobindo further writes about the inertia or fundamental resistance in the human consciousness to change as well as egoism where the mind clings to its own ideas and desires (Sri Aurobindo, 1997).

Thus, while cognitive self-reflection may suggest a different way, it may be difficult for the social worker to follow it due to the unregenerate tendencies of human nature like personal desires, ambitions, egoism, fear, and insecurities. Hence, this calls for the requirement of a discipline that should ensure not merely correction of the flaws in the perceptions and outlook of the individual but a constant evolution of the entire being characterized by unfaltering selflessness and strength to follow the truth in the mind, emotions and action as well as an unshakeable calm and steadiness under all circumstances. The effect of such an evolution will manifest in the external behaviour and most importantly in the professional life of the social worker.

Spiritual masters in India consider *karma-yoga* as a discipline that aims for the evolution of the human nature through the development of the clear understanding of one's own self. Sri Aurobindo (1997) define *karma-yoga* as,

> "transformation of mind and being which will lead to perfect inner state and faculty out of which the right principle of action and the right spiritual and divine results of work emerged naturally like a tree out of its seed".

The theory of *karma-yoga* as taught by Śrī Kṛṣṇa in the *Bhagavad Gītā* view life and its varied engagements as a field or rather a workshop for spiritual development and progress. Apart from the numerous treaties by leaders and scholars like Swami Vivekananda, Swami Sivananda, Mahatma Gandhi, Vinoba Bhave, etc., there have been a number of studies on the concept and applicability of *karma-yoga* in work life. Rastogi and Pati (2015) define *karma-yoga* as a persistent and positive state of mind characterized by a service consciousness and absorption. They point to the perquisite of sense control and equanimity for the practice of *karma-yoga.* The two variables "absorption" and "service consciousness", as mentioned by Rastogi and Pati in their definition of *karma-yoga* is further used by Rastogi, Pati, Kumar and Dixit (2020) to develop scale to study *karma-yoga* in management institutes and workplaces.

In a study about positive psychology, Kumar and Kumar (2013) write about *karma-yoga* and the non-attachment to rewards of work as an effective means for individuals leading to a satisfied life. They suggest that *karma-yoga* may be therapeutic in reducing anxiety and morbidity associated with psychiatric and medical illnesses relating to it. Similarly, Navare and Pandey (2022) investigate the positive association of *karma-yoga* with positive psychological outcomes like thriving, psychological capital, flourishing, and negative impact on job burnout and find empirical validation for these hypotheses. Gupt (2021) finds that a non-attached (*anāsakta*) man is a person who not only enjoys health but enjoys his existence. He lives in a blissful state of intrinsic self-fulfilment. Mulla and Krishnan (n.d.) explore the positive relationship between *karma-yoga* and empathy on the one hand and the moderating effect of personal distress on the relationship. The study finds that the relationship between empathic concern and *karma-yoga* is substantially stronger for persons with low personal distress. The study concludes that *karma-yoga* is similar to altruistic motivation in the Indian context.

Objectives

This chapter explores the *karma-yoga* concept as Sri Aurobindo elaborated in his *Essays on the Gītā* and elsewhere. It tries to delve into the purification or transformative processes brought in by *karma-yoga,* which may help the social worker evolve towards not just simple clarity of knowledge but also refinement and regeneration of emotions and the consequent action. The chapter tries to find out how *karma-yoga* can be incorporated into the professional life of a social worker. The objectives of the chapter therefore are: (i) to understand the concept and transformative processes of *karma-yoga* as elaborated by Sri Aurobindo; (ii) to study the implication of such transformation and practice of *karma-yoga* in professional social work. The chapter is qualitative and exploratory in nature. It draws on the writings of Sri Aurobindo of *yoga* of work, especially his, *Essays on the Gītā*.

Karma-yoga: The Concept

Indian spiritual thinking goes beyond what we now understand as social work and social service. It institutionalizes social service as a comprehensive offering to the divine because it is the divine that manifests itself in the myriad forms of life. This automatically calls for a fundamental transformation of approach to service. The *karma-yoga* for Sri Aurobindo is neither a disinterested performance of duties nor action dictated by egoistic and altruistic motives. "It is the abandonment of all other standards of duty or conduct for a selfless performance of the divine will working through our nature" (Aurobindo, 1997: 31). As the human will become more and more an instrument of the divine power, it will lead to the transformation and elevation of human will towards freedom, power and perfection (Aurobindo,1997: 40). According to Sri Aurobindo, the human mind and emotions depend on the individual's limited life and sensory experiences. Hence, the mental conclusions by human beings are often flawed and misinterpret of the truth. Sri Aurobindo calls for passing beyond to higher realms of perception and knowledge from the present mental and sensory understandings. *karma-yoga* is both the method and result of that transition.

Karma-yoga: The Transformative Process

Like any other human being, social workers are products of natural forces. The *Bhagavad Gītā* V.14 talks of the material energy consisting of three *guṇa*s (modes of nature): *sattva*, *rajas*, and *tamas*. Sri Aurobindo defines *sattva* as the power of possessing and harmonizing knowledge, *rajas* as the power of desire and impulsion and *tamas* as the power of nescience, inertia, and ignorance (Aurobindo, 1997: 429). He states that in

> "... every natural existence here on earth the three *guṇa*s are there in their inextricable working and it is even said that all action of man or creature or force is merely the action of these three modes upon each other, a functioning in which one or other predominates and the rest modify its operation and results.... (Aurobindo, 1997: 463).

Thus, these modes of nature determine the thoughts, emotions and even the physical being. Therefore, it is a mistake to consider human actions as a product of free will. Sri Aurobindo, therefore, insists on disassociating oneself from this nature, stand back, see the thoughts and emotions passing and witness their working.

> "But how can we change this nature of the doer of works in us? By dissociating works from ego and personality, by seeing through the reason that all this is only the play of the *guṇa*s of nature, and by dissociating our soul from the play, by making it first of all the observer of the workings of nature and leaving those works to the power that is really behind them, the something in nature which is greater than ourselves, not our personality, but the Master of the universe.... In Vedāntic language, it sees the spirit, the being; it ceases to identify itself with the instruments and workings of nature.... (Aurobindo, 1997: 255).

Ramdass (2014) writes that the process of stepping back or dissociating from nature takes oneself out of being submerged in one's experiences, thoughts, emotions and into self-awareness. With this self-awareness comes joy and strength. Swami Vivekananda (1896) in his lectures to his disciples on *karma-yoga* in America, highlights the importance of a witness consciousness and non-attachment towards the body and things related to it in order to be free from misery.

Once dissociated, the mind attains calm and tranquillity as it witnesses the movements of the thoughts and the emotions without getting caught in it. With the sense of oneself being the doer eliminated, the individual is liberated from the reactions of his/her work. All work is then carried out as an offering to the universal nature or the Supreme Divine who is the source of that nature.

By doing works in this selfless tranquillity and impersonality, our works cease to be ours, cease to bind or trouble us with their reactions. Nature and her *guṇa*s weave the web of her works without affecting our griefless self-existent tranquillity (Aurobindo, 1997: 255).

The motive for such work according to *Bhagavad Gītā* is *sarvabhuta hite* or as Sri Aurobindo puts it, "for the maintenance and leading of the people" (Aurobindo, 1997: 257).

Implications of the Practice of *Karma-yoga* on Professional Social Work

Drawing from the elaboration on the concept and method of *karma-yoga* by Sri Aurobindo, the following three assumptions can be made regarding its implications on social work profession.

First, it can be assumed that with the identification of the person as separate from the external nature and identification with the soul as the witness to the working nature, any differentiation based on outward appearances or circumstances is likely to lose its effect on the mind. Thus, the concern of critical social work, as discussed by Vareed earlier in this chapter, regarding the effect of the asymmetrical power relation of the social worker with the client can be addressed through *karma-yoga*. Identifying oneself as the inner self same as the client and other beings irrespective of the outward differentiations, will eliminate the egoistic demands of the sense of societal status and power and the consequent behaviour of the social worker.

Second, with the knowledge that the external world is the play of nature, the fruits of which is employed for the use of nature with the soul being a witness, any personal ambitions or egoistic interests is likely to fall off. Social work carried out in such a state of consciousness is likely to be largely free of vested interests and desire for power, fame or money, concerned to the well-being of all.

Lastly, the path of *karma-yoga,* as discussed by Sri Aurobindo is likely to lead towards self-awareness which is insisted upon by Urdang (2010) and Lamming (2000) as important prerequisite for successful social workers. The awareness of one's true being and its relation with nature which comprises the personality is likely to give the person the strength to command the thoughts and emotions rather than being carried out by it. Thus, such a person may have more strength and resilience in his consciousness to absorb the shocks of the professional life of a social worker. As discussed earlier in this chapter, he or she is less likely to face stress or compassion fatigue.

Conclusion

Social work as a profession demands a non-biased, accepting, and unselfish attitude from its practitioners. However, considering the self-centred tendencies of the human mind at the conscious and subconscious level, it is a rather difficult state to achieve. Various studies worldwide have shown high levels of stress, compassion fatigue and burn-out among frontline social workers. In addition, the asymmetrical power relation between a social worker and the client due to social circumstances, its impact on the attitude of the practitioner is also questioned by critical social workers.

This chapter envisages the practice of a spiritual discipline like *karma-yoga* to reorganize our thoughts, emotions, and the consequent actions to exclude egoist desires and efforts to achieve them, thereby empowering us to render service. *Karma-yoga* as discussed by Sri Aurobindo, involves the selfless performance of divine will through our nature. The process involves recognition of the body, thoughts, emotions, and feelings as part of a universal nature while identifying oneself with the soul or the higher self-independent of the nature. Therefore, all actions are seen as being carried out by nature to fulfil the purpose of universal nature. Though carrying out all activities externally, the individual psychologically stands distinct from nature as a witness to all the movements. All actions are therefore performed as an offering to the nature or to a higher force with the intent of goodwill to all beings.

It can, therefore, be assumed that a social worker practising *karma-yoga,* is likely to remain unaffected by the turmoil of the outer circumstances, maintaining a tranquil mind. It shields the social worker from professional stresses and fatigue. Further, the recognition of oneself as the soul separate from the social paraphernalia is likely to eliminate the sense of superiority or inferiority arising out of the social circumstances, hence bringing a sense of equality and oneness with all beings. Thus, the practice of *karma-yoga* by social worker would address the egoistic sense of difference in status and power, bringing in the feeling of equality with the clients. Selflessness, compassion for all beings and empathy combined with mental strength and endurance are the likely results of the practice of *karma-yoga.*

REFERENCES

Aurobindo, Sri (1997). *Essays on the Gītā: Complete Works of Sri Aurobindo.* Sri Aurobindo Ashram Trust.

Aurobindo, Sri (1997). *Letters on Yoga-IV. Difficulties in the Practice of Integral Yoga.* Vol. 31. *Complete Works of Sri Aurobindo.* Sri Aurobindo Ashram.

Aurobindo, Sri (1972). "The Mind of Light", *Philosophy East and West. 22*(2): 237-38. *Complete Works of Sri Aurobindo.* Sri Aurobindo Ashram Trust.

Engelbrecht, Lambert K. (1999). *Introduction to Social Work.* Lanzo.

Gupt, D.K (2021). "Karma *Yoga* as a Pathway to Health and Well-being". *International Journal of Indian Psychology, 9*(3): 661-66. DIP:18.01.063.20210903, DOI:10.25215/0903.063

International Federation of Social Workers (2014). Global definition of social work. International Federation of Social Workers. Retrieved from https://www.ifsw.org/what-is-social-work/global-definition-of-social-work/ (accessed on 8 February 2024).

Kumar, A. and Kumar, S. (2013). "Karmayoga: A Path towards Work in Positive Psychology". *Indian J Psychiatry.*

Laming, H. (2009). *The Protection of Children in England: A Progress Report.* London: TSO.

Mulla, Zubin R. and Krishnan, Venkat R. (2008). *Karmayoga, the Indian Work Ideal, and Its Relationship with Empathy.* Psychology and Developing Societies, *20*(1): 27-49.

National Association of Social Workers (2022). NASW: National Association of Social Workers. (n.d.). Retrieved on 21 July 2022, from www.socialworkers.org/About/Ethics/Code-of-Ethics / Highlighted-Revisions-to-the-Code-of-Ethic

Navare, A., and Pandey, A. (2022). "Karma *Yoga*: Scale Development and Studies of the Impact on Positive Psychological Outcomes at the Workplace". *International Journal of Cross Cultural Management, 22*(2): 271-99. https://doi.org/10.1177/14705958221111239

Ramdass (2014). *Polishing the Mirror: How to Live from Your Spiritual Heart.* Sounds True Publishers.

Rastogi, Ashish and Pati, Surya Prakash (2015). "Towards a Conceptualization of *Karmayoga". Journal of Human Values, 21*(1): 51-63. Management Center for Human Values. Sage Publications.

Rastogi, Ashish, Pati, Surya Prakash, Kumar, Pankaj and Dixit, Jitendra Kumar (2020). "Development of a 'Karma-*Yoga*' Instrument, the Core of the Hindu Work Ethic". *IIMB Management Review, 32*(4): 352-64.

Scholarly Community Encyclopaedia (2024). Sankhara. Retreived from https://encyclopedia.pub/entry/33631 on 8 February 2024.

Stanley, Selwyn, Gnanapragasam, Mettilda B., and Arumugam, Meenakshi (2018). "Resilience as a Moderator of Stress and Burnout: A Study of Women Social Workers in India". *International Social Work.*

Stanley, Selwyn and Gnanapragasam, Mettilda, B. (2022). "Do Stress and Coping Influence Resilience in Social Work Students?: A Longitudinal and Comparative Study from India". *International Social Work*, *65*(5): 927-40.

Swami Vivekananda (1895). *Karma Yoga.* Retrieved from https://www.vivekananda.net/PDFBooks/Karma*Yoga*.pdf on 8 February 2024.

Travis, Dnika J., Lizano, Erica Leeanne and Barak, Micha'lle E. Mor (2016). "'I'm So Stressed!': A Longitudinal Model of Stress, Burnout and Engagement among Social Workers in Child Welfare Settings". *British Journal of Social Work*, *46*: 1076-95.

Urdang, Esther (August 2010). "Awareness of Self: A Critical Tool". *Social Work Education*, *29*(5): 523-38.

Vareed, Baiju P. (2023). "Identity, Power, and Social Work Practice in India". *Critical Social Work*, *24*(2).

3

Application of Social Casework Concepts and Principles in India

Indigenization and Cultural Relevance of Professional Social Work

Safiya, R., *Sheethal, M.J.*, and *Kavitha, R.*

Introduction

Social work is a profession that upholds social justice, human rights, and the empowerment of individuals and communities. Social work has evolved over the years in India, incorporating both Western theories and indigenous cultural values. It is now recognized as an important discipline contributing to social development and welfare (Rahman & Mirshad, 2021).

Social casework is a form of professional social work that addresses the needs and problems of individuals and families through a holistic and person-centred approach. It involves analysing an individual's social, psychological, economic, and cultural background to develop and implement appropriate interventions (Raju *et al.*, 2021). In the Indian context, the principles of social casework have been adapted to suit the country's cultural values and norms. The concept of *dharma* (duty), in Hindu philosophy, for example, emphasizes the importance of helping others and acting in the best interest of the community. This idea of duty and service to others is deeply ingrained in Indian culture and is reflected in how social work is practised in the country (Bhangaokar & Kapadia, 2009).

The indigenization of social casework in India has ensured its cultural relevance and effectiveness. Since its introduction during the colonial period, social casework in India has evolved and incorporated indigenous knowledge and practices. One of the challenges in applying social casework concepts in the Indian context is the recognition of the diverse cultural and social contexts in which individuals and families are situated. India is a country with a rich cultural heritage and a vast array of social customs and practices. Social workers must be sensitive to these cultural differences and tailor their interventions accordingly (Ouedraogo & Wedler, 2019).

The application of social casework concepts and principles in India has had a positive impact on individuals and communities. It has helped in addressing a range of social issues, including poverty, gender-based violence, child welfare, mental health, and disability. By adopting an indigenized and culturally relevant approach, social workers in India have better understood their clients' needs and experiences and provided appropriate support and interventions (Reamer & Nimmagadda, 2017). Indigenizing social casework in India also involves incorporating traditional Indian values and wisdom into practice. This could include drawing on concepts such as *dharma* (duty), *ahiṁsā* (non-violence), and *sevā* (selfless service) to guide ethical decision-making and client-centred practice (Patel, 2013).

Overall, the indigenization and cultural relevance of social casework in India is essential to ensuring effective support and empowerment of individuals and communities in the Indian context. By incorporating cultural sensitivity, local resources, and traditional values into practice, social workers can address the complex social issues facing India and promote positive change in the lives of vulnerable populations (Pawar, 2019).

Historical Development of Social Work in India

The field of social work in India has a long and rich history that dates back to ancient times. During this period, social work was regarded as a social service of charity and social welfare activities, and these were performed using *yajña*s, the most popular mass ritual in Vedic times (Patel, 2013). The privileged class had the duty to serve the poor, not to show superiority but to attain *mokṣa*. The concept of *dharma* emphasized the importance of social welfare and suggested that one's moral responsibility was to help others. However, the caste system that emerged in the late Vedic era seriously threatened the welfare state. Buddhism also acknowledges the *karma* theory and promotes giving *bhikṣa* to the *bhikṣu*s residing in *saṅgha*. Aśoka developed a comprehensive system of social welfare, including women's welfare, rural development, rehabilitation of the poor, regulation of prostitution, and provision of public utilities (Nadkarni, 2007).

Social welfare during the Sultanate and Mughal Rule was essential in maintaining peace, protecting the kingdom against external attacks, and levying and relying on taxes to provide justice to the masses.

> "Certain towns like Delhi, Lahore, Panipat, Kol, etc. became the hubs of welfare. Hospitals, *madrasā*s, mosques, granaries, *jamiatkhānā*s, etc. were well established in these centres" (Simon, 2021).

The modern era of social work can be divided into two time zones: British and post-British times. During British colonization, a more structured approach to social welfare was introduced. The British government established various institutions and policies to address social issues and provide assistance to the needy. Missionary organizations and social reform movements played a pivotal role in addressing issues such as poverty, illiteracy, and social inequalities. They established schools, orphanages, hospitals, and organizations to provide social assistance to marginalized communities (Robinson, 2003).

Following India's Independence from British rule, the country's constitution established well-defined social welfare provisions (Aspalter, 2003). However, as social work was adopted from Western countries, indigenous literature, cultural beliefs, multiplying responsibilities, dynamic normative and pragmatic dimensions, close ties with the welfare state, and a missing ethical framework posed significant challenges to social casework practice. Despite these challenges, social work in India has evolved into a more professional and organized approach over time. The establishment of the Tata Institute of Social Sciences in 1936 and the introduction of this profession through social worker training in the late 1940s were considered significant milestones in the development of social work in India (Jadhav & Rana, 2020).

Professional social work associations were created to promote the field and set standards for practice (Jayaratne, Croxton & Mattison, 1997). The National Association of Professional Social Workers in India (NAPSWI) is one such organization that plays a vital role in encouraging social work practice and education in the country. NAPSWI serves as a platform for social workers to share knowledge and experiences, advocate for the rights and well-being of vulnerable populations, and gather together.

The principles and concepts of social casework, which focus on individual assessment, intervention, and support, have been applied in various contexts in India. Social workers in India use these concepts to assist individuals and families in need, facilitate access to resources, and empower them to overcome challenges (Parker, 2020). This approach is particularly relevant in a country with diverse cultural contexts, where factors such as caste, religion, and cultural norms can significantly affect people's lives.

It is essential to note that using social casework concepts and principles in India requires indigenization and cultural relevance. Indian social workers must consider the cultural context, social norms, and beliefs of the communities they serve (Gore, 1966). This means being sensitive to cultural differences and adapting interventions and approaches accordingly. It also necessitates recognizing and respecting indigenous social welfare practices that have been prevalent in India for centuries. The historical development of social work in India has laid the foundation for applying social casework concepts and principles.

Core Concepts and Principles: A Foundation for Intervention

Social casework is an approach that empowers individuals, families, and groups to enhance their social functioning. It is based on key concepts given by Felix Biestek, such as "person-in-environment", which recognizes the interplay between internal and external factors in a client's well-being; a "strength perspective", that focuses on identifying and mobilizing a client's inherent strengths; "self-determination", which respects the client's right to make informed decisions about their lives, and "confidentiality", which builds trust with clients by maintaining the confidentiality of client information.

Challenges Faced by Social Work in India

Despite its growth, social work in India faces numerous challenges in effectively addressing social issues. India's vast cultural and linguistic diversity, coupled with a hierarchical social structure and economic disparities, presents complex challenges for social work practitioners. The following are some of the challenges:

- **India's Diverse Landscape:** India is a country known for its diverse cultures, languages, religions, and customs. This challenges social workers operating in different cultural contexts to understand the unique needs and challenges of various communities (Marsiglia, Kulis & Lechuga-Peṣa, 2021).
- **Social Inequities:** Social workers in India often encounter deep-rooted stigma and discrimination towards certain communities, such as Dalits, indigenous tribes, and people with disabilities (Vermais & Srivastava, 2021). Addressing these issues requires advocacy and a sensitive understanding of the cultural and social dynamics that sustain such discrimination. Gender inequality is also a significant issue in India, which includes violence against women, limited opportunities for women in the workforce, and traditional gender roles (Saravanan, 2010). Social workers need to address these issues while acknowledging the gender-specific challenges faced by both men and women.
- **Public Perception:** The field of social work is relatively unknown and misunderstood in India. In communities, people are hesitant to share their problems due to the fear of being judged, or ostracized, or to the belief that family problems should be kept private (Wynaden *et al.*, 2005). Many people are unaware of the services and support social workers can provide, leading to underutilization of available resources. Building awareness and trust in social work as a profession is a significant challenge.
- **Policy Pitfall:** Although India has various welfare programmes and policies in place, the implementation and effectiveness of these programmes often fall short.

Social workers face challenges in navigating complex bureaucratic systems and advocating for policy changes that address the root causes of social issues.

- **Linguistic Barrier and Rural Accessibility:** India has a diverse linguistic landscape, with hundreds of languages spoken across the country. This creates communication barriers for social workers, especially when working with communities that speak indigenous or regional languages (Gorter, 2013). India also has a significant rural-urban divide, with most of the population residing in rural areas. Social workers face challenges in providing accessible services and support to remote and marginalized rural communities, including issues related to infrastructure, transportation, and awareness (Hnatkovska & Lahiri, 2013).
- **Workforce Woes:** According to the article "Social Work Profession in India 2023" (ISWR 2024), India faces a shortage of trained social workers, especially in remote and underserved areas, resulting in a lack of expertise and resources for addressing complex social issues and providing adequate support to vulnerable populations.
- **Political Hurdles:** Political interference is a significant challenge for social work in India, which can hinder the autonomy and effectiveness of social workers in addressing social issues (Pawar, 2014). This interference may arise in the form of political pressures, corruption, or biased decision-making processes.
- **Systemic Shortcomings:** There is a severe lack of support from institutions and insufficient funding for social work programmes. Additionally, there is a dearth of standardized education and training programmes, which hampers the development of skilled and competent social workers.

- **Resource Constraints:** India has insufficient availability of resources and infrastructure. A large number of social workers operate in environments that lack adequate resources, and they face limited access to training, materials, and technology. Therefore, it is crucial to invest in the development of infrastructure and provide the necessary resources to support the work of social workers.

Indigenization and Cultural Relevance of Social Work in India

To effectively tackle the challenges of social work faces in India, it is crucial to adopt social work concepts and principles rooted in Indian culture (Reamer & Nimmagadda, 2017). This requires a deep understanding of the cultural norms, values, and beliefs that shape the behaviour of individuals and communities in India. Social workers must be trained in culturally sensitive intervention methods that are tailored to meet the specific needs and aspirations of the people they serve (National Association of Social Workers). Additionally, social work practice should prioritize community participation and empowerment, recognizing the pivotal role that individuals and communities play in bringing about meaningful social change.

Social work in India faces unique challenges due to its diverse cultural, traditional, and social settings. To effectively address the needs of the Indian population, it is vital to apply the concepts and principles of social casework in an indigenous and culturally relevant way.

Indigenization adapts social work to fit local culture by incorporating cultural values and traditions (OED). It aims to align social work with local cultural values and norms in India. On the other hand, cultural relevance emphasizes the need for social work interventions to be sensitive and appropriate to the clients' cultural context (Bodhi & Tripura, 2013). It requires social workers to understand and respect the cultural diversity of India while applying social work principles and methods.

Indigenization of Social Casework Principles

Some of the key principle concepts in social casework given by Felix Biestek, that can be applied in an indigenous and culturally relevant manner are given below:

- **Individualization:** Individualization emphasizes the importance of recognizing and respecting the uniqueness of each client and tailoring interventions accordingly. In the Indian context, this can mean considering the client's religious, caste, and regional differences, as well as cultural practices and beliefs.
- **Self-determination:** In India, where hierarchical structures and collectivist values are prevalent, social workers need to empower clients to make their own decisions and choices while acknowledging and respecting the influence of family, community, and societal norms (Chadda & Deb, 2013). This can be achieved by involving family or community members in the intervention process and fostering a collaborative approach.
- **Social Justice:** The principle of social justice should be applied with an understanding of India's unique socio-political context (Pandey & Upadhyay, 2009). Social workers need to be aware of and advocate for the rights and needs of marginalized communities, such as lower castes, indigenous tribes, and religious minorities.
- **Empowerment:** It should be emphasized in Indian social work practices. This can be achieved by helping individuals and communities build their capacities and resources and promoting their active participation in decision-making processes affecting their lives.

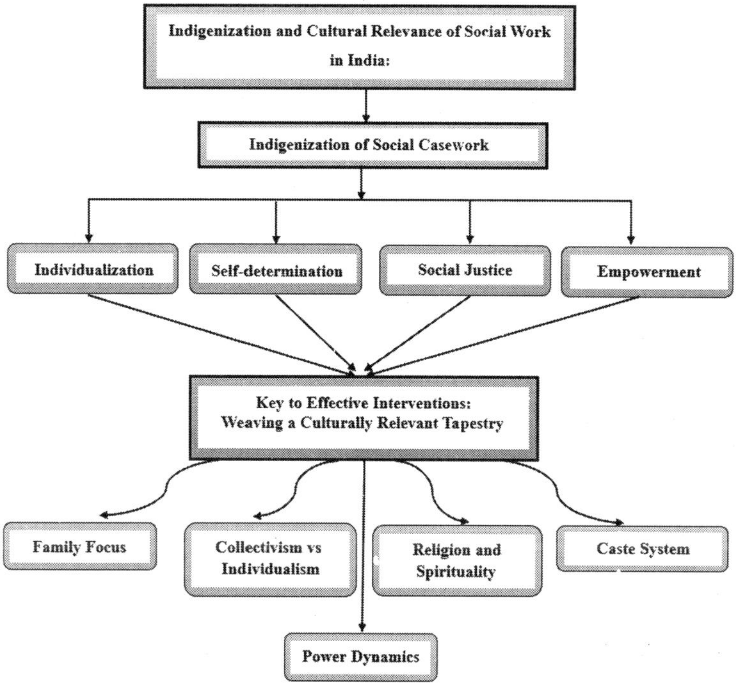

Fig. 3.1: Indigenization and Cultural Relevance of Social Work in India.

Source: By Authors.

Overall, the indigenization and cultural relevance of social work in India require social workers to not only apply the concepts and principles of social casework but also to adapt and modify them to align with the cultural context and needs of the Indian population. By doing so, social workers can effectively address complex social issues and promote social justice and well-being in Indian society.

Key to Effective Interventions: Weaving a Culturally Relevant Tapestry

The effective application of social casework in India requires its adaptation to the country's unique sociocultural context. It has been implemented by the following means:

- **Family Focus: Embracing the Social Unit:** The family unit holds immense importance in Indian culture, as it serves as a crucial support system for individuals and significantly contributes to their identity (Chara Scroope, 2018). Social caseworkers acknowledge the significance of the family and frequently involve its members in the intervention plan. They value the established family hierarchies and dynamics while also assisting in establishing healthy communication patterns.
- **Collectivism vs Individualism: Navigating the Balance:** In Indian culture, there is a significant focus on collectivism, which means that the group's welfare is prioritized over individual needs. Social caseworkers are aware of this but aim to find a balance. They cooperate with individuals to address their requirements while considering the impact on the family and community as a whole (FSU Online, 2020). This approach encourages a sense of shared responsibility alongside individual development.
- **Religion and Spirituality: Integrating Belief Systems:** Religion and spirituality are significant in Indian society (Raju, 1959). Social workers may incorporate spiritual practices or beliefs into their interventions if it is deemed appropriate. They respect religious principles and strive to find common ground for client empowerment.
- **Caste System: Addressing Its Lingering Effects:** Although the caste system has been officially abolished, it continues to influence social interactions and access to resources in many parts of the world (Priyali Sur, CNN). Social caseworkers are essential in addressing

the discrimination faced by people from lower castes. They work tirelessly to promote social justice by advocating for equal opportunities and challenging discriminatory practices.

- **Power Dynamics: Recognizing and Negotiating Hierarchies:** Gender roles and power dynamics can be intricate and multifaceted within families and communities (GGI Insights, 2024). Social caseworkers deeply understand these dynamics and work towards creating a more equitable environment. They empower women to challenge gender stereotypes and advocate for their rights within their families and communities.

Collaboration with Other Professionals

Collaboration with other professionals is an essential aspect of social casework in India (Graham & Barter, 1999). Social workers often work in multidisciplinary teams and build partnerships with professionals from different fields to provide comprehensive and holistic support to individuals and communities.

Collaboration between health-care professionals, social workers, and psychologists can ensure a more comprehensive approach to mental health intervention in India. Social workers bring expertise in addressing social determinants of mental health, while psychologists provide specialized knowledge in diagnosing and treating mental health disorders (Reeves *et al.*, 2011). Together, they can conduct assessments, develop treatment plans, conduct research studies, and advocate for policies that promote mental well-being for individuals and communities.

Social workers may collaborate with educators, legal professionals, NGOs, and community-based organizations (Bronstein, 2003). They identify barriers, develop intervention strategies, and provide support services for individuals and families. They also promote skill development and employment opportunities for marginalized populations. This collaboration helps protect the rights of vulnerable populations by providing legal aid and advocating for social justice issues.

In an Indian setting, cultural competence and sensitivity are decisive in collaborating with other professionals. Social workers must adapt their approaches and practices to account for the diversity and cultural nuances in Indian society (Sundar *et al.*, 2012). They must be aware of and respect cultural norms, values, and practices, and incorporate them into their work. This ensures that interventions are culturally relevant and tailored to the specific needs and contexts of the individuals and communities they serve.

Collaboration with other professionals is essential for social workers in India to effectively address the complex social issues faced by individuals and communities. Professionals from different fields can pool their expertise and resources by working together to provide comprehensive support and bring about meaningful change.

Conclusion

The indigenization of professional social work in India involves adapting and integrating international social work concepts and theories with local cultural norms and values. This process ensures that social work practice acknowledges and respects the diversity of Indian society and addresses the unique challenges individuals and communities face.

The indigenization and cultural relevance of professional social work in India is crucial for addressing the complex social issues. By grounding social work practice in an understanding of Indian cultural norms and beliefs and by collaborating with professionals from other disciplines, social workers can provide adequate support and create positive social change. However, there is a need for continued research and development of context-specific social work theories and practices to further enhance social work's relevance and impact in India.

The indigenization of social work in India has allowed professionals to adapt their practice to the local context and cultural values (Nimmagadda *et al.*, 2012). By incorporating beliefs, customs, and traditions into social work interventions, professionals have established stronger relationships with clients and provided more effective support. Moreover, this approach has helped to overcome barriers such as language and communication differences, leading to improved outcomes for clients.

Applying social casework concepts and principles in India has demonstrated the importance of a holistic and strengths-based approach to social work practice. By focusing on the strengths, abilities, and resources of individuals and communities, professionals have empowered clients and supported their self-determination. This approach has helped to build resilience and promote sustainable change in the Indian context.

The cultural relevance of professional social work in India has also played a significant role in enhancing the effectiveness of social casework. By acknowledging and respecting cultural diversity, professionals have gained a deeper understanding of the social, economic, and political factors that influence clients' lives. This understanding has allowed professionals to tailor interventions that are sensitive to the unique needs of individuals and communities, resulting in better outcomes.

Professional social work's indigenization and cultural relevance in the Indian setting are essential for promoting social justice, equality, and empowerment. Cultural relevance also ensures that social work interventions are tailored to client's specific needs and contexts, leading to more effective outcomes.

Collaboration with professionals from other disciplines is another important aspect of maximizing the impact of social work in India (Atwal, 2023). By working together with psychologists, sociologists, health-care professionals, and others, social workers can gain a broader understanding of complex social issues and develop comprehensive solutions. This interdisciplinary approach also fosters holistic and integrated care, as different professionals bring their expertise to address different aspects of a problem.

However, while indigenization and collaboration are crucial, there is an ongoing need for further research and development of context-specific social work theories and practices. This is because social work is a constantly evolving field, and what works in one cultural context may not necessarily be effective in another. By conducting research and adapting existing theories to Indian realities, social workers can continuously improve their practice and respond more effectively to the social issues faced by the country.

REFERENCES

Aspalter, C. (2003). "The State and the Making of the Welfare System in India". *Journal of National Development*, *3*(1): 149-79.

Atwal, A. (2023). "Reflective Practice for Inter-Professional Co-Produced Social Work Collaboration". *Reflective Practice in Social Work*, 176.

Bhangaokar, R. & Kapadia, S. (2009). "At the Interface of 'Dharma' and 'Karma': Interpreting Moral Discourse in India". *Psychological Studies*, *54*: 96-108. https://doi.org/10.1007/s12646-009-0018-1

Bodhi, S.R. & Tripura, B. (2013). "International Social Work: An Indian Experience". *Indian Journal of Dalit and Tribal Social Work*, *1*(3): 1-24.

Bronstein, L.R. (2003). "A Model for Interdisciplinary Collaboration". *Social Work*, *48*(3): 297-306. https://doi.org/10.1093/sw/48.3.297

Chadda, R.K. & Deb, K.S. (2013). "Indian Family Systems, Collectivistic Society, and Psychotherapy". *Indian Journal ofPsychiatry*, *55*(Suppl 2): S299-S309. DOI: 10.4103/0019-5545.105555

Chara Scroope (2018). *Family, Indian Culture, Cultural Atlas*, https://culturalatlas.sbs.com.au/indian-culture/indian-culture-family

Darrell P. Wheeler & Angelo McClain (2015). *Standards and Indicators for Cultural Competence in Social Work Practice*. National Association of Social Workers.

FSU Online (2020). *The Social Worker Role and Impact on the Community*. Florida State University, https://onlinemsw.fsu.edu/blog/social-worker-role

GGI Insights (March 2024). *Gender Roles: Navigating the Dynamics of Societal Expectations*. Gray Group International, https://www.graygroupintl.com/blog/gender-roles

Gore, M.S. (1966). "The Cultural Perspective in Social Work in India". *International Social Work*, *9*(3): 6-16. https://doi.org/10.1177/002087286600900302

Gorter, D. (2013). "Linguistic Landscapes in a Multilingual World". *Annual Review ofApplied Linguistics*, *33*: 190-212. doi:10.1017/S0267190513000020

Graham, J.R. & Barter, K. (1999). "Collaboration: A Social Work Practice Method". *Families in Society*, *80*(1): 6-13. https://doi.org/10.1606/1044-3894.634

Gupta, D. (2005). "Caste and Politics: Identity Over System". *Annu. Rev. Anthropol.*, *34*: 409-27. https://doi.org/10.1146/annurev.anthro.34.081804.120649

Hnatkovska, V. & Lahiri, A. (2013). "The Rural-Urban Divide in India". *Int Growth Centr Work Pap.*

ISWR (March 2024). "Social Work Profession in India 2023", Institute of Social Work & Research. https://iswr.in/social-work-profession-in-india-2023/

Jadhav, J. & Rana, S. (2020). "Indigenous and Indianized Social Work Education in India: A Way Forward". In *Indian Social Work* (pp. 37-53). Routledge, India. DOI:10.4324/9780429321818-5

Jayaratne, S., Croxton, T. & Mattison, D. (1997). "Social Work Professional Standards: An Exploratory Study". *Social Work*, *42*(2): 187-99. https://doi.org/10.1093/sw/42.2.187

Marsiglia, F.F., Kulis, S.S. & Lechuga-Peṣa, S. (2021). *Diversity, Oppression, and Change: Culturally Grounded Social Work*. Oxford University Press, USA.

Nadkarni, M.V. (2007). "Does Hinduism Lack Social Concern?". *Economic & Political Weekly.*

Nimmagadda, Jayashree & Balgopal, Pallassana (2000). "Indigenisation of Social Work Knowledge: An Exploration of the Process". *Asia Pacific Journal of Social Work and Development.* https://doi.org/10.1080/21650993.2000.9755832

Ouedraogo, S.V. & Wedler, B. (2019). "Westernization-Indigenization in Social Work Education and Practice: Understanding Indigenization in International Social Work". *Recognition, Reconciliation, and Restoration: Applying a Postcolonial Understanding in Social Work and Healing Processes*, pp. 181-200. https://doi.org/10.1007/978-3-031-37712-9_1

Pandey, R. & Upadhyay, C.M. (2009). "Contemporary Issues in Social Justice: (Indian Context)". *The Indian Journal of Political Science*, *70*(3): 853-60.

Parker, J. (2020). *Social Work Practice: Assessment, Planning, Intervention, and Review.*

Patel, C. (2013). *Social Work Practice Religion-Philosophical Foundations.* Rawat Publications.

Pawar, M. (2019). "Social Work and Social Policy Practice: Imperatives for Political Engagement". *The International Journal of Community and Social Development*, *1*(1): 15-27. https://doi.org/10.1177/2516602619833219

Pawar, M. (2014). *Social Work Practice with Local Communities in Developing Countries: Imperatives for Political Engagement.* Sage Open, *4*(2). https://doi.org/10.1177/2158244014538640

Priyali Sur, CNN, *Under India's Caste System, Dalits are Considered Untouchable: The Coronavirus is Intensifying that Slur.* https://edition.cnn.com/2020/04/15/asia/india-coronavirus-lower-castes-hnk-intl/index.html

Rahman, T.M., Mirshad. (2021). *Foundations for Social Work: Basic Concepts in Social Work.*

Raju Lakshmipathi, M.S. Parthasaradhi, Y. Kumar Ashok & Chowdary, Rajesh (2021). *Tenth Edition: Social Casework.* Acharya Nagarjuna University.

Raju, P. T. (1959). "Religion and Spiritual Values in Indian Thought". *Annals of the Bhandarkar Oriental Research Institute*, *40*(1/4): 302-75.

Reamer, F.G. & Nimmagadda, J. (2017). "Social Work Ethics in India: A Call for the Development of Indigenized Ethical Standards". *International Social Work*, *60*(1): 182-95. https://doi.org/10.1177/0020872814559563

Reeves, S., Lewin, S., Espin, S. & Zwarenstein, M. (2011). *Interprofessional Teamwork for Health and Social Care.* John Wiley & Sons. DOI:10.1002/9781444325027

Robinson, R. (2003). *Christians of India.* Sage.

Saravanan, S. (2010). *Violence against Women in India: A Literature Review.*

Simon, R. (2021). *History of Social Work Education in India: Key to Glorious Future.* St. Xavier's College (Autonomous), pp. 13, 76.

Sundar, P. & Sylvestre, John & Bassi, Aman (2012). *Diversity and Social Work Practice.* http://dx.doi.org/10.4135/9781446247648.n24

Vermais, N.M.P. & Srivastava, A. (2021). *The Routledge Handbook of Exclusion, Inequality and Stigma in India.*

Wynaden, D., Chapman, R., Orb, A., McGowan, S., Zeeman, Z. & Yeak, S. (2005). "Factors That Influence Asian Communities' Access to Mental Health Care". *International Journal of Mental Health Nursing*, *14*(2): 88-95. https://doi.org/10.1111/j.1440-0979.2005.00364.x

4

Environment in Our Religious Scriptures and Social Work

Anvita Verma, Mohini Gautam, and *Hareem Fatima Nomani*

Introduction

The question of how the cosmos, or universes, came into being is addressed in almost all religions, but in slightly different ways and with differing levels of precision. However, all religions concur that creation is an act of God and ought to be revered as such. The success of the worldwide solidarity movement for an ethical, moral, and spiritual commitment to conserve God's creation and the environment depends on spiritual leaders at all levels. These leaders have the ability to watch, publicly pledge, tell the tale of their commitments, including the difficulties and rewards of fulfilling them, and extend an invitation to others to join them. They can also demonstrate their sustainable behaviours, acting as role models for the general public and their followers.

The following is a reflection on how religions have addressed religious commitments towards the environment. In Buddhism, the notion of *karma* alone, being an important part of Buddha's lessons, conveys the values of conservation and responsibility for the future. It is said that the morality of our actions in the present will shape our character for the future, an idea close of sustainable development. In Christianity there are approximately hundred verses in the Bible that talk about protection of the environment. Christians therefore have environmental responsibility and encourage behavioural change for the good of the future (Open Bible.info., n.d). Hinduism is a religion deeply rooted in nature. There are numerous allusions to natural deities throughout the sacred texts (the Vedas, Upaniṣads, *Bhagavad Gītā*, and Epics) that are associated with elements like rivers, mountains, trees, animals, and the soil. Hinduism advocates environmental conservation in order to protect them, and there are groups that support environmental protection through campaigns and actions that raise awareness of the need for sustainable development (Green Faith, 2010). Numerous Quranic verses in Islam advocate for environmental conservation. Furthermore, Islam forbids overusing the resources that the earth gives for humankind (Quran 7:31, 6:141, 17: 26-27, 40:34). Wasteful consumption, or *isrāf*, is actually mentioned in the Quran as the thirty-second biggest sin. The Islamic Declaration on Global Climate Change was adopted in 2015 by the Islamic Climate Change Symposium.

The primary doctrine of Jainism, which has its roots in India, is *ahiṁsā* (non-violence) in all facets of life. The philosophical, physical, and mental tenets of Jainism centre on leading a tranquil and orderly existence. Jainas practice vegetarianism, self-control, and avoiding waste. They are also kind to animals. To commemorate the Jaina faith's 1990 admission into the WWF Network on Conservation and Religion, The Jaina Declaration on Nature was also penned (The Jaina Declaration on Nature, 1990). The path of lifelong study in *sikhī* (Sikhism) began to take shape in the Punjab region in the fifteenth century. This new global faith is based on the *gurmat* (eternal spiritual knowledge), that was given to more than thirty Enlightened Ones and has been transmitted down to the present day (*gurbānī*). Every sentient being is seen by *sikhī* as a member of one family. Living a dignified, ethical, healthy, and spiritual life as humble guests in tune with nature and the Divine, while embracing a cyclical world view and reflecting on childhood imprints, separating natural needs from desires, and transcending the diaspora of ephemerality are all made possible by its knowledge.

Environment Education in our Religious Scriptures

Indian culture views nature as a single, all-encompassing entity. The major epics of the *Mahābhārata* and *Rāmāyaṇa* and other ancient Hindu texts, including the Vedas, Purāṇas, and Upaniṣads, have clearly outlined the justification for the protection of and prohibitions against the excessive exploitation of natural resources. For instance, references to ties between humans and the earth abound in the *Atharvaveda*'s Pṛthvī Sūkta. Though only thumbnail sketches, the following verses offer an idea of respect for the environment.

Pṛthvī Sūkta states,

> "The earth supports individuals with a variety of temperaments, both good and bad, but the benefits of the earth are obtained by those who have a fresh perspective and choose the path of moral behaviour."
>
> "O Pure Earth! may we make good use of your soil (for creative production) without hurting or upsetting any of your essential components."

"This universe is the creation of Supreme Power meant for the benefit of all his creation", the *Iśopaniṣad* states. As a result, each unique living form must learn to reap the benefits of joining the system and interacting closely with other species. Never allow one species to infringe on another's rights.

According to a common belief that developed throughout the Purāṇic period (320 BC forward), every tree had its own deity. To safeguard trees, people surrounded them with sacred threads and donated water. The *Narasiṁha Purāṇa* personifies God as a tree. The *Varāha Purāṇa* recommends regular plantations as a way to reach paradise.

According to the *Viṣṇu Purāṇa*, God is happy when someone doesn't hurt or destroy non-verbal animals or other beings. The *Padma* and *Kūrma Purāṇa* indicate that God resides in trees like *pīpal*, *bela*, *bera*, *neem*, etc., and that they should not be cut down. According to *Durgā Saptaśatī*, the human race will persist if there are mountains, forests, trees, plants, etc., on earth. According to *Caraka Saṁhitā*, drought results from the devastation of vegetation. According to the *Padma Purāṇa*, people who sacrifice livestock would ultimately perish.

Animal abuse is completely forbidden in *Manusmṛti*. In order to preserve the equilibrium of the ecosystem, it also discusses making the best use of natural resources.

The *Bhagavad Gītā*'s Environmental Protection

The *Bhagavad Gītā* views nature as a single entity comprising *parā* and *aparā*. *Aparā* is the system's physical component, while *parā* is its conscious component. Two components come together to make the earth a minuscule part of the universe.

Since the conscious component of it is what gives the physical part of its life, everything that is seen is thought to be a manifestation of the one Supreme totality. According to the *Gītā*, nature is the foundation of human civilization, and a man who is devoid of nature is regarded as a soulless being.

Hinduism has numerous local and regional expressions, making it an astonishingly diversified religious and cultural phenomenon. This universe of beliefs contains a number of significant themes. Hinduism's various theologies imply that:

- The earth can be seen as a manifestation of the Goddess and must be treated with respect. The five elements—space, air, fire, water, and earth—are the foundation of an interconnected web of life.
- *Dharma*—often translated as "duty"—can be reinterpreted to include our responsibility to care for the earth.
- Simple living is a model for the development of sustainable economies. Our treatment of nature directly affects our *karma*.

Many of these lessons were demonstrated by Gandhi, whose example still motivates modern environmental, social, and religious leaders to take action to save the environment. Ten significant Hindu environmental precepts are as follows:

1. Pañca-mahābhūtas (The Five Great Elements): The structure and interdependence of the universe and the human body reveal the *Pañca-mahābhūta*s that form a web of life. According to Hinduism, *prakṛti* (primordial energy), is the source of all five major elements that make up the environment: space, air, fire, water, and earth. While each of these components has a unique life and form, they are all interdependent and connected to one another. The relationship between these elements and *Brahman* (ultimate truth from which they originate), is explained in the Upaniṣads as follows: "From *Brahman* arises space, from space arises air, from air arises fire, from fire arises water, and from water arises earth". Hinduism links each of the five elements to a particular sense and acknowledges that the human body is made up of and related to these five components. Humans have relationships with the earth, water, fire, air, and space through their noses, tongues, and ears. This sense-to-element bond is the basis of our relationship as humans with the natural world. Hinduism holds that the natural world and its surroundings are neither foreign nor hostile to humans. They make up our bodies and are essential to who we are.

2. Iśāvāsyam—Divinity is Omnipresent and Takes Infinite Forms: Iśāvāsyam—God exists everywhere and manifests in countless forms. Hindu scriptures like the *Bhagavad Gītā* (VII.19, XIII.13) and the *Bhāgavata Purāṇa* (2.2.41, 2.2.45) make frequent allusions to the Supreme Divinity's omnipresence, which includes both its presence outside and inside of nature. Hindus acknowledge and revere God's existence in the natural world. For instance, the Ganges and other powerful rivers in India are revered by many Hindus as goddesses. The universe and everything in it were made as the dwelling place of the Almighty God and for the benefit of all, according to the *Mahābhārata*. This suggests that each species should be content with its place in a wider system and in relationships with other species.

3. Protecting the Environment is Part of *Dharma*—One of the basic ideas of Hinduism, *dharma*, is translated into English as obligation, morality, cosmic order, and religion. Preserving the natural world is a significant way that Hinduism expresses *dharma*. Indian societies, like other traditional communities, did not have a concept of "the environment" as anything distinct from their other areas of life in previous ages. Numerous rural Hindu communities, including the Bhīls, the Swādhyāya, and the Bishnois, have upheld strict communal customs to preserve the area's ecosystems, including the forest and water resources. These communities carry out these conservation-focused activities as manifestations of *dharma* rather than as "environmental" deeds. Hindu teachings say that when Bishnois guard animals and trees, when Swādhyāyīs construct *nirmala nīra*s (water harvesting sites) and *vṛkṣa mandira*s (tree temples), and when Bhīls perform their rituals in sacred groves, they are really expressing their reverence for creation, not "restoring the environment". These indigenous Indian communities do not distinguish between the domains of religion, environment, and ethics. Rather, they recognize that treating creation with respect is a component of their *dharma*.

4. Our Environmental Choices have an Impact on Our *Karma*—*Karma* is a fundamental Hindu concept that teaches that every action we take has good and negative repercussions and that these consequences make up our *karma*. *Karma* then determines our future destiny, including the role we will play when we reincarnate. Our actions towards the environment carry kārmic repercussions. Even though we may have harmed the environment in the past, we have the freedom to choose to protect it in the future by changing harmful kārmic patterns with beneficial ones.

5. The Earth—'Devī', is a Goddess and Our Mother and Deserves Our Devotion and Protection—Many Hindu rituals recognize that human beings benefit from the earth, and offer gratitude and protection in response. Many Hindus touch the floor before getting out of bed every morning and ask Devī to forgive them for trampling on her body. Millions of Hindus create *kolama*s daily—artwork consisting of bits of rice or other food placed at their doorways in the morning. These *kolama*s express Hindu's desire to offer sustenance to the earth, just as the earth sustains itself. The Chipko movement—made famous by Chipko women's commitment to "hugging" trees in their community to protect them from clear-cutting by outside interests—represents a similar devotion to the earth.

6. Hinduism's Yogic and Tāntric Traditions offer teachings and practices to unite humans with divine energy and recognize the holiness of material existence. The Tāntric tradition of Hinduism holds that holy energy manifests itself across the universe. The word *yoga*, which comes from the Sanskrit word "to yoke" or "to unite", describes a set of physical and mental exercises meant to help a person become more connected to this divine force. All phenomena, things, and people are said to be manifestations of the divine in each of these religions. Furthermore, because the earth is seen as a Goddess in both of these traditions, modern Hindu teachers have drawn upon these teachings to argue against the exploitation of women, indigenous peoples, and the environment.

7. Reincarnation is a Belief that Contributes to the Idea that all Creation is Interconnected—Hindus believe in the cycle of rebirth, which holds that each being experiences millions of cycles of birth and rebirth in various forms based on their past lives *karma*. Therefore, a person may reincarnate as a human, an animal, a bird, or another member of the larger living community. Reincarnation fosters a sense of solidarity between humans and all other creatures as a result, as it is believed that everyone experiences multiple lifetimes *en route* to ultimate liberation.

8. Non-violence (Ahiṁsā), is the Greatest *Dharma*—*Ahiṁsā* (non-violence) is the highest kind of *dharma*. *Karma* is enhanced by *ahiṁsā* toward the land. Astute Hindus believe that inflicting pain or suffering on another person breaks one's *karma* and prevents progress toward *mokṣa* (liberation). To stop the negative energy from continuing to accumulate, Hindus are advised to abstain from violent actions and eat vegetarianism. Many devout Hindus reject the institutionalized raising and slaughter of fish, animals, and birds for human food because they adhere to the *ahiṁsā* ideology.

9. *Saṁnyāsa* (Asceticism) is good for the environment and a means to liberation: Hinduism teaches that asceticism, or abstaining from material possessions and leading a simple life, is a path to *mokṣa* (liberation), which respects the earth. The translation of the well-known Hindu precept *tena tyaktena bhuñjītha* is "Take what you need for your sustenance without a sense of entitlement or ownership". Many Hindus were inspired by the austere lifestyle of one of the most well-known Hindu environmental campaigners, Sunderlal Bahuguna. His numerous fasts and arduous foot marches, which he carried out in order to promote and disseminate the Chipko doctrine, established him as a noteworthy ascetic in our own day. Hindu texts advised people to renounce worldly ambition, and in him, they saw a real example of that renunciation, demonstrated by his willingness to suffer and his self-sacrificing spirit.

10. Gandhi is a Simple Example of Simplicity; his life reads like an ecological manual. His small meals of nuts and fruits, his morning ablutions and daily bodily practices, his periodic observances of silence, his morning walks, his cultivation of the small as much as of the big, his spinning wheel, his abhorrence of waste, his resorting to basic Hindu and Jaina values of truth, non-violence, celibacy and fasting—all of these tiny acts, emotions, and thoughts functioned in this life like a functioning ecosystem. Gandhi's life and words inspire a wide range of people, including moralists, feminists, journalists, social reformers, trade union leaders, peasants, prohibitionists, nature lovers, renouncers, and environmentalists.

The Hindu concept that the entire universe is a sacred forest, signifying the divine quality of totality and the interconnectivity of the whole, guides the harmony and health of the trees and plants in the forest. The following passages from Hindu Religious Scriptures are quoted:

- These trees live their entire lives to serve; they are kind people looking out for one another.
- They exist for the benefit of others through their leaves, blossoms, fruits, branches, roots, shade, scent, sap, bark, wood, and, at the end, their ashes and coal.
- Destruction of forests is seen as the destruction of the state, and reforestation is an act of rebuilding the state and advancing its welfare.
- Trees have five kinds of kindness, which are their daily sacrifice: to families they give fuel; to passersby they give shade and a resting place; to the birds they give shelter; to the animals it offers food; and with their leaves, roots, and bark they give medicine. Animal protection is regarded as a holy obligation.
- The *Bhagavad Gītā* states, "God is the life of all that lives, and everything rests on Him like pearls are strung on a thread".

Viṣṇu is the God who sustains the divine harmony and balance in the natural world. Humanity is responsible for recognizing and upholding this divine equilibrium via sacrifice, perceiving and imitating him. The earth is revered as a mother and Goddess, full of holiness, fertility, compassion, and dependability. Without it, humanity cannot exist, and in order for humanity to continue nourishing the mother earth and receiving nourishment in return, this link must be maintained.

In this perspective, nature is seen to represent the cosmos' feminine creative principle. Mother Earth is the embodiment of these material and spiritual principles that firmly bind everything in our universe together. It is the meeting point of the conscious principle (*puruṣa*), and the creative material principle (*prakṛtī*). "Mother (earth), with your oceans, rivers, and other bodies of water, you give us land to grow grains, on which our survival depends", the ancient Vedas state, cereals, milk, fruits, and water as we must eat and drink.... Please pour a thousand streams of treasure to enrich me like a dependable cow. May the cloud nurture you, our motherland where we grow wheat, rice, and barley, and may the rain show you love. The Vedas describe the *puruṣa*, the male essence, as follows:

> "The rivers are the veins of the Cosmic Person; the hills and mountains are his bones; the air is his breath; the trees are the hairs of his body; the oceans are his waist; His movements are the passing of ages." (*Atharvaveda*)

From Hymn to Mother Earth, therefore, God is viewed as many in one and one in many in Hinduism. Nature in all of its diversity is the material cause, while God is the efficient cause. The two have a harmonious connection.

Every prayer, Hindus recite the phrase *oṁ śānti śānti śānti* three times, meaning "peace". Peace with nature is represented by the first *śānti*, peace with society by the second, and peace within oneself by the third. Hindus believe that the environment embraces social, ecological, and spiritual tranquillity.

Furthermore, it is a fact that only India's constitution has language pertaining to the preservation of the environment. In order to protect wildlife and forests, the Indian constitution supports the idea of sustainability. The state and the people are required under the constitution to preserve biodiversity.

"The state shall endeavour to protect and improve the environment and to safeguard the country's forest and wildlife", according to Article 48A. Every citizen is expected by Article 51A(g) to have compassion for all living things and to preserve and enhance the natural environment, which includes woods, lakes, rivers, and wildlife. Every Indian citizen has the right to clean, healthy air and water under Article 21.

Environmental Sustainability and Social Work

"Natural capital should remain long-lasting, which means natural resources should not be used in excess of their renewal rate" is the definition of environmental sustainability. Non-renewable resources should also be protected and used sparingly. The profession of social work has been mainly dormant in this area. Hence, it is imperative that social work techniques and social work education address this issue.

Mary (2008) predicted that transpersonal elements will become increasingly important in social work values, and that academic coursework, fieldwork, and continuing education in social work must critically examine how social workers can contribute to the literal and figurative improvement of their clients' lives.

In addition, Cowley (1994) has supported social work that adopts a transpersonal perspective rather than a strictly modernist one. The transpersonal assumption is one of the postmodern approaches that suggests introducing social workers to a transpersonal perspective that incorporates the spiritual dimension. The researcher employed this strategy by raising respondents' awareness of their own consciousness through the upgrading of their value systems in relation to the natural world. The exploitation of people is a logical by-product of the exploitation of natural resources. Populations have suffered as a result of environmental deterioration, both directly and indirectly.

According to Coates (2003), social injustice can be seen in the "quest for economic growth and profit". The following are a few environmental issues that are exploitative of both people and the environment in turn:

- The indigenous group has lost their territory due to deforestation, and members of the community are suffering from previously unheard-of disease.
- Environmental prejudice is pervasive, as evidenced by the rubbish that industries discard in impoverished neighbourhoods.
- The waters and the livelihood of those reliant on the sector have been depleted due to overfishing.
- Asthma rates among metropolitan children have increased significantly in recent years, along with other environmental disorders.

According to Coates, "Social injustice has resulted from the senseless exploitation and pollution of the earth". Furthermore, two recent developments in social work that are effectively raising environmental consciousness are conservation and green social work. The social work ecological model known as conservation social work (CSW) is a paradigm that emphasizes persons-in-context and includes consideration of natural physical environments, relationships with non-human animals, careful stewardship of natural resources, and advocacy and skills for environmental resilience and health.

Supporting Environmental Justice

Social work education must consider environmental justice and consider ways that social workers can practically and figuratively make their clients' lives better. More actions centred on the community are required in regard to environmental policy. Social workers can contribute to environmental justice by financially supporting environmental causes and making personal efforts to live sustainably, but greater group activism is required. In order to effectively combine social development with conscientious and prudent environmental management, as well as with sustainable economic growth and progress, social workers must possess the necessary skills and expertise.

These are the fundamental elements of a comprehensive strategy for long-term social work practice in a society that is always changing. Properly integrating environmental education with the three educational components of knowledge, information, and wisdom is recommended. The door to mental development is opened by education. The first entity information focuses on the norms that people need to be aware of in order to improve their knowledge and gain the wisdom to take action to protect the environment.

The basic requirements of people, such as those for food, shelter, water, energy, clothing, jobs, education, health, and other things, are growing along with the population. Therefore, it makes sense for societies in emerging nations to aspire to these degrees of material well-being, consumption habits, and wealth. Progress and growth are inevitable and necessary to meet material demands, consumption patterns, and expectations. The environment and natural resources are essential to development. Therefore, overuse of the environment and natural resources is occurring in the name of development, risking the very survival of all life on earth by deteriorating the sustainable features and potential capability of earth.

As a result, changes must be made to the development pattern, which is predicated on commercial philosophy with an economic focus. It's also essential to conserve and ratify the resources in order to protect the environment and guarantee that future generations can continue to have access to them. Furthermore, efficient and effective resource management is necessary to guarantee distributive justice across generations, nature's survival, all living things—including humans and non-human animals—and their natural habitats.

Conclusion

To address the significant and frequent issues arising from human interactions with animals and the natural world, the multidisciplinary approaches such as conservation and green social work are needed. When used with environmental education, that relationship can help people feel more connected to the natural world. Though perplexing, annoying, and nonsensical, our relationships with the environment and animals are essential to life as we know it on earth. To foster well-being for people in a manner that is similar to that of animals and the natural world, conservation, also known as green social work, offers a cohesive and global approach to problems centred on human-animal, human-nature, and human-human interactions. Social work devoted to conservation cannot succeed until environmental education is separated from humankind and can provide. Social work devoted to conservation won't be effective until environmental education is separated from human society and can restore people's faith in the natural world, as it did in primitive times. It has been logically demonstrated that a balanced attitude toward the environment, as portrayed in our holy texts, maintains the equilibrium between the environment and humans. Now is critical to recognize religious texts' role in preserving the natural world. Nurturing our children with the teaching of these holy scriptures, which is logically proven, can develop a responsible attitude among them through its practice of promoting a healthy environment.

REFERENCES

Dash, Shushil Kumar (2007). "Climate Change: An Indian Perspective". *Environment and Development Series.*

Dass, Sujata K. (2004). *Global Climate and Sustainable Development*, vii.

Environment Education in the Indian School System, Status Report 2007, Centre for Environment Education, Ahmedabad, India.

Flavin, Christopher and Engelman, Robert (2009). *The Perfect Storm, State of the World, Into a Warming World.*

India Environment Portal | News, reports, documents, blogs, data, analysis on environment & development | India, South Asia (n.d.). http://www.indiaenvironmentportal.org.in/

Satapathy, Nityanand (1998). *Sustainable Development* (*An Alternative Paradigm*), Karnavati Publications, Ahmedabad.

Sustainable Development in India (n.d.). *India Brand Equity Foundation.* https://www.ibef.org/pages/sustainabledevelopment

Sustainable Development Learnings and Perspectives from India based on a Nationwide Consultative Process. Ministry of Environment and Forests, Government of India (2002). Available on https://moef.gov.in/wp-content/uploads/wssd/doc4/consul_book_final.pdf

Wizard Social Issues & Institutions, First Edition, 2007, Published by Career Classics, Delhi.

World Development Report 2004, *Making Services Work for Poor People*, A co-publication of the World Bank & Oxford University Press.

5

Spiritual Foundations of Social Work Values

Insights from the *Bhagavad Gītā*

Vaishag Velayudhan

Introduction

Social work's origin has a deeply rooted history in India that stems from various ideologies, beliefs and perspectives. The need for such a profession has been uprooted as a result of human suffering; therefore, the very base of this profession is promoting people's rights by helping them overcome their suffering. The evolution of social work in India can be explored through the ideologies of secularism, humanism, welfarism, rationalism, democracy, liberalism, etc. Social work as a service profession is directly linked to strong ethical and spiritual values that have existed since the early Vedic period (Pandey, Gupta & Patel, 2010).

The very mission of this profession is to enhance the well-being of all humans by helping them to help themselves with the primary attention diverted towards the empowerment and needs of those who are oppressed and vulnerable. The dual role of social work is thus to promote well-being within the social context and ensure the greater well-being of society as a whole (Weiss, 2006). Social workers aim to promote social justice and change by striving to eradicate discrimination of all forms, including oppression, poverty, and social injustice. Social workers have high sensitivity towards cultural and ethnic diversity and, therefore, use their skills to understand and address the specific needs of people in discharging their duties as professional social workers. A profession that thus holds the needs and well-being of society as paramount is bound by a certain set of core values that define and give meaning to the profession (National Association of Social Workers, n.d.).

Core Values of Social Work Profession

Like any other profession, social work too emphasizes professional ethics. It has articulated a certain set of values, principles and standards to guide the professional conduct of social workers. Regardless of one's role, setting or even the people with whom they are associated, every social work professional, including the students of social work, is expected to follow the code of conduct (National Association of Social Workers, n.d.). The core values that reflect the essence of the profession, therefore, include:

1. **Service:** Social workers' primary goal is to empower people and help resolve their problems. The other values of social work profession are derived from the value of service. Social workers give greater prominence to the interests and well-being of others than the self. They make use of their professional skills, knowledge and expertise to help people and the community without expecting any financial gain in return.
2. **Social Justice:** Social workers strive to achieve social justice through social change. They stand for and on behalf of those oppressed and marginalized. The

efforts are focused at eradicating social problems such as poverty, unemployment, homelessness, discrimination and other forms of injustice. Social workers promote change through awareness, spreading and disseminating information about various forms of injustice that exist, and helping people stand up for themselves in times of distress. They contribute to overall health and well-being of people and communities by making efforts to create a support system that help them understand their structural conditions and overcome their problems.

3. **Dignity and Worth of the Person:** Of greater significance is the ability of a social worker to treat their clients in a respectful manner, be caring and to be mindful of the differences among each individual and so respect their individuality. Social workers also need to be mindful of the cultural and ethnic diversity. What the profession demands of a social worker is to help their clients to seek solutions to their problems and support them by being cognizant of their duties and responsibilities towards the individuals and society at large.
4. **Importance of Human Relationships:** Understanding and strengthening human relationships is vital to promoting social change. The role of a social worker emerges from the notion of humanitarianism, which is derived from humanitarian principles, and this demands that a social worker engage in helping people. Social workers thus seek to promote, strengthen and help enhance the well-being of individuals, families and communities.
5. **Integrity:** Social workers must be aware of the profession's mission and ethical standards and act in a manner that is consistent with the profession's mission. Social workers must behave in a calm, composed, and honest manner and must be responsible for promoting the organization's ethical principles to which they are

associated. It is one of the most important values that a social worker must possess.

6. **Competence:** For a social worker, it is always important to keep expanding their knowledge base and competence so as to contribute positively to the profession's mission. Social workers must possess the zeal to contribute to the profession's existing knowledge base. Social work as a field of practice demands the social worker's lifetime commitment to continuously expand their knowledge base and skill sets to make their contributions to the profession more meaningful.

Social Work Values: Reflections from the *Bhagavad Gītā*

Many writers have attempted to trace back within the Indian context the roots of what we call as social work in contemporary times. Banerjee (1973), in this regard, calls social work as "an organized effort" to help man attain the highest growth in terms of physical, social, emotional, cultural, intellectual, and spiritual aspects. Banerjee continues to define social work as a field that focuses on solving the problems of individuals by bringing change through reforms. The social worker's role here has been thus considered as a "service to human beings". Dash (2019), calls the social work profession as a spiritual profession within the Indian context as the traditional Indic values (Indian) very well define the role of a social worker and of the social work profession in dealing with individuals. Dash considers Indic values to be of great relevance to Indian social workers who deal with their clients in a caring and respectful manner. Therefore, much importance is given to the traditional value systems in India that play a vital role in shaping social work as a profession in general and the core values of the profession in particular.

Values are a set of standards or beliefs that guide a person's professional conduct. It is an integral part of any profession and social work is no exception. The modern-day understanding of social work in India rests on the pillar of "service to society" as a value which is depicted in the religious text of Hindus "the *Bhagavad Gītā*" where the various *śloka*s in *Gītā* explain the value systems that are embedded within the beliefs and practices of people (Banerjee, 1973). Hence, the knowledge of *Gītā* becomes very significant at this point as it uncovers the understanding of social work values that are reflective of a social worker. The notions of *dharma, ahiṁsā, niṣṭhā, upekṣā*, and *satya* are all considered to be the Indian social work values that is at the heart of the common beliefs of individuals. These values provide meaning and sense when understood through the lens of universal social work values reflected in the *Bhagavad Gītā*.

I. Society-Focused Values

These values emphasize the larger society as a whole rather than just the individuals. The focus is on bringing systemic changes in the larger social structure and promoting the betterment and well-being of the communities and the society at large (The Florida State University, 2020). The values of service, social justice and integrity clearly define a social worker's ethical responsibility towards the society and their commitment towards the same.

The third chapter, titled "Karma-Yoga" in the *Bhagavad Gītā* speaks about performing one's action devoid of desires as an individual's duty. It emphasizes the importance of *karma* (action) to be performed by every individual (*Śrīmadbhagavadgītā*, 2004). The *Gītā* states that:

> *yajñārthāt karmaṇo 'nyatra, loko 'yaṁ karmabandhanaḥ*|
> *tad arthaṁ karma kaunteya, mukta saṅgaḥ samācara*||
> (BG: 3.9)

> (The word *yajña* here refers to actions performed as a sacrifice to God. It emphasizes on work to be performed as *yajña* to God, otherwise, work done towards one's own gratification tends to cause bondage in the material world.

So, therefore, one must perform their duties and actions without being attached to the results of the same.)

Mukundananda (n.d.) explains one's actions or *karma* by drawing an analogy in this context. He states that a knife as an instrument can be perceived from two different angles. When in the hands of a robber, it is used as a weapon or instrument to instill fear or murder people whereas in the hands of a surgeon, it is an instrument to save lives. One cannot determine or come to a conclusion about a knife by its mere properties rather its effect or impact is determined on the basis of how it is put to use. It is one's perception and mindset that matters rather than judgements on the basis of "good or bad". Similar is the case when it comes to performing one's duties. No work can be termed good or bad rather it is one's state of mind that makes it so. The above verse thus speaks of two modes of work and that any one of the two is inevitable as one cannot live without performing their duties or work. Human minds cannot always remain still; therefore, one has to perform their duties either as work done to fulfil one's own gratifications by developing bondage to the material world or as a sacrifice for the pleasure of God to attract divine grace.

The verse emphasizes on the need for individuals to perform their action (*karma*) which in the context of social work defines the value of "service". Banerjee (1973), in this regard finds it important to quote Swami Chinmayananda's explanation of the word *yajña* in the verse. He defines *yajña* as a complex whole of all social, rational and personal activities that an individual performs in the spirit of service and stands at the forefront towards helping the community members to eliminate all forms of problems. This reinterpretation of the word *yajña* gives a new meaning to social work profession that believes in the value of service to all without being attached to any kind of expectations in form of returns.

Yet another verse in the *Gītā* confirms about the very existence of human race to perform their duties to promote betterment of all. It is stated in the *Gītā* 3.10 that:

> *sahayajñāḥ prajāḥ sṛṣṭvā purovāca prajāpatiḥ*।
> *anena prasaviṣyadhvameṣa vo 'stviṣṭa-kāmadhuk*॥

> (The word Prajāpati here means the creator of mankind, the one who has created it with certain duties to fulfil. It is said that upon fulfilling these duties as a sacrifice towards the betterment of all, mankind attains growth and prosperity.)

Social workers find a sense of achievement and fulfilment in the fact that they contribute positively towards the well-being and prosperity of all by sacrificing and prioritizing the needs of the society as supreme over one's own. Social work, thus holds the value of service as paramount and constitutes the foundation of the profession. It is a value that is closely associated with the Hindu concept of *dharma*. It is an eternal principle that is considered the backbone of Hinduism. The concept has many different understandings contextually but in Hinduism, it refers to the duties performed by an individual towards the well-being of the society, family and the self. It is more of a code of conduct and way of life (Dash, 2019).

Illustration 1

The *Bhagavad Gītā* repeatedly mentions the terms duty, righteousness, compassion, and treating people with dignity and respect, and all these teachings infer to the concept of social justice. It refers to the idea of promoting fairness, equality and equity among all especially the oppressed and the marginalized. *Gītā* 3.20 states:

> *karmaṇaiva hi saṁsiddhim āsthitā janakādayaḥ*।
> *lokasaṁgraham eva api saṁpaśyan kartum arhasi*॥

> (The above verse describes the need for one to perform their duties just like King Janaka and others did to attain perfection. Example setting is very important; one must perform their duties and be a good example. The world follows great

people's actions, which are therefore set as the standards of the world. Common people follow those actions and pursue the standards of these great personalities.)

It is clear that one must perform their actions (*karma-yoga*) and thereby attain perfection through discharge of their duties. King Janaka has performed his prescribed duties as a king towards his people and thus set himself as an example for the world to follow. Such people are termed leaders who have the potential to guide and inspire the masses and be a beacon light. They fulfil their moral responsibility towards society through their words, deeds, and character. They aim towards promoting good and righteousness through principled leadership and solve the problems of the society (Mukundananda, n.d.). Similarly, social work professionals have within them the quality of being a great leader. They set noble ideals before the society and encourage people towards holistic development. Inspiring people, guiding them and setting forth ideals to help a man develop is thus not a mere easy task and is no small social work. Having the innate qualities and skill sets to become a good leader is very important that a social work professional possesses (Banerjee, 1973).

Illustration 2

The field of social work also demands the execution of their duties in an ethical manner. The role of a social work professional is to help people and in doing so must uphold professional ethics and maintain transparency that is in the best interest of the clients. Thus, integrity is an important principle reflected in the *Bhagavad Gītā* emphasizing the moral values of honesty, ethical conduct, beliefs and actions. *Gītā* 2.47 states:

karmaṇyevādhikāraste mā phaleṣu kadācana।
mā karma phala hetur bhūr mā te saṅgo'stvakarmaṇi॥

(One has the right to perform their duties but without the expectation of fruits of the action.

> One must never be motivated by the results of one's actions and also must not be attached to the mindset of not doing the prescribed duties.)

None can exist in this world without having performed their duties or actions. Every living entity has the right to perform their prescribed duties. But what is noteworthy here is the understanding that one must perform their duties without being motivated by the results of the same, and such desire or motivation to the results of one's action will only create bondage to this material world. It is also known that all actions produce some result, but the underlying motive behind performing an action should not be based on the desire for such a result. The action in itself must be the reason for one's motivation (*Bhagavad Gītā*, n.d.).

Performing one's action forms the basis of social work profession. A social work professional is always expected to detach oneself from the results of the action and see his activities as part and parcel of this larger world full of activities. The emphasis is on *niṣkāma karma* that is to perform one's actions or deeds without being attached to the fruit of the action. When a social worker is able to carry out his actions without being motivated by the results, the outcome naturally gets transformed into something unique (Banerjee, 1973).

II. Individual-Focused Values

Although social work by its very nature, gives predominant importance to the welfare of the society as a whole, it also gives importance to the individual. It plays a very significant role in helping the individual client with whom a worker-client relationship is established within the context of social work practice (Kapur, 2018). Individual-focused values are those foundational values that help social workers deal with their clients during interactions and help build a healthy worker-client relationship. It makes the social work practitioner more competent in understanding the clients' problems and respecting their inherent worth and rights. Thus, by instilling the values of inherent worth and dignity, human relationships and competence within self, a social worker is able to understand their clients better, thereby prioritizing their needs and preferences towards empowering them to achieve their goals.

Social work gives predominant importance to the dignity of all human beings. It gives importance to the worth of all and perceives everyone as having an intrinsic value of their own. It is nearly impossible to alter the basic worth of any individual, whether they have been brought up in a bad or unpleasant environment or in a good and secure one. What matters here is whether a person is acting in conformity with his dignity or against it. Either ways such a person still has an innate dignity and worth of his own (Banerjee, 1973). This concept has been explained in *Gītā*. The verse in chapter 6, "Ātmasaṁyama-Yoga" śloka 5 states:

> *uddhared ātmanātmānaṁ nātmānamavasādayet*।
> *ātmaiva hy ātmano bandhur ātmaiva ripurātmanaḥ*॥

> (The verse defines the power of human mind. The mind can be a friend and a foe to the self, and therefore, the person has control over his mind and senses. It is he who has to raise himself to his innate strength rather than to degrade self.)

Banerjee (1973) states that an individual has the innate capacity and strength to raise self to the highest potential by realizing his weakness and overcoming the same. In this context, Banerjee illustrates a text from ancient Indian literature about a robber who turned sage Vālmīki. He was able to analyse the shortcomings within his personality and could change himself for good and later became a renowned sage. This view of bringing change has paved the way for contemporary social workers to deal with wide cross-sections of society to help them recognize and promote innate dignity and worth. The study of social work has thus turned its focus on various domains such as social work with criminals, prostitutes, addicts, etc. The *Gītā* also emphasizes on the significance of self-help. A social worker helps the client by working with them rather than for them. The emphasis here is on social workers helping clients restore their intrinsic dignity and worth by being enablers. Social workers can only guide them and to help themselves. The effort to restore the same must stem from the person himself.

Social work also touches upon the concept of "relationship", which is central to its practice. What is important in the practice of social work is to have genuine love and concern for the people with whom social workers are involved. It is a necessary pre-requisite when entering into a therapeutic relationship with the clients (Banerjee, 1973). *Ahiṁsā* is a concept similar to human relationships and love. The term *ahiṁsā* means non-violence, which is considered one of the most important virtues in Indian tradition. The practice of non-violence has been a greatest virtue of the Jainas and the Buddhists. The Buddhists believe in the practice of *ahiṁsā* through their adherence to the eightfold path of Buddhism. Non-violence constitutes as one of the five precepts of Buddhism. The Jainas also believe in the notion of non-violence, which constitutes one of the five *aṇuvrata*s (vows) that the Jainas follow (Dash, 2019).

Illustration 3

The *Bhagavad Gītā* also emphasizes the need for love for mankind. The *Gītā* 6.9 states:

> *suhṛnmitrāryudāsīna madhyastha dveṣya bandhuṣu*|
> *sādhuṣvapi ca pāpeṣu samabuddhirviśiṣyate*||
>
> (He who is impartial with his intellect and remains indifferent towards his well-wishers, friends, enemies, companions, relatives and others and can distinguish between right and wrong is considered the most superior.)

According to Banerjee (1973), the profession of social work demands passion and love towards people with whom the professionals are associated. A social worker requires clarity of mind and maturity to be calm and composed when faced with challenging situations while dealing with clients. A social worker must remember not to retaliate in provocative situations by the clients. This ability on the worker's part holds together a healthy and positive relationship between the worker and the client. It convinces the client that the worker is concerned about their well-being and also keeps the relationship more open. Banerjee finds it pertinent to mention the terms *maitrī* (friendliness) and *karuṇā* (compassion) as described in Patañjali's treatise on *yoga* to be of great importance in the field of social work. Banerjee yet again quotes Swami Vivekananda's words, saying, "duty is seldom sweet. It is only when love greases its wheels that it runs smoothly: it is a continuous friction otherwise" (p. 21). The service to humanity becomes impossible in the absence of love and compassion for people. Thus, social work professionals are expected to cultivate the capacity to show love and compassion when in a working relationship with their clients.

Professional Self and Social Work

It is essential at this juncture to understand the concept of self before delving into the concept of personal and professional self. Self refers to one's own subjective experience of a phenomena. It involves one's perceptions, emotions and thoughts about that phenomena. In phenomenological terms, an individual's existence is void without any experience of events in one's lifetime. Thus, the concept of self can be understood as one's own perception of one's unique abilities, skills, qualities, beliefs, and nature. It is a collection of perceptions whereby one draws a mental picture of oneself (Ebere, 2016).

Like any other profession, such as medicine, where doctors use various instruments and tools, social work also uses the self as an instrument and tool. Social workers use themselves as a tool and make use of their knowledge, skills and values to promote or enhancing well-being of their clients (Kaushik, 2017). This use of self enables the social worker to deal with and help the clients with their problems more effectively, hereby honouring the ethical principles and values that social work practice holds with high regard (Ebere, 2016). According to (Dewane, 2006), use of self in social work practice involves the use of one's knowledge, skills and values learned through social work education and through the aspects of personal self which includes one's personality traits, beliefs, practices, and experiences.

In the context of social work practice, Banerjee (1973) makes a striking distinction between the personal self and the professional self. According to Banerjee, the professional self includes the understanding of self and the understanding of people as essential ingredients in forming a strong working relationship between the worker and the client. This self-awareness helps the social workers to develop a conscious control over self while dealing with the clients. The development of professional self is thus considered inevitable and is guided by certain ethical principles and values that a social worker has to be aware of at all times. On the other hand, personal self is that part of a person which reflects their personal beliefs, feelings, attitudes, biases and prejudices that the social work profession does not demand.

Illustration 4

The *Gītā* understands this professional self-concept as "an action performed without having any kind of desire or self-gain". The term used in *Gītā* for the same is *niṣkāma karma* (Selfless action). The *Gītā* 2.56-57 states:

> *duḥkheshv anudvigna manāḥ sukheṣu vigata spṛhaḥ*।
> *vīta rāga bhaya krodhaḥ sthita dhīrmunirucyate*॥

(The one who stands unshaken in the most difficult of circumstances and miseries, who does not run behind or crave for pleasures and is free from all forms of attachment, fear and anger, thus qualifies to be regarded as a sage with firm wisdom.)

yaḥ sarvatrānabhisnehas tat tat prāpya śubhāśubham।
nābhinandati na dveṣṭi tasya prajñā pratiṣṭhitā॥

(One who is without any form of attachment and who does not rejoice by good fortune nor is dejected by bad or evil is said to possess the perfect knowledge.)

The above two verses contemplate the meaning of the professional self as regarded in *Gītā* as *sthita dhīra* or *sthita prajña* (sage of steady intelligence). Although this has been explained and interpreted in different ways, the essence of all is one that explains an action performed without having any form of pleasure, fear or attachment to anything. The Supreme Lord Kṛṣṇa speaks about an ideal personality devoid of all such characteristics as pleasures or desires, fear, anger, and attachment, which qualifies as a sage with great wisdom. Such a person is not attached to anything or anyone and does not praise anyone nor blame them and nor does he carry with him the feeling of love or hatred for anyone. One possessing such characteristics within is fit to be called as a person with steady wisdom and knowledge of the transcendental (*Bhagavad Gītā*, n.d.).

Mukundananda (n.d.) explains the meaning of the above verse based on the description given by Lord Kṛṣṇa about three categories of sages with steady wisdom. They are:

(1) *Vīta rāga* (to give up one's desires or pleasures),
(2) *Vīta bhaya* (to be free of fear), and
(3) *Vīta krodha* (one without any anger).

One who is said to be devoid of all forms of pleasure, does not run towards the objects of enjoyment and does not give himself to the material frailties such as anger, lust and greed can be called as an enlightened person and such a person raises to the level of metaphysical.

In social work, this understanding of enlightenment and transcendence relates to one's commitment to one's actions performed without attachment to the fruit of his action. According to Banerjee (1973), the biggest concern in social work is the human beings themselves. When working with an individual or client, a social worker needs to have a good understanding and practice in the "realm of feeling". For a social worker, going in depth into the feelings of the persons they deal with is not objectively possible rather can only be felt when the worker learns to empathize with them through practice and understanding. It is more important for a social worker to be conscious when dealing with people and how he reacts, rather than having the technical knowledge of "know how" which is more prominent in other professional fields. This understanding of the nature of social work profession has led Banerjee to emphasize the notion of *niṣkāma karma*. It is an action performed due to dedication to a particular cause (welfare of people) rather than having attached one's own motive of self-gain in the form of money, power, prestige, etc.

A social worker must possess certain qualities and attributes that go deeper into one's personality, enabling him to establish a good worker-client relationship in a more professional way and make him feel responsible towards the people he works with. Developing such qualities and attributes within self is not merely possible only through intellectual knowledge of people's social situations and problems rather, it requires inner blossoming, growth and development to be able to understand the situation and problems of others. Thus, a social worker must be able to "know", "feel", "do" and be the self along with the conscious understanding and meaningful response to people's problems. This contributes to the growth and development of the professional self (Banerjee, 1973).

Discussion

Although one may not indeed be able to trace the origin of social work values from the *Bhagavad Gītā*, all the modern-day understanding of the profession's core values does resonate in the *Gītā*. The philosophical notions in social work is said to have their roots not only in one particular text but in all religious traditions and cultures. *Bhagavad Gītā* is one such source that emphasizes on the foundational values of social work profession. The *Gītā* is a text with a rich collection of verses that describes the need for virtuous human qualities of duty, compassion, selflessness and the pursuit of knowledge, which are again held as the core of social work profession. These values reflect upon the universal humanitarian principles of human dignity and worth, social justice, integrity, and well-being of all.

India, with a great history of civilization, is shackled under the grip of social problems that are more rampant today. In such a scenario characterized by such issues, a discipline like social work needs to take the initiative towards reforms. In the Indian context, what is of greater relevance to budding social workers is its cultural traditions and values called Indic values (Dash, 2019). These values form the profession's ethical standards in India and have a very exhaustive description in the holy text of *Bhagavad Gītā.*

The *Gītā* explains how the "self" develops certain qualities essential for an ethical life. This self is a social being and cannot live in isolation. Self and society are interconnected; therefore, one also has a duty towards society. The *Gītā* calls this duty "sacrifice or *yajña*" that one makes for society's larger good and well-being. It is regarded as a divine quality; without it, one cannot aspire to serve others. Sacrifice is made without the desire or attachmet to the result. When one performs the duty without a sense of attachment, the outcome of the action automatically turns out positive, contributing to greater good and prosperity (Ghosh, 2018; Bhattacharjee, 2021). Within the context of social work, the value of sacrifice is considered important. Sacrifice in "service" to those in need is the profession's foundation. A social worker uses his knowledge, skills, and intellect to help the persons they deal with to ameliorate their problems without any kind of expectation in return.

Along with service as its foundational pillar, social work also rests on other values closely connected with the service's value. These values include respecting the inherent worth of individuals, integrity, compassion, justice, competency and valuing human relationship. For a social worker to achieve, the profession's objectives and goals must be imbibed within the self following humanitarian principles. Ghosh (2018) mentions the synthesis of values as explained in *Gītā*. According to him, the *Gītā* speaks of the syntheticization of values and describes it as the only means by which the members in the society prosper through mutual cooperation, service, help, sympathy, and empathy towards the others that leads to peace and harmony. The *Gītā* is said to spread the message that the right attitude and action and one's constructive use of knowledge and skills shall contribute to glory and justice. A similar stance is true when it comes to social work practice. With the constructive use of one's competency and bearing in mind humanitarian values, a social worker can realize the profession's ideals.

Conclusion

This chapter identifies the valuable insights that *Gītā* provides about the values of social work. The *Bhagavad Gītā* resonates with the core values of social work by emphasizing duty or service, compassion, selflessness, and knowledge enhancement as the most vital principles of social work. The *Gītā* conveys to its readers the critical message of performing selfless duty (sacrifice), keeping in mind the greater good of both society and self, which closely aligns with the value of service that forms the pillar of the social work profession. Social work demands from its professionals a sense of commitment to their duty of selfless service to their clients. Social workers make use of their theoretical knowledge and skills in synthesis with the humanitarian principles of service, empathy, justice, and cooperation towards promoting harmony. These values and principles are powerful in helping social workers navigate the problems and concerns of individuals and society. In a country like India, where the cultural traditions and ethics hold great significance, the role played by *Gītā* is pivotal. It helps integrate spiritual teachings and professional competencies, which in turn helps social workers achieve the ideals set by the profession, thereby contributing to the well-being of society.

REFERENCES

Banerjee, G.R. (1973). *Papers on Social Work: An Indian Perspective.* Tata Institute of Social Sciences, Bombay.

Bhagavad Gītā. (n.d.). Retrieved on 17 February 2024, from Chapter 2: the Eternal Reality of the Soul's Immortality: https://www.bhagavad-gita.org/*Gītā*/verse-02-55.html

Bhattacharjee, G. (2021, March). "A Study on Karmayoga in *Bhagavad Gita*". *Journal of Research in Humanities and Social Science, 9*(3): 10-19. Retrieved from www.questjournals.org

Dash, B.M. (2019, April 22). "Indic Social Work Values", 2. New Delhi: *New Delhi Times.* Retrieved from https://www.newdelhitimes.com/indic-social-workvalues/?

Dewane, C.J. (2006). "Use of Self: A Primer Revisited". *Clinical Social Work Journal, 34*(4): 543-58. doi:https://doi.org/10.1007/s10615-005-0021-5

Ebere, S.C. (2016). *The Use of Self in Social Work Practice.*

Ghosh, R. (2018). "Values Embdded in the Bhagavadgītā". *The Journal of East West Thought, 8*(1): 27-33.

Kapur, R. (2018, March 11). *Understanding the Significance of Social Work.*

Kaushik, A. (2017). "Use of Self in Social Work: Rhetoric or Reality". *Journal of Social Work Values and Ethics, 14*(1): 21-29.

Mukundananda, S. (n.d.). *Bhagavad Gītā: Chapter 3, Verse 9.* Retrieved on 8 February 2024, from *Bhagavad Gītā the Song of God*: https://www.holy-bhagavad-gita.org/chapter/3/verse/9

National Association of Social Workers (n.d.). *Code of Ethics: English.* Retrieved on 30 January 2024, from National Association of Social Workers: https://www.socialworkers.org/About/Ethics/Code-of-Ethics/Code-of-Ethics-English

Pandey, N., Gupta, M., and Patel, S. (2010). "History of Social Work: State Initiatives". In P.G. Thomas, and P.G. Thomas (Ed.), *Origin and Development of Social Work in India* (pp. 1-54). Indira Gandhi National Open University.

Śrīmadbhagavadgita (1st edn.). (2004). Rajahmundry, Andhra Pradesh, India: Rohini Publications.

The Florida State University (2020, July 27). *The Social Worker Role and Impact on the Community*. Retrieved from Florida State University: https://onlinemsw.fsu.edu/blog/social-worker-role

Weiss, I. (2006). "Modes of Practice and the Dual Mission of Social Work: A Cross-national Study of Social Work Students' Preferences". (135-51) *Journal of Social Service Research, 32*(3).

6

Social Welfare in Ancient India through Professional Social Work Perspective

Sandeep Kumar Morishetty

Introduction

The charity was at the heart of social services. Welfare and service have a long history throughout India. In ancient times, family, caste, religion, and *mandira* were the primary centres for welfare initiatives. Social welfare activities were performed by means of *yajña*s, the most popular mass rituals known in Vedic times. The privileged class had the duty to serve the poor, not to show superiority but in order to get *mokṣa*. *dharma, artha, kāma*, and *mokṣa* can be roughly translated as moral behaviour, wealth, worldly pleasures, and salvation. An individual can have a meaningful, sustained life and even achieve salvation after life by earnestly pursuing these goals. If we unravel the history of social work, we can find that society/state has more or less been taking action to better the needy. Various known and unknown approaches to uplift them have been taken from time to time. Charity was the first form of social work practice in India. Charity means love and compassion for the poor and one's fellowmen on religious grounds. It is practised through rendering service to the needy to attain God's blessing.

Social Welfare

Social welfare is an organized system of social services and organizations that help people and communities achieve satisfactory living and health standards. As a result, social welfare attempts to give services to weaker segments of the population who, due to different handicaps such as physical, mental, economic, and social, are unable to access social services supplied by society or have historically been deprived of these benefits. Social welfare is a set of laws and institutions designed by the government to safeguard and promote its people's economic and social well-being. In other words, social welfare attempts to provide services to the poorest members of society by offering various types of social insurance against poverty, unemployment, disability, and old age.

Professional Social Work

Social work is a profession in which trained professionals are devoted to helping vulnerable people and communities work through the challenges they face in everyday life. Social work is a practice-based profession and an academic discipline that promotes social change and development, social cohesion, and the empowerment and liberation of people. Principles of social justice, human rights, collective responsibility and respect for diversity are central to social work. Underpinned by theories of social work, social sciences, humanities, and indigenous knowledge, social work engages people and structures to address life challenges and enhance well-being (International Federation of Social Workers).

Social work practice consists of the professional application of social principles and techniques to one or more of the following ends: helping people obtain tangible services; counselling and psychotherapy with individuals, families, and groups; helping communities or groups provide or improve social and health services, and participating in legislative processes. The practice of social work requires knowledge of human development and behaviour; of social and economic, and cultural institutions; and the interaction of all these factors (National Association of Social Workers).

Friedlander (1964) states,

> "Social work seeks to assist individuals, groups and communities to reach the highest possible degree of social, mental, and psychological well-being. Its function requires awareness of the dynamic interplay of personal, biological, and psychological elements within the socio-economic forces of the environment of human beings."

Emphasis of Social Work in Ancient India

In India, the nature of social service in the past was charity. It has been found in different Hindu scriptures, such as the Vedas, Upaniṣads, and *Mahābhārata* of the Hindu state of India. The earlier reference to charity is found in the *Ṛgveda* I.13.2, which encourages charity by saying, "May the one who gives shine most". The Upaniṣads, like *Bṛhadāraṇyaka*, *Chāndogya*, and *Taittirīya*, said every householder must practice charity. In *Mahābhārata*, Bhīṣma talked to Yudhiṣṭhira in an interaction describing the essence of eternal religion, non-violence, truth, the conquest of anger and the practice of charity. Next to education, reference may be made to religion, which took precedence over everything else to the people of ancient India. According to *Gītā*, privileged-sections must strive towards the fulfilment of its duty to serve the poor, handicapped and underprivileged. Service is the common part of everybody's life. In ancient Bhārata religion, caste, family plays a major role in a person's life, making him learn and practice Charity. *Mandiras*, *maṭhas* are the centres for different welfare activities. Empires from different dynasties sacrificed everything for the welfare of the society.

The nature of social work was one of compassion. *Yajñas*, the most popular public rites known during Vedic times, were used to carry out social welfare initiatives. The privileged elite had a duty to help the impoverished, not to demonstrate superiority, but to get *mokṣa*. In Vedic times, obligations were exclusively defined in terms of religion; there was no provision for adjudication. However, the caste system that emerged during the late Vedic era severely endangered the state's well-being. Buddhism also embraced *karma* and encouraged providing *bhikṣa* to *bhikṣus* living in *saṅgha*. Aśoka was responsible for constructing a comprehensive social welfare system that included women's welfare, rural development, impoverished rehabilitation, prostitution control, and public utility provision. Kauṭilya envisages a perfect state. Kauṭilya imagines an ideal state in which the king is philanthropic and the ministers are dedicated to public welfare. This ideal state's main objective was to ensure its citizens' well-being. The phrase "welfare" refers to a state or situation of an individual's well-being, good fortune, happiness, or prosperity within a society.

Social Welfare by the Practice of Yajñas

It was the most popular mass ceremony throughout the Vedic period. People gathered in a large shed built for the occasion on the banks of rushing rivers, full of commitment. Their purpose was not for personal gain but for the general good of everyone. *Yajñashalas* were classrooms where men and women learned to work together without ego or egoistical aspirations. People were instructed to carry the spirit of the *yajña* rites and their actions not just on the site, but also in their homes, markets, workplaces, and fields. According to the *Āśalāyana Gṛiyasūtra*, one must execute five *yajñas* known as *pañcayajñas* daily, including serving God, ancestors, animals, and oneself.

Welfare Activities by Farmers

Indian society, which is built on agriculture, serves as an example of welfare. The Indian farmer cultivates not just for himself but also her society. During natural disasters, agricultural failures, and many community celebrations, the farmer distributes his profits to the benefit of society, which is a prevalent tradition in Bhārata. With the development of agrarian civilization with private group ownership of land, the noble concepts of charity and welfare came into existence. *Dāna* and *dakṣiṇā* were practised in response to starvation for the sick, the aged, and the weak, when the tribe had common ownership of property. But when private property and class rule came across (during the late Vedic period and after), the concept of *dāna* shifted from an instrument of social insurance to a privilege of the ruling class.

Kingship: During the monarch's reign in ancient India, the welfare state was an ideal social element. The king was the protector of the law, which came from the notion of *dharma*. The mythology also discussed *karma* theory, which defined the nature of good acts. Decent acts produce delight. During the king's reign, a phrase ran like this: prajñāsukheṣu khamrājña (the king's happiness is linked to the happiness of his subjects). Most kings also thought that the well-being of the people was the primary responsibility.

Welfare Activities by Different Empires and Dynasties

Bimbisāra: As agricultural civilization evolved, a new sort of polity emerged in early Kosala and Magadha states. Bimbisāra became king of Magadha in 300 BC He was the first of the Indian rulers to establish an effective administrative structure. He focused on road and agricultural development and societal protection via crime reduction.

Aśoka: A welfare state is one in which the government actively ensures and promotes its citizens' economic and social well-being. Aśoka believed in the king's policy as the father of his people and made several initiatives for them.

The welfare measures by Aśoka can be listed as follows:

- After the Kaliṅga War, Aśoka dedicated himself to the welfare of his people. He appointed *dhammamahāmātras* to spread his message across the empire and advise people to follow the *dhamma*.
- He built roads and planted shady trees on both sides of roads for travellers.
- He built several rest houses for the travellers.
- He dug numerous wells to provide clean water to its citizens.
- He arranged for medical treatment for both human beings and animals.

Social Work during the Gupta Period

The Gupta period witnessed further philanthropic activities, with wealthy merchants and individuals contributing to constructing temples, *stūpa*s, and other public structures. Educational institutions like Nālandā and Taxila flourished during this era, thanks to patronage from the ruling class and affluent citizens.

Kanishka: Like Aśoka, the Great, he took an active interest in the welfare of society. He made generous gifts and subsidies to construct Buddhist *vihāra*s, monasteries, *stūpa*s, and other institutions that served as centers of learning and assistance to the destitute. Kaniṣka appointed administrative officers Gopa and Gramika to address people's concerns in rural and urban regions.

Coḷas: Coḷas not only built gorgeous temples and fine idols but also developed a wonderful system of government and administration. While it was a monarchy, like most other kingdoms of that age, there was a significant endeavour to decentralize and offer self-government at the local level. The empire was divided into provinces called *maṇḍala*s, and each of those *maṇḍala*s was further divided into *koṭṭam*s, which again had districts called *nāḍu*s that had *tehsīl*s, usually a group of villages. While Tanjore and Gaṅgaikoṇḍacoḷapuram were the main capitals, there also existed regional capitals at Kāñcī and Madurai, where courts were occasionally held. Their major achievement though was the local self-government during their times, where villages had their own self-governance. The village units had the power to administer justice at the local level, and for most crimes, fines were imposed, which went to the state treasury. The death penalty was given only for crimes that amounted to treason. Through the Panchayati Raj System, Coḷas assured the representation of weaker sections in local governments and the decision-making process.

Vijayanagara Dynasty: Land was held not only by the crown and individuals but by temples also. Some prominent temples became landowners and the state-appointed officers to gather and supervise proper spending of the money collected from Devadana villages. During this period, the temples became important centres of economic and welfare activity. The travelogues of contemporary foreign travellers testify that local and long distance trade flourished under the Vijayanagara regime. The state provided reasonably good roads and facilities for travellers between towns. For short distance transport, carts were in vogue. Large number of temples came into reality during the Vijayanagara rule. It is said that the temple acted as an integrative factor and a central place for voluntary operations.

Professional Social Work Perspective

Helping the community and society is a way of life in India. Agriculture accounts for 90 per cent of people's occupations. When comparing India to other nations, the concept of agriculture in India is different. It is not for profit but rather as a part of culture, and farmers indirectly provide services to society and people experiencing poverty. Families, temples, and *maṭhas* serve as hubs for charity operations. During festivals, ceremonies, and other occasions, families participate in many types of volunteer activities like food, clothing, and *dāna* distribution. Temples and *maṭhas* are service centres that are registered under the Trust Act and have trustees, which are professional bodies that carry out various voluntary operations professionally and transparently. Most dynasties have an approach to the poor. From Candragupta Maurya to Śrīkṛṣnadevarāya, all empires had distinct ministries and welfare bureaus to carry out volunteer operations. Coḷas established the Panchayati Raj System, held elections, and included all groups in decision-making process. King Aśoka has initiated many assistance projects for the underprivileged. Kings like Harṣavardhana, Kaniṣka, and Bimbisāra built temples and Baudhārāms which served as hubs for charity services and education. All dynasties established professional bodies to assist the people.

Conclusion

Ancient India had a rich tradition of philanthropy and altruism deeply rooted in its religious and cultural practices. The concept of *dāna* (charity) played a significant role in Hinduism, Buddhism, and Jainism, where individuals were encouraged to give to people in need as a moral duty. In recent years, two essential fronts have emerged in Indian social work: mental health and human rights. The history of social work in India is a testament to the power of compassion and altruism in transforming lives and societies. From ancient philanthropy to modern-day professional interventions, social work plays a vital role in addressing India's complex social challenges.

The professional social work education in India since its inception in 1936 has remained Eurocentric, which looks down upon the Indic knowledge systems in every field. As a result, most of the universities in India have adopted the

Western model of social work education. Western social work theories and ideologies were introduced in India, assuming their universality without examining their relevance or adequacy of addressing the social problems in the Indian context. The cultural, economic and political differences of our contexts were ignored. There have been initiatives to replace indigenous wisdom with imported Western stuff without properly examining their appropriateness, application, and feasibility in the Indian setting (Dash, 2020). From the Vedas to the present day, individuals have extended their support to society as part of their daily duties. Unlike other countries, in India, social institutions play a significant role in service activities, but this has never been discussed or popularized. Family and caste provide their help at all times across society. The fact that temple and *maṭha*s are in the forefront of assisting people is not explained in any textbooks. It's a necessity of the hour for people to return to their origins, and academicians, particularly in social work, must reform the curriculum and include the Indian model of the welfare system in all UG and PG courses.

REFERENCES

"Aśoka established a Welfare State based on the Idea of Paternalistic State". Defines the terms welfare state, paternalistic state and describes in detail the welfare measures taken by Aśoka. (2022, July 4). BYJU'S Online Learning Programmes For K3, K10, K12, NEET, JEE, UPSC & Bank Exams; BYJU'S. https://byjus.com/question-answer/ashokas-established-a-welfare-state-and-based-on-the-idea-of-paternalsitic-state-define-the/.

Choudhary, A.S. (2021). "Welfare State in Kauṭilya's Arthashastra: An Analytical Study". *Maharshi Dayanand University Research Journal ARTS.*

Dash, B.M. (2018). "Bhāratīyakaran of Social Work: Understanding the Meaning and Concept". *New Delhi Times*, India's Only International Newspaper, Empowering Global Vision, Empathizing with India. (7 December). New Delhi Times. https://www.newdelhitimes.com/bhāratīyakaran-of-social-work-understanding-the-meaning-and-concept/

Dash, B.M. (2020). "Movement towards Indianization of Social Work Education". In *The Palgrave Handbook of Global Social Work Education*. Palgrave, New York, pp. 393-405.

Datta, S.R. (2019, December 5). *Bimbisara: World History Encyclopedia*. World History Encyclopedia;https://www.worldhistory.org#organization.https://www.worldhistory.org/Bimbisara/.

Glory of Vijayanagara empire, their contribution to art, literature and culture, Velpu.com. (n.d.). Velpu. Retrieved on 16 June 2024, from https://velpu.com/blog/glory-of-vijayanagara-empire,-their-contribution-to-art,-literature-and-culture/NzI=

History of Social Work in India 2023—Institute of Social Work & Research. (2023, August 7). Institute of Social Works & Research. https://iswr.in/history-of-social-work-inindia/#:~:text=Ancient%20India%20had%20a%20rich,needy%20as%20a%20moral%20duty.

Rana, V. (2014, July 31). *Vijayanagara-Bahmani Kingdoms: Polity, Law and Other Details*. History Discussion—Discuss Anything about History. https://www.historydiscussion.net/history-of-india/vijayanagara-bahmani-kingdoms-polity-law-and-other-details/2026

Simon, R. (2021, February). "History of Social Work Education in India: Key To Glorious Future". *Aviskaar*: A Xaverian Journal of Research.

Social Work Education : Social Welfare Activities during the Ancient Period in Indian Subcontinent (n.d.). Social Work Education. Retrieved on 27 March 2024, from https://swpust2015.blogspot.com/2016/07/social-welfare-activities-during.html

Social Work in Team (2023, June 17). *Development of the Social Work Profession in India*. SocialWorkin; Blogger. https://www.socialworkin.com/2023/06/development-of-social-work-profession.html

The Coḷas: Maritime activities in Sourth-east Asian countries. Coḷa administration, art & architecture. CGPCS Exam Preparation. (2016, November 9). CGPCS Exam Preparation; https://www.facebook.com/ChhattisgarhPCSNotes1796262557296021/. https://chhattisgarh.pcsnotes.com/prelims-notes/economy/the-cholas-maritime-activities-in-sourth-east-asian-counturies-chola-administration-art-architecture/

SECTION TWO
Indian Social Work Practice

7

Humanistic Approach in Indian Social Work Practice

Rama Srivastava

Introduction

The obliteration of humanity in society has led to colossal deterioration in the sociocultural and economic domains. To deal with this obstruction, we must pursue Pt. Deen Dayal Upadhyaya's view of Integral Humanism. Before attaining a comprehensive picture of essential humanitarianism, we need to know the basics of humanism. Even though the word humanitarianism registered the sight as an artefact of the Western renaissance, the construct endured in Indian culture much earlier to that. While Westerners define humanism according to their culture, in India, the scope and essence of the concept is different. The Indian viewpoint on humanitarianism is based on the notion of *vasudhaiva kuṭumbakam*, indicating "the world is one family", highlighting the relation of all beings and the necessity for kindness and respect concerning all life forms indicating co-existence. Indian humanism also points out the theory of *dharma*, which mentions to the moral way of living and performing one's obligations towards humanity and the surroundings. It fosters people to pursue learning, promotes responsiveness and kindness, and follows non-violence in every aspect of life. Additionally, Indian humanism emphasizes *sevā*, or noble service to others, utilizing one's abilities and resources to facilitate individuals in hardship and uphold the well-being of humanity. Furthermore, Indian humanitarianism agrees that the vital purpose of human existence is not just material accomplishments or individual contentment, but rather the fulfilment of sacred illumination and freedom from the sequence of birth and demise. Indian humanitarianism approaches a comprehensive assessment of social well-being and persuades people to dwell in congruence with themselves, others, and their environment.

Humanitarianism in India

Humanitarianism is a viewpoint or a way of reasoning about the world. It is a set of moral code or concepts regarding in what way people should live and behave. People who hold this set of moral belief are regarded as humanists. The view of humanism examines predominantly to an approach of concept, which aims at the self-sufficiency of the individual. Ever since the Vedic period, the Indian culture has been characterized by the simple yet very important values like safeguarding the self-respect of people and creating conducive environment for them to progress towards their betterment.

Integral humanism, a model explained by Pandit Deen Dayal Upadhyaya, emphasizes the importance of individuals as the essential elements of a country. Like cells in a human body form organ, people unite to form unique shared systems. The nation consists of numerous structures such as family, religion, educational institutions, workplaces, court, and government that function based on the state's self-awareness or persistent influence recognized as *dharma*. The self-consciousness created by *dharma*, is what endures India as a country. The collective self-consciousness acts as the self-consciousness of the universe, which embodies the vision of oneness of humanity known as Integral Humanism. Deen Dayal Upadhyaya gave this thought as a novel vision of development for India, accentuating culture and spirituality, the linkage of persons and culture, and the necessity for a entrusted and independent country encouraging societal and pecuniary righteousness. This model of humanitarianism tempted to those in India who were disheartened with the Western notions of mechanization and transformation ruling the progress representations at the time, offering an exceptional way of thinking that underlined the relevance of human well-being and social justice.

Integral Humanism and Radical Humanism

In India, Radical Humanism was a honest and common drive that surfaced in the mid-twentieth century in India. It was started by M.N. Roy, a pronounced Indian political theorist and activist. The prime philosophy of this Activist Humanism is the authority of the individual over all institutions, involving the state, religion, and society. It emphasizes triggers, moral code, and autonomy, and removes faith and false notion. Radical humanism supports for the formation of a secular and symbolic humanity based on the concepts of equality, justice, and humanitarianism. But Radical Humanism did not gain as much recognition as Integral Humanism in India. One explanation for this could be that Activist Humanism was contemplated as too strong and stirred only on distinctiveness, not considering the considerable shared and cultural perspective. Whereas Integral Humanism points out the connection of the individual and culture and the importance of social and spiritual values along with definite independence.

The Beginning of Humanism in India

The evolution of humanism in India dates to the time of Vedas and Upaniṣads since 200 BC *sarve bhavantu sukhinaḥ sarve santu nirāmayaḥ*. The *śloka* signifying the Welfare of all as its primary concern. Further, the humanitarian philosophy can be traced back to 563-483 BC, the era of Gautama Buddha. "Man, the measure" is the earliest declaration of humanistic outlook. Humanists confirm that man is the maker of his own destiny and social change. Humanists enjoy the open-endedness of a quest and the freedom of discovery. The human progress depended on progress in the direction of liberty and truth, with change human mind.

The latter half of the nineteenth century authenticated Hindu Resurgence initiated by Brahma Samaj of Raja Ramamohun Roy and Arya Samaj of Dayananda Saraswati, finally flourishing into Vedāntic Hinduism of Vivekananda. Vedāntic Hinduism, highlights the significance of assistance to the weak and the needy as its applied viewpoint. That society is the greatest where the highest truths become practical. Humanism has undergone significant development assuming variety of forms in the West and in the East. Western humanism is atheistic in content because Christianity conceives of God as the Creator, unlike Vedāntic Humanism which is not atheistic.

Gandhian Humanism

In the ocean of humanity, a human is a rarity, Gora writes of Gandhi: "In spirit he was not a Hindu, he was fundamentally a Human". Gandhi's great influence on humanism depends on in imagining a religion that focuses nearly surrounding man and his life. His humanism is integral, discussing all the aspects of human life and has rationalist attitudes which differ from Romantic Humanism as well as Radical Humanism and yet synthesizes the two. He believed religion, should permeate all our actions, it cannot be practised in isolation from life's other activities and fellow beings. The counterpart for religion is *dharma* in Sanskrit which means moral commitment and implies individual's honesty as well as social cohesion.

Resurgence of human-centred pursued to unite the mankind in common pursuit of rightfulness and formation of a ethical order in the society. Integrity for him was not a substance of apparent compliance but of deep realization, of deep faith achieved by reasonable acts. The right thought must result into right action. Gandhi's greatness lies in translating one's noblest thoughts into action which is the highest achievement of man. Einstein said that the challenge of getting peace to the world on global basis will be resolved only by using Gandhi's approach on a huge magnitude. Gandhi firmly believed that non-violence must be lived in day-to-day life.

Manavendra Nath Roy another humanist in India, his original name was Narendra Bhattacharya, well known as M.N. Roy in his book *New Humanism*, which suggested a systematic, humanist philosophy. He drew morality to its natural roots and indicated that human advancement depended on improvement concerning freedom and truthfulness. Roy had envisaged a scientific, rational, independent, egalitarian, and humanist Indian society. But for the few liberated thinkers, the nation was not open to his diverse approach to life. Technology and its affected advances were to influence the lives of the people. Roy was much fast of his paces and denied negotiating with technically unreasonable or morally unreliable views of applied politics. We live in an age where creation is splendid, but dispersal is incomplete, where knowledge has seized irrationality but religion is transmitting myths and irrational belief, where technology has brought human race closer, but separatism is prompting conflicts and violence. Philosophers and thinkers have influenced to the improvement of human wisdom; science and technology have bestowed resources of relief and ease to human survival, but deceptions and dishonesties have tried to ruin genuine human development in all areas of the world's existing human race. The quest of non-aggressive and non-violent tactics for determining the world's highest dreadful clashes of eras which frequently result in massacre, hostilities, and dictatorship, is vital for human existence and advancement.

The voyage from Indian humanism to Integral Humanism echoes an expanding understanding of the necessity for a more universal and assessed attempt to progress that reflects people's social and spiritual significances. Integral Humanism embodies a distinctive mix of conventional Indian humanist values with progressive dogmatic and economic reasoning, and it maintains to impact Indian thought and practice today. However, while examining the practice methodology, situation, and theoretical perspectives of implied postulation that social work is humanistically oriented reveals several inconsistencies, glitches, and probable possibilities. There are many definitions of humanism but for a social worker it is a society in which each individual human being is regarded as a human with essential worth and dignity society where everyone has evenly balanced opportunities to extend to his/her highest human capability.

In general, the focus of social work practice is largely on individual and family thereby ignoring the impact of its consequences of a very apparent yet vital attribute of our society, i.e., its socio-economic disposition. This practising profession is often portrayed as unpolitical. It is disappointing to admit that all social work practice is politically influenced and there exists some pertinent paradoxes among social work and humanism. All social work practice occurs within social institutions. These institutions, whether publicly financed or privately financed through united ways, are designed to provide services so that the existing social arrangements and social order may be maintained, (Piven and Cloward, 1971; Goroff 1973; Mandell, 1973).

The opinion that social work system is driven by political activity and thus holds the promises. Social workers who execute their services contained by these established structures are presenting a political act, whether that act is appeared at trying to transform the influential measures or to retain and support them (Galper, 1975). As far as our society and its institutions are based on guarantees, it will put the social work practitioner in an enigmatic situation questioning their professional stance of humanism in non-humanistic social institutions.

Numerous linkages instituted connecting the social worker and the individual taking assistance within this major construct exhibit, "the vocabulary of motives". In these settings, the social expectancies from the client and practitioner are inherent to the culture. Commonly there is a philosophy of interventionism and non-exchange permeating the cultures of the bureaucratic structured social service institutions. The imbalance in power and authority exhibited in the upright relationships (Freire, 1973) can be theorized as a political relationship parading as a professional relationship. In a bureaucratic setting social worker act like a soft cop and an agent of social control thereby reinforcing the conformism and *status quo*. This is in contradiction to the basic role of social worker to contribute towards the just society adhering to the non-oppressive inherent nature of the profession.

Another relationship explained by Friere was a horizontal relationship. In this relationship there is a commitment to equality, to the abolition of privileges, and to non-elitist forms of leadership by exercising special qualifications.

Challenges of Humanistic Approach to Social Work

Some of the theoretical understanding that social workers apply exhibits some inconsistencies for the humanist social worker. Social workers have used various psychological frames to understand the human situation. Seldom, have the political consequences of the diverse psychological theories been investigated (Sternberg, 1977). The effect of these framework is to place the origin of the problem in the individual, overlooking how the social arrangement is affecting the person. It is true that the discomfort ensuing from the problem the individual is undergoing lies inside the individual, conversely the source is commonly in the social arrangement. The consequence is to focus on the individual rather than on the socio-economic arrangements.

There are several psychological and sociological assumptions which are prefaced on the "individual deficit model". To the point that social workers apply these frames as a foundation for understanding the human circumstances, they often impose their views upon those seeking their assistance. The irony here for the social worker who is trying to be a humanist is that the individual becomes an "object to be examined and diagnosed" for his/her flaws rather than an individual to be understood.

As social work developed gradually more "professional" with appropriate professional concerns, graduate schools, there has been an associated rise in perplexity. An eminent attribute of aiming to place assertion to field of practice as one's confined sphere, i.e., become professional, is to develop an expertise. The "expertise" in social work as in most "professions" is such as to require a considerable degree of bafflement. Disorientation is a major constituent of dehumanization (Lee, 1976). Again, to legitimate the assertion of social workers that we are a profession we have constructed a contradiction for the humanistic social worker. We have muddled ourselves.

Many interpreters have long recognized the relationship of language, thought and actions. The fact that words denote class gaps, power associations and differential access to resources have not been appropriately highlighted in many of the helping occupations including social work. Since the most common stance is to examine social work as a compassionate serving occupation, the use of semantic is not essentially seen as defining political realities, but significantly the dynamics of the "helping process" (Edelman, 1974). Social workers seldom try to enforce their will on clients; it is the client that usually resist help. Social workers do not try to correct people, rather only set limits for people. Social workers do not refuse people what clients want; they do not reinforce "demanding behaviour". When social workers use other semantic to alter realism and hence make additional enigmas for the humanist social worker. Perhaps one of the more serious ironies for the humanistic social worker is the use of social science theories to insist on drawing meaning of the behaviour of people instead of finding out how people are explaining their ecosphere and what they are trying to accomplish. The need to comprehend the realistic world of the performer to understand the actor was stressed by Blumer (1969) and others. Yet, in the likelihood of winning validity in the intellectual world, social work has become a scientistic profession instead of a scientific one. The application of theories as norms for deciding the rationality or familiarity of human conduct look like a turnaround of what should be. There is the postulation that if the individual's behaviour does not match with the theoretical construct, then there is something wrong with the person and not the theory.

It is likely to continue to validate the contradictions a humanistic social worker faces because of how social work services is delivered, how social workers apply theories, the conventional conceptual inferences of many of the psychological and sociological concepts (Zettlin, 1968) borrowed from these disciplines and the failure to recognize social work activities as radical actions.

The challenges encountered by the humanistic social worker can often be trailed to the characteristics and construct of the social service organizations. Most organizations are hierarchically structured, i.e., have vertical patterns of dealings. The organizational restraints exercised over the social worker create circumstances which results in contradiction between "professional sovereignty" and organizational controls. Mostly, the organizational restraints start from the necessity of the organization to sustain itself instead than granting assistance to those who need it.

The dilemma between the demands of the people for service and the society to preserve itself may place the social worker in the dilemma. Generally, these disagreements are between factions with uneven authority. The social worker who undertakes to hold a unbiassed view is essentially covering the more influential organization for neutrality in conflicting situations.

When the social worker teams with the someone looking for help, he/she is often perceived by others as a mischief-maker; not team player, etc., since he/she is against the others.

Problems may arise for the humanistically oriented social worker because of being involved with graduate social work education. There have been studies which tried to examine the impact of graduate education for social work on students' values. Admittedly, there is little correlation between the answers people give on paper and tests and their actions in the actual situations. Nevertheless, there is sufficient data to raise questions whether social work education supports humanistic orientations or whether it educates bureaucrats.

Another hindrance is observed in the relativistic views of humanism *vis-a-vis* an oppressive situation. When one assumes that contrasted to the existing unjust circumstances what "I do is better and consequently humanistic" without genuinely finding that. Determining aspirations for others is non humanistic. Judging people on their behaviour as maladaptive is not right may be the behaviour is just non-conforming or challenging the authority, and hence labelled as maladaptive. May be at times just creating more tolerable situations for people in distress is humanistic in the given time and context.

The assurance for a human-centred social work is in the perception that social work practice is influenced by the external environment. In this framework one can no longer exhibit as an apolitical or neutral social worker. It is not indicating to the point that our action as social workers either retain the existing social arrangements and unbalanced allocation of resources and thus resulting inadequate life risked for people or seek out to help prevent these arrangements. The promise for a humanistic social work practice lies in the acknowledgement by social workers that we are either tyrants or are being repressed. It is also essential to accept that we can be oppressed while hounding others. This implies a shift in awareness to develop more critical of the socio-economic basis of our society and the cultural belief system (Gil, 1977).

The potential for a humanistic social work practice lies in the recognition that all social theories make convinced assumptions about the nature of the human being, the nature of the social sphere and the relationship between the individual and the social sphere (Goroff, 1973). There are political concerns which result from these theories that are important for social workers to analyse with critical understanding.

The aptitude for a humanistic social work practice lies in the inclination of social workers to give up arrogance which permits us to validate our planning or setting goals for clients and to identify that we are like the people, looking for self-actualization which can only be attained in a society that is classless supportive and unoppressed. Only in such a society can all human beings achieve self-actualization.

The vow for a humanistic social work practice will be succeeded as we engage in the practice of making a just and humane social directive. The social order that we are presently sharing is not devised to meet the conditions. Humanists validate that man is the creator of his own fate. Gandhiji also gave great significance to freedom. His entire life was spent for the countryman and national freedom. However, for him free will was "rational self". Once you condition yourself with "rational self" you are free to move in those limits.

The humanist style maybe more demanding for university students to comprehend as it is more advanced since it breaks several biases that are well embedded in common sense. To pursue this approach, one must surrender the desire of homogenizing existence. Students and teachers seeking for fix guidelines will not like this methodology much. It is a more contextual view, where human beings are valued more over words. In communication, it is not significant which means we use, but the effect we get. The objective of the semantic theory is to regulate the linguistic procedure into persistent forms; whereas the humanistic approach says that you can not regulate the language. The semantic approach is technical; the humanistic approach is aesthetic.

There is no standalone realism in the "structure". Structures are not universal. Two people happen stances, they converse and, by their connecting and talking, they create their peculiar construct. The structure was not there earlier than the development of communication, but it is formed using communication. So, every group rebuilds its peculiar arrangement, based on collective standards, but adjusted in order to create their own uniqueness.

Humanism is not a founded school of philosophy but is a recognized rational viewpoint. It accentuated the worth and dignity of fellow by discarding other materialism and transcendental philosophy. It is this sophisticated, man-centred earthly rational viewpoint. It argues that the individual is self-contained and can understand the sphere occurrences and operates in a specified shared order. It is an attitude towards and an approach to man's worldly life and values. It is characterized by curiosity in individual, concern for fellow beings. Humanism as the rational approach observes the analysis of human experience as the prime.

REFERENCES

Bauman, Richerdn (1997). *Human Rights in Anc Rome*. Routledge Classical Monographs.

Blau, Peter and Scott, Richard W. (1962). *Organizations*. San Francisco, California, Chandler Publishing Company.

Blumer, Herbert (1969). *Symbolic Interactionism Perspective and Method.* Englewood Cliffs, New Jersey, Prentice-Hall, Inc.

Das, Ratan (2002). *Gandhi in 21st Century*. Sarup & Sons, New Delhi 2002.

Davis, Tony (1997). *Humanism the New Critical Idiom*. Drakakis, John, Series Editor, University of Stirling, UK. Routledge, ISSBN 0-415-11052.

Easton, Loyd and Guddlt, Kurt H. (1967). *Writings of the Young Marx on Philosophy and Society*. Garden City, New York, Doubleday and Company Inc.

Edelman, Murray (1974). "The Political Language of the Helping Professions". *Politics and Society*.

Freire, Paulo (1973). *Education for Critical Consciousness*. New York, Seabury Press.

Galper, Jeffry (1975). *The Politics of Social Service*. Englewood Cliffs, New Jersey, Prentice-Hall, Inc.

Gandhi, M.K. (1949). *Non-violence in Peace and War*. Vol. II. Ahmedabad. Navajivan Publishng House.

Gandhi, M.K. (1959). *Truth is God*. Ahmedabad, Navajivan Publishing House.

Gil, David G. (1977). "Overcoming Cultural Impediments to Human Survival". *Humanity and Society*, *1*(1), Summer.

Gil, David G. (1976). "Resolving Issues of Social Provision". In *The Challenge of Social Equality*. Cambridge, Mass, Schenkman Publishing Company, Inc.

Goodman, Lenn Evan (2003). *Islamic Humanism*, Oxford University Press, ISBN 0-19-513580.

Gora (1951). *An Atheist With Gandhi*. Navajivan Publishing House, Ahmedabad.

Goroff, Norman N. (1973). "Ideology, Sociological Theory and Public Policy". *Journal of Sociology and Social Welfare*, *1*(1).

Goroff, Norman N. (1974). "Social Welfare As Coercive Social Control". *Journal of Sociology and Social Welfare*, *2*(1).

Johnson, Paul (2000). *The Renaissance*, New York: the Modern Library.

Jones, W.M. Morris (December 1959). *The Exploitation of Indian Political Life*. Pacific Affairs.

Kristeller, Paul Oskar (1961). *Renaissance: The Classic, Scholastic, and Humanist Strains*. New York, Harper and Row.

Kristeller, Paul Oskar (1979). *Renaissance Thought and its Sources*. Colombia University Press, ISBN 0-231-04513-1.

Lee, Alfred McClung (January 1976). "Humanism As Demystification". *Journal of Sociology and Social Welfare*, *3*(3).

Mandell, Betty Reid (1975). *Welfare in Amerika*. Englewood Cliffs, New Jersey, Prentice-Hall, Inc.

Piven, Frances and Cloward, Richard (1971). *Regulating the Poor*. New York: Random House.

Rao, K. Narayana (2017). "Indian Thought of Humanism Answer for Cheerful Human Life". *Global Journal for Research Analysis* (*GJRA*), *6*(9), Special Issue (September), ISSN No. 2277-8160.

Roy, M.N. (1981). *New Humanism: A Manifesto*. Delhi: Ajanta Publication.

Seeman, Melvin (1959). "On the Meaning of Alienation". *American Sociological Review*, Vol. 24, December.

Steinberg, David Joel (1977). *Radical Sociology: A Critical Introduction to American Behavioural Science*. Hicksville, New York, Exposition Press.

Zeff, Shirley B. (June 1977). "A Humanistic Approach to Helping Underachieving Students". *Social Casework*, *58*(6).

Zeitlin, Irving (1968). *Ideology and the Development of Sociological Theory*. Englewood Cliffs, New Jersey, Prentice-Hall, Inc.

8

The Role of Street Theatre in Social Work Practice

R. Belinda

Introduction

One of the main goals of the social work profession is to empower and liberate people while also fostering social development, social cohesion, and social transformation. The initial stage in introducing the community/target group/public to new services, programmes, facilities, or activities is often through awareness campaigns. Its goal is to increase familiarity with a desired behaviour, for example, encouraging vaccination or enhancing public health. To positively influence a community's attitudes, behaviours, and beliefs toward the accomplishment of a certain purpose or objective, awareness-raising is thus intended to educate that community (Sayers, 2006).

Social Work

Social work is defined as "a practice-based profession and an academic discipline that promotes social change and development, social cohesion and empowerment and liberation of people" by the International Federation of Social Workers (IFSW) and the International Association of Schools of Social Work (IASSW). Social work is based on the fundamental values of social justice, human rights, group responsibility, and respect for diversity. Social work involves people and structures to address life difficulties and increase well-being, and is underpinned by theories of social work, social sciences, humanities, and indigenous knowledge (www.ifsw.org, 2014).

Social workers have the power to change people's lives individually and have a positive knock-on effect on the community, inspiring and motivating future generations. Social workers operate as advocates to bring attention to the needs of their clients and connect them to resources and programmes that provide solutions to help them deal with life's obstacles (Mimi Abramovitz, 1998).

A thorough grasp of human behaviour and the systematic planning of actions to implement the intended change in people's behaviour are prerequisites for implementing attitude and behaviour modifications, which are very intricate and difficult processes. To do this, it is necessary to support individuals as they progress through several phases to arrive at a placc where they can adapt and sustain new behaviours. Social workers have contributed to this process for many years by addressing important challenges. Less often recognized, awareness campaigning can be thought of as a widely coordinated attempt to alter norms, regulations, or behaviours.

Being an ever-evolving profession, social work necessitates adapting fresh, cutting-edge methods, tools and approaches to help people with problems impeding their current and emerging social functioning. A discipline like social work, demands constant enhancement to assist individuals, groups, and communities from a variety of backgrounds.

Folk Media

Every society's lifeblood is communication, which is the

transfer of information from one person to another through various mediums. Every human community has evolved its own native and customary communication channels and forms that define its existence, structure, etc. As a result, there is a kind of cultural variation in indigenous and traditional communication styles and channels.

These traditional communication channels and modalities are recognized, evaluated, and comprehended within the framework of the specific culture and its set of values. Communication begins when the sender or source makes symbolic noises anchored in the environment and relating to past experiences. We claim that communication is possible if the audience or receiver has had comparable experiences that are anchored in the environment and have been conditioned to identify the provided sounds with those experiences and attach a common meaning. If the intended reaction happens, the message is successful.

Communities, particularly rural communities, policymakers, planners, and administrators who wish to implement functional economic and social changes must first identify these community communication modes and channels and make use of them to give the public as much information as possible about these changes. Because it is practical, interpersonal, and grounded in context, traditional performing arts can convey messages of transformation, advancement, and expansion. Traditional folk forms have been used in programmes over electronic media in addition to these live programmes with in-person interactions.

According to Balwant Gargi (1991),

> "Folk media portrays people in their natural environment, with all their paradoxes and diverse activities. It provides a peek of their speaking, dancing, music, attire, and knowledge. It contains chivalric tales, medieval romances, mythological heroes, societal mores, beliefs, and legends. To fully grasp India's vibrant diversity and cohesion, it

> is imperative to witness folk theatre in its authentic environments."

The accessibility and affordability of folk media contribute to their growing popularity in rural areas. Their exceptional capacity for spontaneity, participation, and involvement sets them apart in the media for any significant and impactful change. It absorbs customs, beliefs, and social structures. Although it has strong religious and ceremonial elements, it can also portray secular issues, social life, and universal principles.

The traditional folk media in India has been utilized to speak to the masses and has shown to be quite successful and powerful in conveying the most recent developments in the nation, igniting demonstrations, and raising public awareness. The norms and traditions of traditional folk performing arts have a lasting effect on society and culture. Even though folk media, folk performing arts, traditions, and cultural heritage have all been greatly impacted by globalization, economic liberalization, and contemporary forces of change, folk media continues to play a vital role in promoting social integrity, cultural diversity, and nation-building (Gargi Balwant, 1966).

Street Theatre

Indian folk theatre is a hybrid art form that combines music, dance, and theatre and aims to satisfy its viewers' aesthetic, emotional, and intellectual demands. It is a whole emotional experience that goes beyond simple amusement and fosters a condition of receptivity where messages are most effectively conveyed. Folk theatre has served as a social reform, protest, and awareness vehicle. It is well recognized that regional rural drama performances can effectively and persuasively effect change by serving as a link between various rural communities and between rural and urban locations.

Socially conscious art is a valuable tool for encouraging marginalized communities to communicate their struggles

(Johnson, 1990), and it can be used with all age groups—from young children to the elderly. Both adults and children can benefit from it (Talerico, 1986).

Street theatre is a style of theatrical presentation and performance that happens in unpaid public areas for the general population. It serves as a channel of communication for disseminating political and social messages and educating the general public about urgent social issues. Amateur street theatre productions have become increasingly popular worldwide in public health projects, education campaigns, and community organizing. Street plays have covered a wide range of topics over the years, including themes of national consciousness, capitalism, labour and peasant movements, the environment, community activism, sexual harassment of women, domestic violence, issues pertaining to children's rights, child abuse, HIV/AIDS, corruption, etc. (Deshmukh Vishal & Jadhav Aaishwarya, 2021).

Street theatre (plays), are a crucial component of social work. It's a creative method used on public and communal platforms that works well to illustrate different social messages and societal problems. Five to ten people congregate in a bustling complex or market area, and they utilize attention-grabbing phrases to draw people in. After that, a prepared performance that illustrates a social message is executed. It's a laborious process that necessitates much practice and dialogue preparation (Vidushi Srivastava & Sayantani Guin, 2021).

According to Dr Harish Kumar, UNESCO suggested integrating folk theatre and mass media in family planning communication programmes. This was the first significant international recognition of the traditional media in developing countries' communication and development strategies. This sparked interest, and efforts to emphasize folk media as powerful platforms for developmental messaging led to several international seminars and workshops (Kumar Harish, 2006).

Augusto Boal, a Brazilian dramatist, theatre director, and activist, promoted theatre-based pedagogy, social work, and therapeutic approaches to support the disadvantaged and empower them in cooperative yet innovative problem-solving techniques through his book *Theatre of the Oppressed* (Halonen, 2018). According to the *Theatre of the Oppressed*, there are different theatre forms:

1. Image theatre is a technique where participants portray themselves as statues that represent oppression in some way. Individuals engage in this process through analysis, personality alignment with various characters, critical evaluation, and creative response.
2. Forum theatre as community-based theatre. Usually, community people who are dealing with issues like marginalization and injustice carry it out. In this version, the entire play is performed several times, and the audience is asked to identify and freeze the specific instances in which they see oppression.
3. Invisible theatre is performed in public spaces to maximize audience participation and provocation.
4. Readers' theatre is one in which the performer reads passages from poetry and short stories to portray repressive realities in that particular community.

Street theatres or *nukkaḍa nāṭaka*, commonly known in Hindi, are a crucial component of social work. It is an artistic approach used in communal and public forums. It helps illustrate a range of social themes and circumstances. Five to ten people gather in a bustling complex or market area, and they utilize attractive slogans to draw others in. After that, a rehearsed performance that illustrates a social message is executed. It's a laborious process that needs a lot of practice and dialogue preparation.

In the 1990s, street theatre was employed by non-governmental organizations (NGOs) to raise awareness of family planning, AIDS, and the environment. Although didactic in intent, the majority of this work has a mediocre theatrical quality. NGO theatre for development is typically funded by donor agencies, many of which are foreign, in contrast to leftist street groups, who ask for voluntary contributions from the public to pay costs after their performances.

The street theatre should know its community, identify the issues of concern, intertwine communal expression with entertainment, invite audience participation and call for action (Banerjee, 2013). One of the key characteristics of street theatre is the performers' deliberate and purposeful use of their bodies (turning and twisting, shivering, facial emotions, voice texture, raising and lowering, bodily motions, haircut, clothing, etc.) to elicit a response from the audience and to portray particular play themes and moods. The audience's participation in the performance, its interactive aspect, and the opportunity for improvisation in the performative script through discussions are other important aspects of street theatre. The artists involve the audience in a conversation by letting them speak up in a variety of ways. This is accomplished by having the performers first introduce sociocultural political issues (using a problem-posing technique) and arouse the audience's emotions through various reflective performance tools. The line between performers and viewers is blurred when the audience is also encouraged to act, as mere critical thought is insufficient to effect change. Through this exercise, the actors co-create the play to raise public awareness of social concerns and promote conscientization (Datoo & Chagani, 2011).

When people engage in street theatre, they are immersed in a performance that portrays social issues in context and projects lived experiences; individuals are able to visualize a scene from their lives being acted out in a new body but with a comparable spirit. Through this process, they revisit a past experience, leading to catharsis. After achieving catharsis, onlookers are freed from social and personal anxieties. This psychological respite enables people to examine societal issues from perspectives or terrains they have never ventured into before (Datoo & Chagani, 2011).

Through stage plays, the Prosperity Project in Bangladesh employs this captivating technique to raise awareness of numerous social, health, rights, and climate change issues. The street plays' subjects are chosen with the current issues in the community in mind. These topics relate to several project components, including gender parity, disaster management, nutrition, resilient livelihoods, and service accessibility. Street plays also tackle other societal topics, such as the dangers of underage marriage, the need for dowries, and the avoidance of drug addiction. The 20-25 minute performances are held in public spaces to guarantee maximum exposure. In addition to guaranteeing community ownership, community engagements provide issue-based plays a local voice. Every performance is followed by an interesting audience conversation that, by sharing and mutual learning, helps to emphasize the play's theme more effectively (www.ppepp.org, 2022).

Satya Special School organized street theatres in several villages to increase awareness about disabilities, particularly those pertaining to people with intellectual disabilities, and the need to create an inclusive society for them that starts with an inclusive education system for a rural population at Puducherry. They chose this media because it is a well known, customarily accepted, and acknowledged instrument for raising awareness in rural communities. It made the message widely accessible to the public and encouraged them to learn about inclusion and disabilities. This experiment showed that it was feasible to implement an intervention promoting inclusiveness and disability awareness through street play. This project communicated the content in a way that was culturally relevant to the audience while considering the participants' sociocultural and language backgrounds. This project aimed to serve 35 villages' rural and semi-rural residents. Additionally, it touched roughly 35,000 individuals indirectly and about 11,000 people directly in the target villages. This endeavour suggests that street plays might serve as a helpful medium for disseminating knowledge and raising awareness of any additional intellectual disabilities or aspects of emotional health. When viewers were asked for their opinions on this kind of intervention (using street theatre), they responded favourably. The state should investigate this possibility, and primary health-care providers should make use of these resources as a potential tool to raise awareness in rural areas (Satya Special School, 2018).

AWAG, an NGO in Ahmedabad, fights against violence against women. To use street theatre as a tool to raise awareness of issues such as appropriate and inappropriate touching, sexual harassment in public and at work, sexism, and girls' education, AWAG has produced a street play called *Hun Puchun Chu, Kem?* (I ask, Why?) that centres on the injustices that women experience in society. Over 2,000 individuals saw the play performed in various Ahmedabad locations and educational institutions. This has created awareness among the viewers and empowered them (AWAG, 2021).

Street theatre does not only benefit the community watching it but also helps the actors performing it. In 2007, the administration of a Seville (Spain) municipal shelter for the homeless came up with the concept of hosting a theatrical workshop for the destitute. This session was designed to assist a group of fifteen shelter residents in learning social skills and dispute-resolution methods. This approach was unique because it applied complementary methods from social work and theatre methodologically to a learning and interaction process that was formed within the group. These experiences were guided by a group of homeless people who became actors through this programme, and they were part of an applied research study that employed theatre as a tool to help social work. It was called the "Theatre of Inclusion". This initiative artistically exposes the needs of this collective and creates spaces where they can regain their dignity through the use of applied theatre techniques and group social work.

This initiative demonstrated how theatre can be useful for individual and group social work. It presents the opportunity to collaborate with individuals and groups using horizontal relational and interaction patterns. This methodological approach fosters cooperative learning-based collaboration processes by fusing social work techniques with the cultural practice of theatre. Theatre enables us to confront personal and social issues more flexibly, open, and non-intrusively by demonstrating different creative dynamics (Nuria Cordero Ramos & Manuel Muñoz Bellerin, 2017).

The practical domain of social work is complemented by the creative plane created during theatrical rehearsals. One example that stands out is the employment of methods like discussion groups, which allow for analysis where each member offers an opinion about how the theatre performance materializes and about things that concern the artistic process in all its details. The destitute actors use it as a way to communicate their emotions, insecurities, loneliness, etc. In the different versions given, people re-signify contexts (personal, societal, and cultural) and the reasons and effects of each act and scenario.

People are empowered by theatre because of their capacity for creativity and invention. By creating a reality/fiction dichotomy through discursiveness and corporeality, rehearsing imagined dramatic circumstances alongside everyday situations allows people who have experienced realities like oppression, prejudice, inequality, violence, etc., to reevaluate them. Ultimately, this discursiveness is reflected and representative when it is told in a theatrical play on stage. In addition to representing a group of individuals within a particular civilization, it is portrayed through the staging and performance of a collective creation. It is representative because the actors presenting the performance are people who have personally experienced the (fictitious) scenario they are portraying. Lastly, these discourses are directed in part at the society/audience in an effort to get acknowledgment and a re-evaluation based on a revised perception and sensitivity. For those who are homeless, the chance to get this acknowledgement is a turning point in their ability to identify with themselves and to become more socially and personally empowered (Nuria Cordero Ramos & Manuel Muñoz Bellerin, 2017).

The above literature review shows that street theatre is a powerful tool for practising social work. It will help in practising all the methods of social work:

(1) *casework:* clients can be taught street theatre and their performance can give a cathartic effect for them, which will aid in treatment;

(2) *group work:* it will be helpful for individuals as well as the group. As a group they can perform to help in the treatment of others, which will definitely bring the treatment of self and others;

(3) *community organization, social action, social welfare administration:* creating awareness on policies, programmes, problems, etc.;

(4) *social work research:* it will be a great tool for building trust among the respondents as the first phase, mobilization of respondents thus aiding data collection.

Thus, street theatre will be an influential instrument in social work practice.

Suggestions and Conclusion

A diverse range of artistic mediums contribute significantly to human welfare. Any performing arts paradigm enables people to express their decisions, frustrations, and feelings freely. Social workers should employ dance, theatre, drama, music, and other forms of creative expression to assist their clients in their professional practice. Through the use of the arts in communities, we can bring about the desired change for the community and the actor. It works well as a proactive method to build people up.

The use of creative arts benefits social workers and service consumers by encouraging critical thinking in the practitioners and pushing them to design activities that yield the desired outcomes. It's an approach that uses several approaches to elicit information from social workers in order to reach their goals. Through art, several art educators are utilizing social justice, community involvement, individual and collective growth, and social action themes. A lack of practice and connection between the two frequently hinders social workers' ability to contribute to art-based platforms. Different aspects of professional practice must be consistently aligned with classroom instruction and fieldwork experience. The creative arts is a discipline unto itself. Performing arts are offered as degrees and courses in several nations, including India. Psychologists and counsellors now frequently incorporate performing arts therapy into their practices. Social workers must recognize the value of creative art treatments and incorporate them into their curricula. It is a useful tool for improving student's skill sets and giving them a flexible outlook on the scenarios they encounter. These methods ought to be welcomed in social work practice to maintain its professional cadence and foster its expansion. The greatest way for social workers to achieve their goals is to expand the scope of how they assist the underprivileged. It is suggested that the social workers (educators and practitioners) start this merger to support the profession's survival and its wide variety of clients.

REFERENCES

Anonymous. (2012, December 12). *Indian Street Theater*. Retrieved on 13 September 2013, from India Net Zone: http://www.indianetzone.com/5/indian_street_theatre.htm

Banerjee, Ankita (2013). "Evaluating the role of street theatre for social communication". *Global Media Journal-Indian Edition*. Winter Issue *4*(2).

Datoo, A., Chagani, Z.M. (2011). "Street Theatre: Critical Pedagogy for Social Studies Education". *Social Studies Research and Practice*, *6*(2): 21-30.

Deshmukh, Vishal, & Jadhav, Aaishwarya (August 2021). "Street Play: A Medium of Social Communication". *Journal of Emerging Technologies and Innovative Research (JETIR), 8*(8).

Gargi, Balwant (1966). *Folk Theatre of India.* Seattle: University of Washington Press.

Halonen, D. (2018). "Theater, Drama, and Performance". In T.H. Heinonen & E. Krahn, *Expressive Arts for Social Work and Social Change*. New York: Oxford University Press.

Johnson, L. (1990). "Creative Therapies in the Treatment of Addictions: the Art of Transforming Shame". *The Arts in Psychotherapy*, *17*(4): 299-308.

Kumar, Harish (July-December 2006). "Folk Media and Rural Development Indian Media Studies". *Journal*, *1*(1).

Mimi Abramovitz (November 1998). "Social Work and Social Reform: An Arena of Struggle". *Social Work*, *43*(6): 512-26, https://doi.org/10.1093/sw/43.6.512

Nuria Cordero Ramos & Manuel Muşoz Bellerin (2017). "Social Work and Applied Theatre: Creative Experiences with a Group of Homeless People in the City of Seville". *European Journal of Social Work*, DOI: 10.1080/13691457.2017.1366298

Srivastava, Vidushi & Guin, Sayantani (2021). "Performing Arts and Social Work: Initiating Creative Amalgamations". *Global Journal of Enterprise Information System*, *13*(1): 78-86. Retrieved from https://gjeis.com/index.php/GJEIS/article/view/631

Talerico, C.J. (1986). "The Expressive Arts and Creativity as a Form of Therapeutic Experience in the Field of Mental Health". *The Journal of Creative Behaviour*, *20*: 229-47.

Wehbi, S., McCormick, K. & Angelucci, S. (2016). "Socially Engaged Art and Social Work: Reflecting on an Interdisciplinary Course Development Journey". *Journal of Progressive Human Services*, *27*(1): 49-64.

9

Disrupting Eurocentrism in Social Work Pedagogy

Apoorva Patel

Introduction

Social work education (hereafter SWE) is pivotal in shaping future practitioners who will navigate the complexities of addressing societal issues and promoting social justice. However, India is at a crossroads, facing the pressing need to decolonize its pedagogy and embrace an integrative and Indianized approach to curriculum development. This imperative arises from the acknowledgement of the pervasive influence of Eurocentrism in SWE and its implications for perpetuating colonial legacies and marginalizing Indigenous perspectives, values, and knowledge systems (Kumar, 2019; Dash, 2018 & 2022; Chougule, 2016; Jaswal & Pandya, 2015; Tamburro, 2013; Desai, 1985) often failing to adequately address the unique cultural, social, and political contexts of the country. This Eurocentrism in social work pedagogy has perpetuated a disconnect between the curriculum and the realities faced by Indian communities, particularly marginalized groups (Imran & Zabi, 2018; Jaswal & Pandya, 2015; Hall, 2005).

Statement of the Problem: Eurocentrism in Social Work Education and Its Implications

Eurocentrism in SWE manifests in various ways, including privileging Western theories, methods, and frameworks at the expense of indigenous knowledge and cultural contexts. This hegemonic approach not only reinforces power imbalances but also undermines the diversity and richness of Indian society, hindering the development of culturally responsive social work practices (Clarke *et al.*, 2012; Hall, 2003). Therefore, it is essential to recognize the implications of Eurocentrism in SWE and take proactive steps towards decolonization.

Decolonizing SWE is a pressing imperative, ensuring the profession remains relevant, responsive, and allied with the requirements and aspirations of the Indian people. Decolonization in this context refers to the critical examination and transformation of Eurocentric frameworks that have historically dominated SWE (Jaswal & Pandya, 2015; Razack, 2009). By adopting an integrative and Indianized approach to curriculum development, we can address the limitations of Eurocentrism and create a more inclusive and culturally responsive educational environment.

Purpose of the Paper: To Propose Strategies for An Integrative and Indianized Approach to Curriculum Development

This chapter advocates for an integrative and Indianized approach to social work curriculum development that draws upon the rich tapestry of indigenous knowledge systems and world views while selectively incorporating relevant Western theories and practices. By reimagining social work pedagogy through an Indianized lens, we can foster a more inclusive and culturally responsive curriculum that equips social work practitioners with the tools to address the diverse needs of Indian society.

This chapter proposes strategies for decolonizing SWE in India, emphasizing incorporating indigenous knowledge systems, community-based learning, and critical reflexivity. By disrupting colonial legacies and centring indigenous perspectives, we aim to transform social work pedagogy and practice to endorse social justice, fairness, and empowerment for all.

Decolonizing SWE: A Review of Literature and Theoretical Frameworks

In India's SWE realm, rising literature delves into the imperative of decolonizing pedagogy and addressing the impact of Eurocentric frameworks. This review explores the latest and most relevant literature, focusing on key themes such as disrupting colonial legacies, centring indigenous perspectives, and drawing insights from postcolonial theory and critical pedagogy.

Decolonizing SWE is a pressing issue, as Eurocentric frameworks have historically dominated the profession. The literature on decolonizing SWE underscores the need to move away from Eurocentric frameworks that have historically shaped the profession. Further, the impact of Eurocentric frameworks emphasizes the need for a transformative shift towards more inclusive and culturally responsive practices.

Studies have highlighted how Eurocentrism perpetuates a disconnect between the curriculum and the lived realities of Indian communities, particularly marginalized groups (Batra, 2021; DaCunha, 2016; Crampton, 2015; Desai, 1985). The literature emphasizes the importance of recognizing and addressing the implications of Eurocentrism in SWE to foster a more comprehensive and culturally responsive learning environment. The literature highlights the need to disrupt colonial legacies and centre indigenous perspectives in social work pedagogy.

Scholars cited in this chapter and others have advocated for disrupting colonial legacies and centring Indigenous perspectives in social work pedagogy. By challenging dominant Western paradigms and incorporating indigenous knowledge systems, educators can create a curriculum more aligned with the diverse needs of Indian society. This literature underscores the transformative potential of centring indigenous perspectives in SWE to promote inclusion, equity, and empowerment for all.

Postcolonial theory and critical pedagogy are vital concepts in understanding the impact of Eurocentric frameworks on SWE. Postcolonial theory emphasizes the importance of recognizing colonialism's historical and ongoing impacts on indigenous peoples and communities (Spivak, 1988). Critical pedagogy, on the other hand, emphasizes the need to challenge dominant power structures and promote social justice (Freire, 1970).

The introduction of postcolonial theories by Ambrose (2024) stresses the close relations between literature and cultural studies, highlighting the significance of H. Bhabha's *Third Space and Hybridity*, G.C. Spivak's *Subaltern Voices*, and A. Nandy's *Psychological Impact of Colonialism*. These concepts, along with P. Chatterjee's *Nationalist Thought,* and A. Ahmad's *Eurocentrism*, provide a framework for understanding and addressing the implications of Eurocentrism in SWE.

Drawing on postcolonial theory and critical pedagogy, researchers like Kumar (2019), Tamburro (2013) and Ponnuswami, and Harris (2020) have explored theoretical frameworks that can inform the decolonization of SWE in India. These concepts provide a lens to critically examine power dynamics, knowledge production, and educational practices within decolonizing pedagogy. By integrating key concepts from postcolonial theory and critical pedagogy, educators can develop strategies that challenge Eurocentric norms and promote a more inclusive and justiciable approach to SWE in India.

The literature also highlights the importance of centring Indigenous perspectives in social work pedagogy. It involves recognizing colonialism's historical and ongoing impacts.

Tamburro (2013) highlights the importance of decolonization in SWE, urging social workers to consider the effects of colonization when working with indigenous peoples. This approach calls for a postcolonial theoretical lens to critically examine and address colonization's historical and ongoing impacts on social work practice.

In the context of African Caribbean perspectives, scholars have underscored the importance of decolonizing SWE from an intersectional lens (Hackett, 2015). The continued challenge of discriminatory actions against indigenous children in child welfare underscores the urgency of disrupting colonial legacies and advocating for the inclusion of Indigenous perspectives in social work pedagogy (Hackett, 2015).

Postcolonial theory and critical pedagogy offer valuable frameworks for understanding and addressing the complexities of decolonizing SWE. These theoretical perspectives emphasize the need to historicize, politicize, and depathologize social work practices, focusing on centring indigenous and African Caribbean experiences (Moss, Rowen & Lee, 2022; Jaswal & Pandya, 2015). SWE can move towards a more equitable and inclusive approach by challenging the naturalization of representations and disrupting the binary positioning of knowledge holders (Bodhi, 2014 & 2011).

The concept of "settler colonialism" is also relevant to the discussion of decolonizing SWE. It refers to the ongoing process by which European colonizers dispossessed indigenous peoples of their land and established their own legal and social structures (Evans, 2009). It emphasizes the enduring effects of colonialism on indigenous peoples and communities in terms of also that settler-colonial legal systems are inherently violent, legitimizing the dispossession and subjugation of indigenous populations (*ibid.*). The literature highlights the need to decolonizing social work practice, and education is essential for fostering a more inclusive, equitable, and culturally competent approach to social work that respects and uplifts the voices and experiences of indigenous peoples and marginalized communities (Fortier & Hon-Sing Wong, 2018).

However, Tuck and Yang (2012), in their seminal work, "Decolonization is not a metaphor", argue for a critical understanding of this term, emphasizing that it transcends a mere metaphor for social justice initiatives or educational improvements. The authors posit decolonization as a distinctly political project with a core objective of repatriating indigenous land and life. They critique the tendency to misuse or appropriate decolonizing language within educational scholarship and advocacy. They caution against trivializing decolonization by reducing it to a catch-all phrase for various initiatives that don't confront the fundamental issues of settler colonialism.

Tuck and Yang (2012) emphasize the intertwined complexities of settler colonialism. They argue for acknowledging decolonization's unique and sovereign nature as a project that actively challenges existing power dynamics and dismantles the concept of "settler futurity"—the idea of a future dominated by settler colonial structures. This distinction between metaphor and political project is crucial. Deemphasizing the symbolic understanding of decolonization, it pushes for a more rigorous approach that necessitates addressing the historical injustices and ongoing effects of settler colonialism. This perspective is particularly relevant when considering the decolonization of social work education in India, a nation with a complex colonial history.

McNabb (2019), through a treaty-based framework, particularly relevant in *Aotearoa*, New Zealand, argues for decolonizing social work education while partnering with indigenous knowledge holders to ensure social work practice reflects indigenous communities' unique needs and contexts. This approach facilitates the co-creation of new knowledge and promotes culturally relevant practices in SWE.

The chapter "Disrupting colonization in the Social Work Classroom: Using the Obuntu/Ubuntu Framework to Decolonize the Curriculum" by Tusasiirwe (2023) explores how the Ubuntu philosophy, an African philosophy emphasizing humanity, interconnectedness, and communal responsibility, can be used as a framework for decolonizing the social work curriculum.

The literature underscores the need to decolonize SWE by centring indigenous perspectives and knowledge. It involves recognizing colonialism's historical and ongoing impacts and promoting social justice and equity. SWE can advance decolonizing practices and foster culturally relevant approaches by engaging in truth-telling and critically reflecting on existing practices.

Application of Theoretical Framework(s)

In the context of decolonizing SWE in India, drawing upon a theoretical framework(s) that challenges Eurocentric perspectives and centres indigenous knowledge systems is crucial. The frameworks are rooted in postcolonial theory, which critiques colonization's historical and ongoing impacts on indigenous peoples and cultures (Tamburro, 2013). Postcolonial theory emphasizes the need to decolonize knowledge production and dissemination, recognizing the integral theoretic colonization rooted in Western concepts and teaching (*ibid.*).

Decolonization is central to such frameworks, involving the critical examination and transformation of Eurocentric frameworks that have historically dominated SWE (Udah, 2020). Decolonization in education involves radically transforming the curriculum, pedagogy, and institutional structures to promote cultural relevance, inclusivity, and social justice.

Critical pedagogy is crucial in challenging dominant discourses and promoting transformative learning experiences in SWE (Bhabha, 1994). By encouraging critical reflection, dialogue, and action, critical pedagogy can help social work educators and students to disrupt colonial legacies and promote decolonized practices (*ibid.*).

The discussed framework(s) for decolonizing social work pedagogy draws on postcolonial theory and critical pedagogy insights. They involve a commitment to centring indigenous perspectives, challenging Eurocentrism, and promoting culturally responsive and inclusive learning environments (Tusasiirwe, 2023; McNabb, 2019; Tamburro, 2013; Asakura *et al.*, 2023; and Udah, 2020). By adopting this framework, social work educators can work towards creating a more equitable and just profession that is receptive to the issues and responsive to the aspirations of Indian communities.

The theoretical framework for decolonizing social work education can be applied to social work practice in India in the following ways:

1. **Centring Indigenous Perspectives:** By centring indigenous perspectives in social work practice, practitioners can challenge the dominance of Western theories and approaches. It incorporates indigenous knowledge systems, values, and practices into social work interventions.
2. **Promoting Culturally Responsive Practice:** Decolonizing social work requires a commitment to culturally responsive practice grounded in the lived experiences and cultural contexts of Indian communities. It involves adapting interventions to be relevant and meaningful to the communities being served.
3. **Challenging Eurocentrism:** Social work practitioners must critically examine the Eurocentric assumptions and biases embedded in social work practice. It involves deconstructing the whiteness and colonial legacies inherent in social work practice and promoting more inclusive and equitable approaches.

4. **Engaging in Critical Reflection:** Decolonizing social work practice requires ongoing critical reflection on one's biases, assumptions, and power dynamics. Practitioners must be willing to engage in difficult conversations about race, power, and privilege and their impact on social work practice.
5. **Collaborating with Indigenous Communities:** Decolonizing social work involves working with indigenous communities and knowledge holders. It requires a commitment to shared decision making, community empowerment, and co-creating knowledge and practice approaches.
6. **Promoting Social Justice:** Decolonizing social work practice is inherently linked to promoting social justice and equity. Practitioners must be willing to challenge systemic oppression and work towards the liberation and self-determination of marginalized communities in India.

By applying this theoretical framework to social work practice in India, practitioners can work towards creating a more inclusive, equitable, and culturally responsive profession that is responsive to the needs and aspirations of Indian communities.

Understanding Eurocentrism in Social Work Pedagogy

Eurocentrism in social work pedagogy implies the domination of European and Western perspectives, frameworks, and methodologies in the curriculum and teaching practices. This dominance often marginalizes and overlooks non-Western societies' rich, diverse cultural, social, and historical contexts, particularly in postcolonial regions like India. Eurocentric frameworks prioritize Western theoretical models and practices, which may not resonate with or apply to local populations' lived experiences and needs (Razack, 2009). This overemphasis on Western paradigms can lead to a disconnection between the education provided and the social realities faced by students and communities in India.

Colonial legacies are deeply embedded in social work education, influencing the curriculum's content and delivery. These legacies manifest in several ways:

1. **Historical Narratives:** Social work history often centres on the profession's development in Western countries, such as the UK and the USA, while neglecting the contributions and practices of indigenous and non-Western societies. It creates a skewed understanding of the field's evolution and overlooks the rich traditions of community support and social welfare outside the West (Gray, Coates & Yellow Bird, 2008; Gray *et al.*, 2013).
2. **Theoretical Dominance:** The curriculum predominantly features Western theories and models of social work, such as psychodynamic theory, systems theory, and ecological models. While these theories offer valuable insights, they may not fully address the cultural, social, and economic realities of Indian communities. Indigenous knowledge systems and practices, which could provide more relevant and effective frameworks, are often underrepresented (Smith, 2012; Kapoor & Singh, 2002).
3. **Pedagogical Approaches:** Teaching practices in SWE frequently adopt Western pedagogical methods, which may not align with the learning styles and cultural contexts of Indian students. It can create barriers to effective learning and engagement, as students may find it challenging to relate to or apply these methods in their local contexts (Freire, 1970).

Identification of the Limitations and Challenges Posed by Eurocentrism

The Eurocentric orientation of social work education poses several limitations and challenges:

1. **Cultural Irrelevance:** Eurocentric curricula can be culturally irrelevant and fail to address local populations' specific needs and realities. This cultural mismatch can lead to ineffective practice and alienation of students and service users (Prasad *et al.*, 2021; Mathebane & Johanna, 2018; Healy, 2001).
2. **Marginalization of Indigenous Knowledge:** By prioritizing Western knowledge systems, Eurocentric curricula marginalize indigenous knowledge and practices. It undermines the value of local traditions and wisdom and limits the development of a more inclusive and holistic approach to social work (Gray, Coates & Hetherington, 2007; Gray *et al.*, 2013).
3. **Reinforcement of Power Imbalances:** Eurocentrism in education perpetuates colonial power dynamics by positioning Western knowledge as superior and authoritative. It reinforces existing inequalities and inhibits the development of a more equitable and just social work practice (Battiste, 2013).
4. **Lack of Critical Engagement:** Eurocentric frameworks often discourage critical engagement with colonialism's historical and ongoing impacts. This lack of critical reflection can prevent students from understanding and addressing the root causes of social issues, thereby limiting the transformative potential of social work (Rankine, 2013; Mullaly, 2010).

To overcome these challenges, there is a need for a concerted effort to decolonize social work pedagogy. It involves integrating indigenous perspectives, adopting culturally responsive teaching methods, and fostering critical engagement with the colonial histories and power structures that shape social work practice. By doing so, SWE can become more relevant, inclusive, and effective in addressing the diverse needs of Indian society.

Reimagining Pedagogy through an Indianized Lens

An Indianized curriculum in SWE involves the incorporation of indigenous perspectives, values, and knowledge systems into the teaching and learning process. This approach recognizes India's rich cultural heritage and diversity. It seeks to integrate these elements into the curriculum to create a more contextually relevant and culturally responsive educational experience. An Indianized curriculum moves away from the Eurocentric frameworks that have historically dominated SWE and embraces indigenous ways of knowing and being.

Integrating indigenous perspectives, values, and knowledge systems into SWE is crucial for several reasons. First and foremost, it acknowledges the unique histories, cultures, and world views of indigenous communities in India. By centring indigenous voices and experiences, SWE becomes more inclusive and respectful of diverse ways of knowing and being. Additionally, incorporating indigenous perspectives enriches the curriculum by offering alternative insights and approaches to addressing social issues. It fosters a deeper understanding of the complexities of social work practice within the Indian context. It equips students with the skills and knowledge to work effectively with diverse populations.

Several initiatives in India have successfully implemented Indianized approaches to SWE. For example, some institutions have developed specialized courses or modules focusing on indigenous perspectives and practices in social work. Others have integrated indigenous content throughout the curriculum, weaving it into existing courses and assignments. These initiatives often involve collaboration with indigenous communities and leaders to ensure authenticity and cultural relevance. By showcasing these examples, we can demonstrate the feasibility and effectiveness of Indianized SWE and inspire further innovation.

Reimagining pedagogy through an Indianized lens can potentially transform SWE in India. By centring indigenous perspectives and knowledge systems, educators can create a curriculum that is more inclusive, culturally responsive, and relevant to the needs of Indian society. Indianized pedagogy emphasizes experiential learning, community engagement, and reflective practice, providing students with opportunities to learn from and with indigenous communities. This approach fosters a deeper appreciation for diversity, social justice, and equity and equips students with the skills and knowledge needed to navigate complex social realities in India.

By embracing an Indianized curriculum and pedagogy, SWE can better prepare practitioners to address the diverse needs of Indian society. Indianized approaches emphasize the importance of cultural competence, humility, and reflexivity in social work practice. They encourage practitioners to critically examine their biases and assumptions, challenge dominant narratives, and advocate for social change. By equipping students with a deep understanding of indigenous perspectives and practices, SWE can empower them to work collaboratively with diverse communities, promote social justice, and create positive change in Indian society.

Strategies for Decolonizing Social Work Pedagogy

Several strategies are proposed to decolonize social work pedagogy. First, there is a need to incorporate indigenous knowledge systems into the curriculum. It involves recognizing and valuing indigenous ways of knowing and being, integrating indigenous perspectives into course content, and inviting indigenous community members to share their knowledge and experiences with students. Community-based learning is another crucial strategy which emphasizes the importance of engaging directly with communities to understand their needs, strengths, and challenges. This hands-on approach allows students to understand social issues better and enhances their ability to work collaboratively with diverse populations.

Critical reflexivity is also essential in decolonizing social work pedagogy. Educators and students alike must critically reflect on their own biases, assumptions, and positionalities, as well as colonization's historical and ongoing impacts on social work practice. This self-awareness enables them to challenge dominant narratives, question power dynamics, and advocate for social justice. Additionally, culturally responsive teaching methods are crucial in decolonizing social work pedagogy. It involves adapting teaching strategies to reflect diverse student populations' cultural backgrounds, learning styles, and lived experiences, creating an inclusive and supportive learning environment for all.

The proposed strategies aim to transform social work curriculum and pedagogy by centring indigenous perspectives, promoting community engagement, fostering critical reflexivity, and embracing cultural responsiveness. By integrating these transformative strategies into SWE, educators can create a more inclusive, equitable, and socially just learning environment that prepares students to address the diverse needs of Indian society.

Community-based learning is emphasized to bridge the gap between theory and practice, providing students with real-world experiences and opportunities for hands-on learning. Critical reflexivity is highlighted as a fundamental skill for social work practitioners, enabling them to critically examine their assumptions and biases and engage in continuous self-reflection and learning. Culturally responsive teaching methods are also emphasized to ensure that teaching practices are accessible and relevant to all students, regardless of their cultural background or identity.

Educators play a crucial role in promoting decolonized pedagogical practices. They are responsible for designing and implementing a curriculum that reflects indigenous perspectives, facilitating meaningful community engagement opportunities, fostering critical reflexivity among students, and adapting teaching methods to meet the diverse needs of learners. Educators must also be role models for ethical and culturally responsive practice, demonstrating a commitment to social justice, equity, and inclusion in their teaching and student interactions.

Conclusion

The chapter uncovers the imperative of decolonizing social work pedagogy in India and the potential of an integrative and Indianized approach to curriculum development. Reviewing the literature on decolonizing social work scholarship highlighted the limitations of Eurocentric frameworks and the need to centre indigenous perspectives and knowledge systems. The findings underscore the transformative potential of decolonizing social work pedagogy for social work curriculum and practice in India. Educators can create a more inclusive, culturally responsive, and contextually relevant curriculum by challenging dominant narratives, disrupting colonial legacies, and integrating indigenous perspectives, values, and knowledge systems. The implications of decolonizing social work pedagogy extend beyond the classroom, shaping how social work practitioners engage with diverse communities and address complex social issues. SWE can foster social justice, equity, and empowerment by equipping students with a deep understanding of indigenous perspectives and practices.

Looking ahead, there is a need for further research and development in decolonizing social work pedagogy. Future studies could explore innovative teaching methods, curriculum designs, and assessment strategies that promote decolonization and Indianization in SWE. Furthermore, there is a need for continuing discourse and association between educators, practitioners, and indigenous communities to ensure the authenticity and effectiveness of Indianized frameworks to SWE. In conclusion, decolonizing social work pedagogy is essential for advancing social justice, equity, and empowerment in India. Educators and institutions must embrace an integrative and Indianized approach to curriculum development to create meaningful and transformative student learning experiences. By centring Indigenous perspectives and knowledge systems, SWE can contribute to a more just, inclusive, and equitable society for all.

REFERENCES

Asakura, K., Miller, J., Nakash, O. & O'Neill, P. (2023). "Toward 'Decolonizing' Clinical Social Work Practice and Education". *Smith College Studies in Social Work*, *93*(2-4): 73-82. https://doi.org/10.1080/00377317.2023.2279389

Batra, P. (2021). "Re-imagining Curriculum in India: Charting a Path beyond the Pandemic". *Prospects*, *51*(1-3), 407-24. https://doi.org/10.1007/s11125-020-09518-6

Battiste, M. (2013). *Decolonizing Education: Nourishing the Learning Spirit*. Purich Publishing.

Bhabha, H.K. (1994). *The Location of Culture*. Routledge.

Bodhi, S.R. (2011). "Professional Social Work Education in India: A Critical View from the Periphery". *Indian Journal of Social Work*, *72*(2): 289-300.

Bodhi, S.R. (2014). "On the Politics of Social Work Curriculum and Pedagogy: Reflections of a Social Work Educator". *Indian Journal of Dalit and Tribal Social Work*, *2*(2), 6th ser., 71-83 [Transnational Institute for Cultural Interchange. (2020). "Social Work Lectures on Curriculum and Pedagogy". *TICI Journals*. https://www.ticijournals.org/wp-content/uploads/2020/02/Social-WorkLectures-on-Curriculum-and-Pedagogy.pdf]

Chougule, M. (2016). "Indigenising Social Work Education: An Analysis". *Social Work Chronicle*, *5*(1) DOI: 10.21863/swc/2016.5.1.012

Clarke, J., Aiello, O., Chau, K., Atcha, Z., Rashidi, M. & Amarla, S. (2012). "Uprooting Social Work Education". *LEARNing Landscapes*, *6*(1): 81-105. https://doi.org/10.36510/learnland.v6i1.577

Crampton, A. (2015). "Decolonizing Social Work 'Best Practices' through a Philosophy of Impermanence". *Social and Cultural Sciences Faculty Research and Publications*, 159. https://epublications.marquette.edu/socs_fac/159

DaCunha, J.C.M. (2016). "Disrupting Eurocentric Education through a Social Justice Curriculum". *International Development, Community and Environment* (*IDCE*), 25. https://commons.clarku.edu/idce_masters_papers/25

Dash, B.M. (2018). "Revamp Social Work Education". *Pioneer*. https://www.researchgate.net/publication/324586828_Revamp_Social_Work_Education

Dash, B.M. (2022). "The Need for Decolonizing Field Work Training in Social Work in India". In B.M. Dash (Ed.), *The Routledge Handbook of Social Work Field Education in the Global South* (1st edn.). Routledge.https://www.taylorfrancis.com/chapters/edit/10.4324/9781003270119-9/need-decolonizing-field-work-training-social-work-india-bishnu-mohan-dash

Deepak, A.C. (2012). "Globalisation, Power and Resistance: Postcolonial and Transnational Feminist Perspectives for Social Work Practice". *International Social Work*, *55*(6): 779-93. https://doi.org/10.1177/0020872811414038

Desai, A. (1985). "The Foundations of Social Work Education in India and Some Issues". *The Indian Journal of Social Work*, *XLVI* (1): 39-56.

Evans, J. (2009). "Where Lawlessness is Law: the Settler-Colonial Frontier as a Legal Space of Violence". *Australian Feminist Law Journal*, *30*(1): 3-22. https://doi.org/10.1080/13200968.2009.10854413

Fortier, C. & Hon-Sing Wong, E. (2019). "The Settler Colonialism of Social Work and the Social Work of Settler Colonialism". *Settler Colonial Studies*, *9*(4): 437-56. https://doi.org/10.1080/2201473X.2018.1519962

Freire, P. (1970). *Pedagogy of the Oppressed*. Continuum.

Gray, M., Coates, J. & Hetherington, T. (2007). *Indigenizing Social Work*. Ashgate Publishing.

Gray, M., Coates, J. & Yellow Bird, M. (Eds.). (2008). *Indigenous Social Work Around the World: Towards Culturally Relevant Education and Practice*. Ashgate Publishing.

Gray, M., Coates, J., Yellow Bird, M. and Hetherington, T. (Eds.) (2013). *Decolonizing Social Work* (*Contemporary Social Work Education Studies*), England, Surrey: Ashgate Publishing Company.

Hackett, V.C.R. (2015). "African Caribbean Presence: Decolonizing Social Work Education". *International Journal*, 1-16. DOI: https://doi.org/10.48336/IJZEFD2904

Hall, R.E. (2003). "The Hegemony of Eurocentrism in Social Work Practice: From Race to Culture as Ecological Perspective vis-à-vis Southeast Asian Populations". *The Indian Journal of Social Work*, *64*(3). Retrieved from https://ijsw.tiss.edu/greenstone/collect/ijsw/index/assoc/HASH0145/3f2f5518.dir/doc.pdf.

_____(2005). "Eurocentrism in Social Work Education: From Race to Identity Across the Lifespan as Biracial Alternative". *Journal of Social Work*, *5*(1): 101-14. https://doi.org/10.1177/1468017305051238

Healy, L.M. (2001). *International Social Work: Professional Action in an Interdependent World*. Oxford University Press.

Imran, M. & Zabi, Z. (2018, November). "Social Work Education in India: A Decolonial Perspective". Paper presented at the 6th Indian Social Work Congress, New Delhi, India.

Jaswal, S. & Pandya, S. (2015). "Social Work Education in India: Discussions on Indigenisation". *Indian Journal of Social Work*, *76*(1): 139-58. doc.pdf (tiss.edu)

Kapoor, K. & Singh, A.K. (2002). *Indian Knowledge Systems: Nature, Philosophy and Character*. Indian Institute of Advanced Study.

Kjær-Rasmussen, Lone Krogh, *et al.* (2019). *Towards Indigenous Social Work Practice: Addressing Professional Challenges in Working with Homeless Greenlanders in Aalborg*, Denmark, https://core.ac.uk/download/304609499.pdf.

Kumar, A. (2019). "Ideas Old and New: Bharatiyakaran/Indianization of Social Work". *The International Journal of Community and Social Development*, *1*(3): 254-63. https://doi.org/10.1177/2516602619878353

Mathebane, M.S., and Johanna, S. (2018). "Decolonizing the Curriculum That Underpins Social Work Education in South Africa". *Southern African Journal of Social Work and Social Development*, *30*(1):19. https://doi.org/10.25159/2415-5829/2360.

McNabb, D. (2019). "A Treaty-based Framework for Mainstream Social Work Education in Aotearoa, New Zealand: Educators talk about their Practice". *Aotearoa New Zealand Social Work*, *31*(4): 4-17. doi:http://dx.doi.org/10.11157/anzswj-vol31iss4id667

Moss, M., Rowen, R. & Lee, A.D. (2022). "On the Other Side of the Rabbit Proof Fence: Decolonizing Social Work Education: A Framework for Change". *Social Work Education*, 1-17. Advance online publication. https://doi.org/10.1080/02615479.2022.2147157

Mullaly, B. (2010). *Challenging Oppression and Confronting Privilege: A Critical Social Work Approach*. Oxford University Press.

Nadkarni, Vimla V., and Sandra Joseph (2014). *Envisioning a Professional Identity: Charting Pathways through Social Work Education in India*. https://core.ac.uk/download/212693260.pdf.

Ponnuswami, I. & Harris, N. (2020). "Decolonizing Social Work Research Education: Reflections from India and Australia". In I. Ponnuswami & A. Francis (Eds.), *Social Work Education, Research and Practice: Perspectives from India and Australia* (pp. 73-81). Springer Nature, Singapore.

Prasad, S., Actovin C.A. and Dash, B.M. (2021). "A Study on Relevance of Social Work Curriculum in Selected Social Work

Institutions in India". *African Journal of Social Work, 11*(6): 344-53. ajol-file-journals_551_articles_220355_submission_pro_of_220355-6493-540369-1-10-20220124.pdf

Rankine, M. (2013). "How Critical are We?: Revitalising Critical Reflection in Supervision". *Advances in Social Work & Welfare Education, 15*(1): 1-12.

Razack, N. (2009). "Decolonizing the Pedagogy and Practice of International Social Work". *International Social Work, 52*(1): 9-21. https://doi.org/10.1177/0020872808097748

Smith, L.T. (2012). *Decolonizing Methodologies: Research and Indigenous Peoples*. Zed Books.

Tamburro, A. (2013). "Including Decolonization in Social Work Education and Practice". *Journal of Indigenous Social Development, 2*(1): 1-16. Retrieved from https://scholarspace.manoa.hawaii.edu/server/api/core/bitstreams/af0157d6-fdda-409c-9a27-1e887cd0567a/content

Tuck, E. & Yang, K.W. (2012). "Decolonization is not a Metaphor". *Decolonization: Indigeneity, Education & Society, 1*(1), 1-40. PDF.

Tusasiirwe, S. (2023). "Disrupting Colonisation in the Social Work Classroom: Using the Obuntu/Ubuntu Framework to Decolonise the Curriculum". *Social Work Education*, 1-15. https://doi.org/10.1080/02615479.2023.2246499

Udah, H. (2020). "Decoloniality and Social Work Education and Practice". In: Ponnuswami, I., Francis, A.P. (Eds.) *Social Work Education, Research and Practice*. Springer, Singapore. https://doi.org/10.1007/978-981-15-9797-8_10

10

Nature-Culture Entanglements and Indigenous Ethics of Care

Reflections on Community Practice in Aarey Colony, Mumbai

Hemant Patange and *Sunil D. Santha*

Introduction

Indigenous communities such as the Adivasis in Aarey are deeply connected to their natural environment. They share the same world view of oneness, interconnectedness or harmony between humans and the natural environment. This is usually identified through their rituals, practices, belief systems, and other cultural components. An essential element of this can be understood through their modes of worship and sacred groves, which all bolster the idea that their lifeworld exists only if forests exist. However, these communities are at the margins today due to development, displacement, and dispossession. This chapter reflects on the pathways that social work education and practice could possibly undertake towards working with indigenous communities caught up between diverse, complex forces such as urbanization, deforestation, and displacement. Further, this chapter highlights the relevance of indigenous epistemologies in shaping sustainable development in eco-fragile regions such as Aarey Forests in Mumbai.

This chapter is guided by a posthumanist perspective that offers a new ethics of engagement for education and practice. It recognizes nature-culture entanglements as the ontological base of social work practice, considering the indigenous epistemologies of the Adivasis rooted in their forests and related cosmologies. Contemporary posthumanism stands on par with certain indigenous philosophies, which consider existence in multi-species entanglements and relationalities. One could draw similarities to such posthumanist thought in some of the prominent Indian world views, such as *vasudhaiva kuṭumbakam* or *lokaḥ samastaḥ sukhino bhavantu*, with almost all of them focusing on the goal of the oneness of the world. These perspectives shape our lifeworld with trust in the harmony between humans and the rest of nature.

Similarly, Gandhian philosophy reminds us to engage with the universe in all its relationalities, showing deep respect for mother nature and co-crafting an economic system based on preserving the natural environment rather than destroying it. The African philosophy of Ubuntu, which means "I am because we are", believes in a universal bond of sharing that connects all humanity. Indigenous communities in India value the significance of such human-non-human or nature-culture relationalities.

Post-humanism is an invitation for us to think beyond anthropocentric models of growth and development. It is built from a radical critique of dualisms—nature/culture, mind/body, micro/macro, and tradition/modern, enabling us to engage with practices of knowing-in-being and ecologies-of-repair (Blanco-Wells, 2021). Indigenous knowledge systems are more embedded in the relationality of entangled beings, humans, and non-humans, rather than the thing or identity usually dominant in Cartesian knowledge frames (Bellingham,

2022). Meaning-making embedded in indigenous world views emerges in a relational context, where land, water, and other entities have stories to tell, exercising agency in the emergence of situated knowledge (*ibid.*). Post-humanist perspectives thus shift the conceptualization of a human being from a singular, separate, independent entity with a continuing essence or substance bounded by its skin and rooted in rationality to a much more open, relational, and bodily sense of being (Fox, 2021). It further offers a new understanding of engaging with ethics and social and environmental justice (Bozalek & Pease, 2021).

Engaging with a posthumanist perspective, Mūnster (2014) narrates how, through diverse capitalist resource extraction strategies, including the exploitation of cheap labour, indigenous ecological knowledge, and non-human life forms, the colonial regime controlled the everyday lives of both Adivasis and non-human beings in the forest of Wayanad. Reviewing the story written by Mahasweta Devi on the "Death of Jagmohan, the Elephant", Ray (2023) explores how the symbolic and subjective perceptions of non-human life are entangled with the exploitation of Adivasis and other forest beings in post-Independence India. Ray argues that one could witness a "slow violence" (Nixon, 2011) of environmental degradation and social discrimination, which represents not only a kind of temporal unevenness between the state, civic institutions, and tribal constitutional rights but also the disenfranchisement of Adivasis in a more-than-human world. We can see that the situation today is not that different regarding the case of Adivasis in Aarey when they are forced to move out of their forests in search of work. The colonial practices of extraction and dispossession continue today (Badri, 2024).

The following sections narrate the everyday challenges that Adivasis in Aarey face and the diverse forms of non-violent resistance they engage with. The arguments presented in this chapter are part of the corresponding author's doctoral research work. Data was collected through ethnographic fieldwork, mainly through observation, in-depth interviews, and oral histories.

Urbanization and the Challenges of Indigenous Communities

Often referred to as the "Lungs of Mumbai", Aarey Colony is a lush, forested area on the city's outskirts, initially inhabited by diverse tribes such as the Warli, Kokna, Mallar Koli, and Katkari. Currently, there are twenty-seven *pāḍā*s or Adivasi hamlets in the Aarey colony. Traditionally, the Adivasi communities in Aarey rely on the forest for all their dietary needs and livelihood practices. Most Adivasi families in Aarey cultivate grains, vegetables, and fruits to sustain themselves and sell any excess in markets. Nowadays, they also grow paddy and vegetables. They have also planted fruit trees around their homes, including banana, guava, jackfruit, mango, and sapodilla (chikoo). They also catch fish, prawns, and chimbori (soft-shelled crabs) from the Tulsī and Vihār lakes near their forests.

Aarey colony, at present, is spread over 3,165 acres, having twenty-seven Adivasi hamlets with a total population of around 10,000 (Bhalerao, 2019). The Adivasis worship nature. Their lifestyles and festivals are also connected to nature. For instance, Vāgh Baras (which celebrates the power of tigers) and Gāoṅ Devī Pūjā (the Goddess of villages) are some of their important festivals. Archaeologists have discovered relics and tribal artefacts dating back to the Shilahara dynasty/ Sheelar Yadav period (765-1029 AD) in Aarey. They also found remains of old settlements and a Kuladevī worship spot of the Malhār Kolī community at Ultan Pada. They also unearthed five Gāodevī statues, a Wāghobā statue, and a Kīcaka (pillar bracket) worshipped as a Gaṇeśa statue. These findings provide evidence of the historical existence of tribal communities and their cultural significance. Many relics were used as statues of local deities, which the locals worshipped (Bose, 2016 & Johari, 2017).

The Adivasis living in Aarey are strongly bonded by their land, forests, rest of nature, and traditional way of life. A woman tribal artist and activist from Maroshi Pada in Aarey, explains that "their lives are so intimately connected to the jungle: like how fish cannot survive without water, Adivasis cannot survive without the jungle". Although most people now cultivate their land and work outside the forest to supplement their income, urbanization continues to spread, causing the jungle to shrink and making these communities increasingly insecure and vulnerable. Nevertheless, the community's connection with the land, forest, and nature remains strong. Many young people are pursuing higher education while continuing to farm. The unique arts, crafts, music, and cuisine of the Adivasis, which are the products of their traditional wisdom passed down from generation to generation, are also intricately entangled with nature. Warli art, Adivasis cuisine, and Tarpa dance are some of these.

In the 1940s, the government acquired nearly 1,600 ha of forest land of eight villages, including Aarey, to set up the Aarey Milk Cooperative. The aim was to industrialize and boost dairy production to meet the growing city's needs. The Aarey Milk Colony was officially established in 1949 by Prime Minister Jawaharlal Nehru (Sunavala, 2018; Nath, 2019). However, when the Aarey Milk Colony was established, some tribal settlements were displaced to set up dairy farms, with the promise of employment in the dairy farms. Subsequently, some people from these hamlets began to work at the cattle sheds. The colony also permitted tribals to grow fruits and vegetables. According to a 1956 letter from the Chief Officer of Aarey Milk Colony, tribals were asked to pay Rs. 1 per *guṇṭhā* cultivated (Sunavala, 2018).

Nevertheless, the unplanned, complex forces of urbanization slowly began to seep into the pristine Aarey to accommodate the exponential growth of Mumbai city. Over time, the deciduous forests and lands that once solely belonged to the tribal communities gave way to the development of various infrastructural projects, ranging from a Film City to Metro railway projects. A social activist from Adivasi Vanhakk Samvardhan Samiti (AVSS) commented,

> "Various development projects such as the Aarey Milk Colony in 1949, a State Reserve Police Force camp in 1974, the Film City in 1977, and the Bombay Veterinary College in 1978 have forced the Adivasis to move from their original lands and forests, confining them to smaller areas".

There are other complexities as well. For example, a tribal leader mentioned,

> "The state had established a commando unit in 2009-10. The unit was allocated 96 acres of land adjacent to the villages of Kelti Pada, Chafecha Pada, and Damu Pada. However, the presence of the unit has restricted the freedom of the families living in these hamlets. They cannot even repair their homes or construct additional extensions without obtaining permission from the unit. Despite owning the land, they cannot repair their homes for the monsoons without the unit's consent, as the land is now under their control!"

Before 2014, the land (around 33 acres) allotted to Metro Car Shed was under a No Development Zone. Despite strong protests from local communities, various organizations, and environmentally sensitive citizens from Mumbai, the trees were cut overnight, and agricultural plots were confiscated by constructing barricades to construct the Metro Car Shed. Leaders of the tribal communities believe that the status of the land of Aarey forest has been changed from the "No Development Zone" to the "Development Zone for Commercial purposes" in the new Development Plan to benefit the builder lobbies in the city. Consequently, diverse political, state and non-state actors collaboratively engage to develop and perpetuate non-Adivasi settlement in the Adivasi hamlets and their fringes, forcing the Adivasi hamlets to be reinterpreted as slums so that the whole hamlet comes under the purview of the Municipality's slum rehabilitation policy. However, such strategies are aimed at appeasing some big builders in the name of development, at the cost of these Adivasi communities being displaced, dispossessed, and alienated from Aarey.

The Forest Rights Act (FRA) of 2006 provides much scope to undo the historical injustice on Adivasi communities whose lifeworlds are entangled with Forests. In 2015, the government issued a notification stating the applicability of the FRA in Municipal areas where there is scope for recognition. Aarey Colony comes under the Municipal Corporation of Greater Mumbai, and various studies prove that the land and area of the Aarey Colony is Forest. This act enables Adivasi communities to claim their rights over land and to preserve their land from getting into the hands of the real estate and builders' lobbies. The AVSS persistently facilitates the claim of their rights via the FRA. However, there is much delay in processing the claims, and some reluctance is observed among the politicians and the bureaucracy. Consequently, despite strong evidence, the government is not ready to recognize Aarey as a Forest area. The AVSS has not received any positive response since 2016.

The barriers to getting valid documents to prove their identity and nativity are another challenge these communities face. For example, a caste certificate is an essential document for the recognition of various rights and benefits bestowed by the constitution, laws, and schemes formed by the government. It is a crucial document for Individual Forest Rights under the FRA 2006, where a family gets the legal right to reside and cultivate forest land. Further, they need to produce their caste certificates to receive support in education and jobs. It has been observed that despite providing the required documents to get the caste certificate, there are significant bureaucratic delays in receiving these documents. The AVSS leaders comment,

> "Most of the time, officials do not entertain our people in such matters. They intentionally do this to prevent us from claiming our rights and legitimizing our claim to continue living in Aarey. We are prevented from renovating our home or extending a roof or room. At the same time, there is lots of back-door encouragement for non-Adivasi populations to carry out illegal constructions in Aarey. In return, the officials take bribes. Though we have complained about such illegal constructions, no action is seldom taken. In contrast, on many occasions, the state has often attempted to define the Adivasi hamlets as slums. We are also denied basic rights such as electricity in some of our homes."

Such activities push Aarey into the epicentre of urbanization, depleting nature and destroying the Adivasis' culture. Efforts are still on to designate slums and send the Adivasis to Slum Rehabilitation buildings or else declare them as encroachers on their land.

Adivasis and Their Ways of Everyday Resistance

The Adivasis in Aarey have been non-violently fighting for their rights for the last forty years. They have employed various non-violent protest and demonstration strategies to resist the dispossession of their land and livelihoods. They organize protests, rallies, and demonstrations to raise awareness about their plight and garner support from the public and media. These protests involve marches, sit-ins, and road blockades. During such events, they showcase banners with messages such as "Save Aarey Forest" and chanted slogans calling for action to prevent the area from being handed over to builders.

They insist that Aarey is a forest, home to wildlife and Adivasi communities, and appealed to stop the destruction of the forest for the sake of infrastructure projects such as the Metro car shed. Recently, the Adivasi residents of Habale Pada and Nagarmudi Pada organized a sit-in protest to block the survey task for the Goregaon-Mulund Link Road (GMLR). They protested against the construction of twin tunnels that will pass beneath the Sanjay Gandhi National Park (SGNP) hills.

A recent incident occurred in Habale Pada, adjacent to Film City. The Film City administration expanded their landholdings without informing the families in Habale Pada. One day, the administration began filling an Adivasi's farmland with debris using bulldozers. The government provided police protection to continue this activity at that time. However, when the Adivasis found out, they mobilised other Adivasis and directly sat in the farming land to stop the work. The resistance was so strong, with the presence of women, that the police and administration had to stop the work. The Adivasis in Aarey often form alliances with other marginalized groups, activists, and non-governmental organizations (NGOs) to strengthen their resistance movements. Solidarity campaigns at the local level help amplify their voices and increase pressure on the authorities. There have been several incidents where Adivasis from Thane, Palghar, and nearby districts have come to support the concerns of Adivasis in Aarey Colony.

The Adivasis often engage in legal battles to challenge the government's land acquisition policies. They file lawsuits, petitions, and court appeals to assert their rights and protect their land. The Adivasis in Aarey formed AVSS to initiate the Forest Rights Act process. They have filed claims for individual and community forest rights, which means the government cannot start any work until they make a final decision on the claims. Petitions and legal battles like these are ways to resist such development projects. On certain occasions, they directly negotiated with government officials and project developers to seek fair compensation, resettlement packages, or alternative land options. For example, concerning the FRA, the leaders of AVSS are engaged in direct negotiation to establish a ward committee and speed up the process. A few civil society organizations also work with Adivasis in the Aarey Colony to facilitate these legal routes.

The Adivasis represent themselves on many platforms to speak up about their struggle to preserve their land, water, and forests. Universities and colleges in the city have invited Adivasi people from Aarey to speak about their cultural identity, legacy, and contemporary livelihood struggles. Additionally, many civil society organizations organize workshops and invite Adivasis to share their understanding of nature, culture, and development. Further, the Adivasis in Aarey use traditional and social media platforms to highlight their struggle and reach a wider audience. They share stories, videos, and testimonials to garner public support and sympathy for their cause. For example, the leader of AVSS and the hip-hop group Swadeshi came together and released a song called "The Warli Revolt" to stop cutting trees in the Aarey forest for a metro car shed. In February 2023, Vikalp Sangam released the "Song of Resistance: Aarey", which discusses Adivasi's symbolic relationship with nature and animals in the forest. Additionally, there are Facebook and Instagram accounts named Aarey Conservation Group and Aarey Forest, where Adivasis post everyday happenings regarding Aarey and Tribal people's struggles. Despite facing challenges from several quarters, they continue their music and non-violent struggles, making us ponder the mainstream ideas on development, livelihoods, and the environment.

Recognizing their cultural identity in their ongoing struggles is an important aspect that helps strengthen their collective identity and resilience against forces of dispossession and displacement. For example, in every protest, they wear traditional outfits and sing traditional songs during rallies. Also, they have a unique instrument called *tarapa*, on which they carry out group dance. Also, most of their rallies start with worshipping historical temples at Habale Pada or the Gaondevi Pada, proving the Adivasi's presence in Aarey for more than 1000 years. Also, Warli Painting is unique to the Warli Adivasi community, and it is done in their house to showcase and preserve culture and identity. By employing these diverse strategies, tribal communities in the Aarey Colony strive to protect their land, livelihood, culture, and way of life from the encroachment of developmental infrastructure projects.

Indigenous Epistemologies and Implications for Social Work Education and Practice

Conventional, Eurocentric social work paradigms seldom engage with nature-culture and multi-species entanglements (Bell, 2013). Modernism is at the core of Eurocentric social work, propagating anthropocentrism as its organizing principle in much of contemporary social work theory and practice (Bell, 2013; Santha *et al.*, 2023). Social work is constrained by a dualistic framework that dichotomises the social and natural. It is constrained by dualisms such as nature-culture, material-discursive, subject-object, human-animal, man-woman, and north-south—that structure modern thinking (Bozalek and Pease, 2021). Such dualisms are hierarchical and legitimize all forms of oppression and human mastery of nature. Braidotti (2018) insists that a post-human pedagogy of the oppressed must focus on the missing people (such as Adivasis) by recognizing real-life subjects whose knowledge never made it into official cartographies. This chapter suggests a way forward that social work education, instead, should inculcate an ethical sensibility that values the mutual entanglements and relationalities of Adivasis' life with their natural and multi-species environment. Attentiveness to these relationalities becomes crucial for social work education and practice, where we are among the many agents involved in knowledge co-production and change-making (Gale, 2016).

Engaging with indigenous communities is always a relational process, not a standalone practice (Higgins, 2016). The Adivasis world-making is a process of knowing-in-being entangled with their external and internal worlds. While the external would include relationships with other-than-human or more-than-human bodies, internal relationships are linked to the heart, mind, body, and spirit (*ibid.*). Social workers guided by a post-humanist perspective could be entangled with these communities in everyday world-making through "seeking, making, sharing, and celebrating" (Cajete, 2000: 178). Entanglements reveal an alternative world view on matter and aliveness (Barad, 2007). Studying entanglements also implies that we are self-aware and sensitive to multiple ecologies of becoming and belonging (Braidotti, 2019). Such a post-human understanding would strive towards affirmative action with a communal and distributed subjectivity amidst complex technological development, urbanization, or hyper-capitalism (*ibid.*).

The modern development narratives mete out injustices on the Adivasis, cheapening and categorizing them along with the rest of nature. The practices of othering perpetuate their everyday living, alienating and dispossessing them from their natural environment. There is a kind of dehumanization of the Adivasis that occurs amidst the plundering of their natural world under the pretext of development (Bera & Singh, 2021). Thus, while the Adivasis recognize their entanglements and responsibilities in a more-than-human world, modern development pushes them into the margins along with their livelihoods, knowledge systems and cultural diversity (*ibid.*). Further, the resistance strategies of Adivasis are also grounded in multi-species entanglements and non-violent ethics of care. Social workers need to recognize this strength of Adivasis and engage with these strengths in shaping a just and sustainable world.

The practices of care and resistance also showcase the relational and contextual nature of problems impacting

Adivasis' everyday life. Their ethics of care emphasize the virtues, practices, and knowledge associated with the Adivasis' way of caregiving and receiving in this world (Whyte and Cuomo, 2017). It emphasizes the relational dimensions of Adivasis with and in their natural environment, the Aarey Forests, and how their acts of love, empathy and compassion shape their everyday livelihood practices. In every agential action, the Adivasis showcase certain ethical elements of care, namely "attentiveness, responsibility, competence and responsiveness" in nurturing and sustaining their multi-species entanglements (Tronto, 1993). All these elements are crucial for just transitions in city spaces such as Mumbai. Further, we should recognize the historical and intersectional drivers of exploitation and oppression of Adivasis and the ethics of care and healing that these groups practice in their day-to-day lives (Ranganathan and Bratman, 2019).

Conclusion

The uncertain future humanity and non-human life face in today's ecological crisis is both a unifying factor and a prospect of unequal fallout, further threatening to displace and dispossess more precarious life forms, including those of the Adivasis, their land, homes, and forests (Bignall & Braidotti, 2019). This chapter has highlighted the challenges indigenous communities face due to urbanization, using the example of the Adivasis in Aarey Forest, who are at risk of being displaced due to development projects. It is essential to view the current world of the Anthropocene epoch through a post-humanist perspective that recognizes the interconnectedness between humans and the natural environment. Insights from this chapter could offer a new ethic of engagement for social work education and practice, which recognizes nature-culture entanglements as its ontological base. Indigenous knowledge systems are more embedded in the relationality of entangled beings, humans, and non-humans, rather than the thing or identity usually dominant in Cartesian knowledge frames. By engaging with a post-humanist perspective, social work can shift from an anthropocentric model of growth and development to a more open, relational, and bodily sense of being.

Acknowledgements

We are deeply grateful to the people associated with Adivasi Vanhakk Samvardhan Samiti, Amrita Bhattacharjee, and all the Adivasi people who provided us with the opportunity and the information we used for our research chapter. We extend our heartfelt thanks for their support and willingness to provide crucial insights, without which this study would not have been possible. Their dedication to preserving cultural heritage and openness in sharing perspectives greatly enriched this research.

REFERENCES

Badri, A. (2024). "Feeling for the Anthropocene: Affective Relations and Ecological Activism in the Global South". *International Affairs*, *100*(2): 731-49.

Barad, K. (2007). *Meeting the Universe Halfway: Quantum Physics and the Entanglement of Matter and Meaning*. Durham: Duke University Press.

Bell, K. (2013). "Post-conventional Approaches to Gender, Climate Change and Social Justice". In M. Alston & K. Whittenbury (Eds.), *Research, Action and Policy: Addressing the Gendered Impacts of Climate Change* (pp. 53-61). Dordrecht: Springer.

Bellingham, R.A. (2022). "A Diffractive and Decolonizing Reading Methodology for Education Research". *Australian Journal of Environmental Education*, *38*(3-4): 375-87.

Bera, S. & Singh, R. (2021). "Appeal for Embracing Post-humanist Perspectives in Orijit Sen's the River of Stories". *Journal of Graphic Novels and Comics*, *13*(4): 536-53.

Bhalerao, S. (2019, October 20). "How Tribal Residents of Mumbai's Aarey Milk Colony Built A Cuisine Around What the Forest

Provides". *The Indian Express*. https://indianexpress.com/article/express-sunday-eye/how-tribal-residents-of-mumbais-aarey-milk-colony-built-a-cuisine-around-what-the-forest-provides-6076133/

Bignal, S. & Braidotti, R. (2019). "Post-human Systems". In S. Bignal & R. Braidotti (Eds.), *Post-human Ecologies: Complexity and Process After Deleuze* (pp. 1-16). London: Rowman and Littlefield International.

Blanco-Wells, G. (2021). "Ecologies of Repair: A Post-human Approach to Other-than-human Natures". *Frontiers in Psychology*, 12. https://doi.org/10.3389/fpsyg.2021.633737

Bose, M. (2016, July 30). "Relics, Caves put Mumbai in Different League". *Deccan Herald*. https://www.deccanherald.com/content/561203/relics-caves-put-mumbai-different.html

Bozalek, V. & Pease, B. (2021). "Towards Post-anthropocentric Social Work". In V. Bozalek & B. Pease (Eds.), *Post-Anthropocentric Social Work: Critical Post-human and New Materialist Perspectives* (pp. 58-94). London: Routledge.

Braidotti, R. (2018). "Foreword". In V. Bozalek, R. Braidotti, T. Shefer & M. Zembylas (Eds.), *Socially Just Pedagogies: Post-humanist, Feminist and Materialist Perspectives in Higher Education* (pp. xiii-xxvii). New Delhi: Bloomsbury Academic.

Braidotti, R. (2019). *Post-human Knowledge*. Cambridge: Polity Press.

Cajete, G. (2000). *Native Science: Natural Laws of Interdependence*. Santa Fe, NM: Clear Light Books.

Fox, J. (2021). "Feeling the 'Weight of the Body': Post-humanism and Deliberalising Social Work". In V. Bozalek & B. Pease (Eds.), *Post-anthropocentric Social Work: Critical Post-human and New Materialist Perspectives* (pp. 58-65). London: Routledge.

Gale, K. (2016). "Theorizing As Practice: Engaging the Post-human as Method of Inquiry and Pedagogic Practice within Contemporary Higher Education". In C.A. Taylor & C. Hughes (Eds.), *Post-human Research Practices in Education* (pp. 242-57). Hampshire: Palgrave Macmillan.

Higgins, M. (2016). "Decolonizing School Science: Pedagogically Enacting Agential Literacy and Ecologies of Relationships". In C.A. Taylor & C. Hughes (Eds.), *Post-human Research Practices in Education* (pp. 186-205). Hampshire: Palgrave Macmillan.

Johari, A. (2017, August 21). "In Mumbai's Nooks and Crannies, Researchers are Uncovering 1,000-Year-Old Fragments of History". *Scroll*. https://scroll.in/magazine/847711/in-mumbais-nooks-and-crannies-researchers-are-uncovering-1000-year-old-fragments-of-history

Mūnster, U. (2014). "Invisible Labor: Adivasi Workers in the History of South Indian Forest Conservation". *RCC Perspectives*, (3), 53-58.

Nath, S. (2019, November 1). "Warli Art on Dried Mushrooms?: Peek Inside a Unique Tribal Hamlet in Mumbai's Aarey". *The Better India News*. https://www.thebetterindia.com/201937/mumbai-mushrooms-paintings-save-aarey-forest-milk-colony-tribal-cuisine-culture-india/

Nixon, R. (2011). *Slow Violence and the Environmentalism of the Poor*. Harvard University Press.

Ranganathan, M. & Bratman, E. (2019). *From Urban Resilience to Abolitionist Climate Justice in Washington, DC*. Antipode. https://doi.org/10.1111/anti.12555

Ray, S. (2023). "'Forced Renegades': Interspecies Relationalities, Historiographic Violence, and Zoopolitical Realism in Mahasweta Devi's 'The Death of Jagamohan'". *ISLE: Interdisciplinary Studies in Literature and Environment*, *30*(4): 889-910.

Santha, S.D., Mandhare, K.V. & Gajbhiye, D. (2023). "In Search of the Native: A Post-humanist Approach to Community Practice". *Glocalism: Journal of Culture, Politics and Innovation*. https://riviste.unimi.it/index.php/glocalism/article/view/22471

Sunavala, N. (2018, March 18). "Deep Inside Aarey: These Mud Huts are Still a World Removed from the Concrete Jungle". *Times of India*. https://timesofindia.indiatimes.com/city/mumbai/deep-inside-aarey-these-mud-huts-are-still-a-world-removed-from-the-concrete-jungle/articleshow/63350018.cms

Tronto, J.C. (1993). *Moral Boundaries: A Political Argument for An Ethic of Care*. London: Routledge.

Whyte, K.P. & Cuomo, C. (2017). "Ethics of Caring in Environmental Ethics: Indigenous andFeminist Philosophies". In S.M. Gardiner & A. Thompson (Eds.), *The Oxford Handbook of Environmental Ethics* (pp. 234-47). New York: Oxford University Press.

11

Balancing the Spirit

Understanding Indian Indigenous Healing and Traditional Healers in Mental Health Practice

Fayaz Ahmad Paul, Priyanka Saikia, Arif Ali, and *Wakar Amin Zargar*

Introduction

Health refers to a person's physical, mental, and social well-being, which was earlier described as the ability of the body to function well. A person is considered to be in excellent health if they don't have any physical illnesses, are not under any mental stress, and have positive interpersonal interactions. When a person maintains good health, everything else falls into place. Nonetheless, sustaining excellent and positive health depends upon several elements, including physical, social, spiritual, and emotional aspects; each has equal significance, and an individual cannot achieve total health by ignoring anyone of them (Manjunatha *et al.,* 2022). The primary aspect of health is physical fitness, which is the absence of any bodily illnesses; on the other hand, social health is the ability to communicate with people on an interpersonal level, which is equally crucial to sustaining good health. Spiritual well-being is essential for maintaining physical and mental well-being and can aid in navigating difficult circumstances like rejection, death, or adversity. Good health, which encompasses an individual's emotional and psychological well-being, also involves being cognitively sound (Mark, 2019).

Mental health is all about enhancing people's and communities' capacities and empowering them to realize their objectives. It is, therefore, appropriate for everyone to be concerned about mental health, not only those who have a mental illness. There exist several mental health conditions, each with unique symptoms that impact individuals' lives in diverse ways (Kua, 2019). People with mental health issues represent a significant proportion of the world's population. Because one in four individuals will have a mental illness at some point in their lives, millions of people worldwide suffer from mental health issues. Even though not everyone will receive a diagnosis of mental health issues during their lifetime, the effects of poor mental health are often overlooked or ignored. A person's mental health can be significantly impacted by common difficulties, including stress, trauma, the death of a loved one, troubles at home, feelings of anxiety or sadness, problems in interpersonal interactions, and excessive concern and worry.

Seeking traditional or religious healers to treat mental health issues significantly impacts patient access to effective mental health care, delaying the treatment of major mental problems by requiring psychiatric consultations. Together with the physical, verbal, and sexual abuse of the patients, it may result in murder or suicide, health issues, social issues, and/or financial exploitation (Okasha, Karam & Okasha, 2012). Mental health practitioners need to pay sufficient attention to the role that cultural influences play in managing mental diseases. Cultural and traditional approaches to conceptualizing and treating mental diseases should be taken into account since patients' desire to seek and adhere to therapy might be influenced by their ideas about mental illness (Younis, Lafta & Dhiaa, 2020). It is essential for the successful use of mental health-care treatments to comprehend cultural perspectives on mental disease (Viswanath & Chaturvedi, 2012). Traditional healing has traditionally included therapeutic modalities. It is said that faith healing, a type of conventional medicine, is practised as an alternative medicine in nearly every country on earth (Chadda *et al.*, 2001). The sudden death of infants and children is explained as resulting from the attack of blood-sucking witches; death from malaria is interpreted as witchcraft, and other deaths are attributed to the agency of ghosts (Fabrega & Nutini, 1993).

Burden of Mental Disorders

In India, where neuropsychiatric disorders account for 14 per cent of the world's illness burden, mental health is a major concern, and progress in providing mental health services is slow (Srivastava, Chatterjee & Bhat, 2016). While the prevalence of serious mental and behavioural problems is 65/1,000 persons at anyone moment, the overall prevalence of mental illnesses in India is 58 per 1,000 people, 48.9 per 1,000 in the rural population, and 80.6 per 1,000 in the urban population (Ranjan & Asthana, 2017). A breakdown of support networks, fast-paced lives, stress, complexity of living, and difficulties with unstable economic conditions may all contribute to the much greater frequency of neurotic or stress-related disorders, schizophrenia, and mood disorders (Yasmeen, 2016).

As per the 2020 report by the India State-Level Disease Burden Initiative Mental Disorders Collaborators (IMDC), approximately 197.3 million individuals in India experienced mental disorders in 2017. Of these, 45.7 million had depressive disorders, and 44.9 million (41·2-48·9) had anxiety disorders. In addition to depression and anxiety, which account for 10.8 per cent of intellectual disability, the highest percentage of mental disorders, Disability-Adjusted Life Year (DALYs), was caused by schizophrenia (9.8%), bipolar disorder (6.9%), conduct disorder (5.9%), eating disorders (2.2%), autism spectrum disorders (3.2%), and attention-deficit hyperactivity disorder (0.3%). In India, the provision of adequate mental health care consistently fails to meet the demands that are both explicit and implicit. This is mostly because mental illness is still stigmatized, poorly understood, frequently disregarded, and considered taboo. Individuals with mental health issues, together with their loved ones and caregivers, as well as health-care providers, continue to face significant stigma. A standard association between the idea of mental health issues and the threat posed by those who suffer from such conditions is dread. The outcome of all of these may impact the patient's physical health demands (Kishore *et al.*, 2011).

Mental illness often has two sides: on the one hand, persons who suffer from it must cope with the symptoms and limitations of their condition; on the other hand, stigma, discrimination, negative attitudes, and hostility are commonplace (Kapungwe *et al.*, 2011). The stigma attached to mental health concerns stands in the way of significant progress in the field of mental illness and health (Abdullah & Brown, 2011). Erroneous perceptions about mental disease lead to prejudice and stigmatization against a large number of individuals who have serious mental disorders. As a result, people with mental health issues are denied opportunities for a high-quality life, including access to safe housing, decent employment, and social connections with a diverse range of people (Corrigan & Kleinlein, 2005). Higher levels of self-stigma are associated with decreased hopefulness, low levels of self-efficacy and self-esteem, and a major stigma that prevents them from getting the treatment they need for their symptoms (Turner, 1991).

Culture and Mental Health

Every community is heavily influenced by its "culture", or way of life, which is adhered to by every member of that specific culture (Biswal, Subudhi & Acharya, 2017). The views and behaviours of people who seek assistance are heavily influenced by their culture, which makes it possible to forecast the etiology of a disease and the best course of treatment. Additionally, it also shapes the expression of mental illness and pathways to health care. Mental illness and culture are viewed as two sides of the same coin, with culture playing a significant role in identifying the many causes of mental illness and influencing the course of therapy by those findings (Alarcon, 2009). Paranjpe (2012) contend that cultural factors explain the reasons behind people's suffering and possible solutions. Cultural perspectives on mental illness vary widely, and these differences have an impact on the phenomenology, treatment, outcome, and epidemiology of mental health issues and problems.

Castilo-Lorente, Rivera-Fernandez & Vazquez-Mata (1997) have also mentioned a few significant ways that culture affects mental health, including the individual's personal experience with the illness and its associated symptoms, within the context of their cultural norms, how the individual expresses his or her experience or symptoms, how the expressed symptoms are interpreted and therefore, diagnosed, and how mental illness is treated, as well as the outcome of this treatment. In India, health and well-being are closely linked to religious and spiritual healing. Over two-thirds of individuals with mental health issues and their family members strongly believe that supernatural forces cause mental illness; as a result, they seek traditional forms of treatment before seeking modern medical care (Biswal, Subudhi & Acharya, 2017). Numerous cultures attribute mental illnesses to phenomena like spirit possession, ancestral spirits or evil spirits' actions, enemy curses, upsetting ancestors, or being cursed. The cultural explanations for mental illness compel people to turn to priests, mystics, shamans, and diviners for assistance. These individuals utilize magic, sorcery, and rituals to aid people through complex moral, social, and economic situations/crises.

Mental Health Practice and Indigenous Healing

The term "mental health practice" refers to the many therapeutic approaches used by indigenous healers to address mental health issues. According to Marks (2009) traditional healers do not know how to treat mental illness properly, so they treat patients using conventional methods like making ritual offerings to the *pīr*, making wishes (*mannata māṅganā*), tying sacred threads, lemons, bangles, or other artefacts for wish-fulfilment, bathing and cleansing oneself, lighting incense, circumambulation (*pradakṣiṇā*), performing selfless service at the *dargāh*, wearing locked chains around one's hands or ankles in the *pīr*'s name (*bābā kī bedī*), petitioning the *pīr* (*arẓī*), trancing, mediumship, going through physical ordeals, and exorcism from spirit possession and witchcraft (Subudhi *et al.*, 2020). One of the studies showed that the participants' phenomenological world and their external social environment include normative norms, values, emotions, and social ties, all symbolically represented in the healing process. In South Asia, faith healing practice persisted despite increased access to modern medicine, according to Sarkar, (2014). There, traditional healers performed various tasks such as carrying out complex rituals, suggesting amulets, wearing particular rings, branding with rods, chaining in temples, exorcising ghosts and *jinn*, and considering animal sacrifices to treat mentally ill patients (Subudhi *et al.*, 2024).

Understanding Indigenous Healing in India

Humans have developed a complex system of religious, magical, and indigenous healing practices over thousands of years. These practices were developed to appease the God and goddesses who appeared to heal and relieve humankind of their illnesses (Moodley & Stewart, 2010; Subudhi & Biswal, 2021). The belief that worshipping a God or Goddess brings health, while hostility brings illness and disease, means that even in modern societies, religion, magic, and supernatural healing are an essential part of the experience. Rituals and celebrations are held to honour the God or Goddess. People turn to religion, magic, and supernatural healing for support when they suffer from illness, disease, or suffering, individually or collectively. However, religion tries to address society's more general social and cultural problems, whereas magic is employed to negotiate on behalf of people with supernatural powers (Moodley, Sutherland & Oulanova, 2008).

People with mental health issues are not the only ones who frequently seek therapeutic practices, such as therapies provided by priests, astrologers, black magicians, and others (Raj, Saleem & Vidyadharan, 2019). These practices serve not only therapeutic and preventive functions but also educate those in need of assistance about the secrets of illness and healing processes. Indigenous healing places more emphasis on the possibility of assistance and a sense of optimism than it does on the precision of the diagnosis and the effectiveness of the therapy, both of which directly contribute to the patient's recovery. The traditional forms of treatment reflect the local understanding of man's nature, which creates close connections between the spirit world and an individual's ancestry. According to Avasthi, Kate, and Grover (2013), patients view their condition as something that needs to be understood and recognized rather than something that has to be treated or managed (Subudhi, 2021).

The foundation of indigenous healing is essentially the belief in the supernatural. It is used in a group setting and involves individuals with mental health issues, their families, the healer, and the mediator. Indigenous healing encompasses a range of health-related practices, knowledge, beliefs, and methods that include spiritual and religious practices used to promote health and identify and address a variety of health-related issues. Indigenous or folk medicine, which includes ancient knowledge systems that evolved over centuries throughout many communities far before the advent of modern medicine, is another way to conceptualize it (Tischendorf, 2009). Individuals who provide healing rituals and engage in indigenous healing practices are referred to as indigenous. Most traditional healers are men rather than women, have lower levels of education, and work mostly in rural regions.

Indigenous healing has long been recognized as a non-invasive medical approach, and many people continue to value this alternative medical approach, even in the face of modern professional therapies (Benedetti, 2020). Sarkar and Seshadri (2015) define indigenous healing as rituals recognized community individuals perform to alleviate distress symptoms. It encompasses beliefs and practices related to illness that are a result of indigenous cultural development rather than directly drawn from the theoretical underpinnings of modern medicine. Indigenous healing is the idea that healing may be affected by religious belief or faith. This can be achieved by rituals or prayers that, in the words of followers, invoke a divine presence and power to cure disease and disability (Bathla *et al.*, 2011). Religious belief is linked to the belief in divine involvement in medical matters. Indigenous healing techniques include prayers, offerings to temples, counter-magic, talismans, physical removal of disease-causing objects, exorcism, holy ash, etc. (Bathla *et al.*, 2011).

The residents of the community where these individuals reside are aware of their qualifications as health-care professionals due to their shared social, cultural, and religious backgrounds, as well as their shared knowledge and views about the causes of illness and disability and the state of physical, mental, and social well-being. Some terms used to refer to traditional healers include faith healers, witch doctors, medicine men, shamans, herbalists, and other similar titles. Almost 90 per cent of Indians have used traditional healers' services at some stage (Hollenberg & Torri, 2013). Even though there is access to modern medical care, people still turn to faith healers in hopes of finding a miraculous solution to everyday issues like marriage, career, money, health, arranging favourable movements for new endeavours, losing loved ones or family members, or domestic animals, among other issues, as different specialists offer services in these varied areas (Rao *et al.*, 2015).

Perspective of Asian Countries towards Indigenous Healing

Based on common knowledge of human nature and the causes of pain, every community or society has established its healing institutions and practices. The Indigenous system so evolved has weathered the vagaries of time and still thrives in the present times on popular support. Indigenous healing in China combines Daoism, animistic belief, Buddhism, superstitious ideas, and other cultural beliefs. These beliefs include calling back a lost soul, banishing a ghost or other supernatural being thought to cause illness, seeking divine assistance to prevent disasters or heal illnesses through rituals, giving patients specific substances to eat, hypnotizing patients, and more. People who are known as witch doctors, shamans, and religious figures like monks and Daoist priests are typically the ones who do indigenous healing in China.

According to Kuruppuarachchi and Rajakoruna (1999), Sri Lankan's hold the belief that the influence of ghosts or spirits of deceased relatives can cause mental illness. To combat this belief, healers engage in a range of religious activities and rituals, from applying a chanted or charmed thread to exorcism, which involves drumming and dancing to drive out any suspected evil spirits from the patient's body or soul. In Pakistan, people's mental processes and belief systems are shaped by their culture, and as a result, health-related practices are influenced by religious and cultural traditions. Because many of Pakistan's customs and rituals are based on Islamic ideology, the country's people hold a variety of superstitious beliefs. These include the existence of ghosts, *jinn*s, demons, and apparitions, as well as the spirits of good and evil, miracle healing, saints, good or bad luck, health or illness, witchcraft, and pilgrimage. Sufis, an indigenous healer, is said to be able to conduct both medical and spiritual healings, communicate with the spirits of nature through sorcery, and gain supernatural abilities through fasting and ecstasy. Certain individuals hold a strong belief in the existence of supernatural powers and a divine role in the manifestation of mental illness. These beliefs include exorcism, ancestor worship, voodoo, charms, and the supernatural abilities of certain people, known as *pīr*s and black magicians, who possess the ability to cast spells, cast magic, haunt, or have "second sight" (Farooqi, 2006).

Nepal's culture and traditions have blended with indigenous healing practices (Baniya, 2015). Dhami-Jhankri, Pandit Lamagubhaju-Pujari, and Jyotishi are the names of Nepal's traditional healers. Nepalese healers function as intermediaries between the spiritual realm and the material world. In Nepal, several spirits are thought to be the cause of common illnesses. Healing practitioners identify the kind of spirit present and then use a spirit bone, often the femur of a person, to either suck the spirit from the patient's body or make a gift to appease it. Healing practitioners appear to be dressed in vibrant clothes during shamanic rituals. They also drum, chant, dance, sing, and sometimes sacrifice a black goat or a rooster, depending on how serious the patient's condition is (Shankar, Paudel & Giri, 2006).

Indian Perspective of Indigenous Healing

The Indian health-care system is impacted by the nation's cultural diversity, which dates back to ancient times and is linked to spiritual customs from many different religions. India is often referred to as a sea of all religions. There are several contemporary and native healers spread around the nation to treat mental health issues (Padmavati, Thara & Corin, 2005). Numerous civilizations in India have long engaged in indigenous healing, and the nation is home to a vast array of therapeutic locations, including temples, shrines, monasteries, local deities, and more (Dalal, 2010). Indigenous mental health healing in India, which individuals still practice without significant changes to methods or approaches, is a reflection of their cultural beliefs. The widespread usage of these healing techniques raises the question of whether they are merely superstitions employed by the healers to take advantage of their clients or if they really improve mental health and aid in the health-care system in any manner.

In India, where over two-thirds of people with mental health issues and their family members firmly believe that supernatural forces cause mental illness, indigenous healers and their healing practices currently play a significant role in the field of mental health. As a result, people in India first consult healers before seeing mental health professionals (Hunter & Whitten, 1977). Several motivating reasons influence people's choices for healing practices, even when they contact several healers to get relief from their sickness (Kar, 2008; Ram, 2017). List of these elements is given below:

I. Psychiatric consultations are stigmatized in society.
II. Strong belief in family members or relatives who decide types of healing.
III. People lack awareness of mental health services.
IV. The healers are easily available and approachable.
V. Deficiencies in the mental health services that are currently available.

A unique philosophy, spirituality, soteriology, and medicine are outlined in the ancient Indian literature, along with instructions on how to alleviate human suffering. Some of these writings are the Upaniṣads and Vedas, the theory and practice of *yoga*, the Brāhmaṇas, the Āraṇyakas, Tantra and alchemy, Āyurveda, and Siddha traditions (Chakravarty, 2015). All items in the world were thought to have souls by the Vedic people, who also believed that magico-religious methods could be used to treat physical illnesses. Through their *mantras*, doctors possessed magical power over gods and utilized that ability for healing in addition to their job of facilitating communication between humanity and the gods (Saini, 2016).

In *Ṛgveda*, fire, or *agni*, is thought to be the medium via which the gods communicate with the sacrificer. As a result, priests of the Agni cult, like the Atharvans, Aṅgīras, and Bhṛgu (one of the seven great sages), were regarded as specialists in the use of magico-religious force for healing. They are also credited as the writers of the *Atharvaveda*, which included information about illnesses, disorders, and how to treat the human body. During this time, people also thought that consuming *soma-rasa* (juice made from the *soma* plant), after it had been offered in a fire sacrifice could grant immortality. This belief in *soma*'s ability to grant immortality also helped to recognize the remarkable qualities of other plants mentioned in the *Atharvaveda*. Indigenous healing is present in Āyurveda, the traditional Indian medical science that promotes positive health. Known as "Aṣṭāṅga Āyurveda", this branch of Āyurveda, which focuses primarily on treating psychological disorders in people, includes *bhūta vidyā* (study of the spirits), which treats diseases acquired or inherited for unexplained reasons.

Characteristics of Indigenous Healing

Different regions have different indigenous healing practices, and different regions have different regional specializations. The several aspects of indigenous healing that S.R. (2018) noted are listed below:

I. **Sacredness:** The significance of sacredness is one of the elements that sets apart the healing customs of rural India. Sacred treatment incorporates the entirety of the community's religion, mythology, and history as the therapist works to activate powerful psychic forces both within and outside the patient. The *tāntrika*, priests, *fakīrs*, *swāmīs*, and *gurus* who oversee them preserve the reverence of these locations. The reverence may be found in various forms, including the regional representations of Lord Śiva and Hanumān, ancestral spirits, and demon rituals.

II. Holistic Approach: The patient's total well-being is the focus of indigenous healing/treatment. A person's values, beliefs, interests, social interactions, and spiritual orientation are all taken into account by the holistic approach while practising treatment. Indigenous healers frequently have an innate understanding of the strong symbiotic link between the body and the mind: when one is ill, the other does not remain well. Indigenous healing places more emphasis on the individual than the issue. While some healers focus on certain issues, many individuals seek healing from them for a variety of crises, including physical or mental disease, family conflicts, business setbacks, marital trouble, or the fury of spirits (Parks, 2008).

III. Healers as Diviners: It is said that healers who can communicate directly with supernatural forces obtain their healing abilities from the divine. Healers are both feared and respected by the local communities. Healing professionals often get intense instruction rather than formal education and frequently inherit the right to practice. Since obtaining physical and mental purity requires years of interior preparation, the background of the healer is rarely given much thought. Although the healers do not charge for their services, their consumers must pay for the services rendered (Kakar, 2003). The majority of healers serve as mediators between the metaphysical and physical worlds.

IV. Cultural Compatibility: The local communities' beliefs and practices are fundamentally shaped by healers and their healing modalities. Healing practitioners use a therapy strategy that often aligns with popular belief systems. Beliefs in such healing rituals are more widely accepted since they have been developed and confirmed in numerous situations over the ages. Mental health issues are treated by a variety of healers in India, but each healer's approach to treatment is unique based on how the patient or his family members express their condition. In addition, some healers recommend treatments like *bālā* (ring), casting charms, or *tābīẓa* (amulet), which they believe will shield the patient from evil forces. They also offer handmade pills or powders made from particular herbs, oils, or unidentified chemicals meant to lessen mental health problems' severity (Neumann *et al.*, 1971).

Types of Indigenous Healing in India

There are two key components to the Indian health-care system, i.e., traditional and modern, wherein the folk sector, religious sector, and classical sector may all be used in the traditional health-care system. Every health-care sector explains sickness differently and uses a different therapeutic technique (Kapur, 1979). In India, the folk and religious sectors are seen as prime suppliers of health-care services, diagnosing mental diseases based on supernatural etiology. Both sectors have different healing processes from one another. The main causes of mental illness include personal sin, bad purpose, enraged deities, soul loss, intrusion by numerous elements, sorcery, and taboo (misdeed) breaches committed by the victim or by his ancestor in this life or a former one (Trivedi & Jilani, 2011).

Sāttvika and *tāmasika* are the general categories under which indigenous healing falls. In healing, they employ different techniques and supplies. Higher caste members are more likely to practice the *sāttvika* style of healing. They are knowledgeable about the Vedas and have a strong Sanskrit background. They make use of amulets as well as prayers, incantations, offerings, and penance. They use sandal paste, *kumakuma*, rice, grains, holy water, coconut, etc. as an offering and give ash gourd as *bali* (sacrifice) to the spirits of gods. Healing practices are conducted on certain auspicious days or times. The healers worship gods of higher cadre. The lowest classes worship spirits (*bhūta*s) using the *tāmasika* healing style. Their rituals are mostly concentrated on animal sacrifice.

The majority of these healers engage in violent practices, are ill-read, and their little information may be out of date or misconstrued for practical purposes. On new moon days or after midnight, they engage in occult rituals in locations such as cemeteries (Tischendorf, 2009). Depending on the ritual they conduct, the healers go by different names depending on the location and circumstances. Muslim healers are called *pīr* or *sayānā*, whereas Hindu healers could be termed *tāntrika* healers, *bābā*, or *ojhā*. One possible treatment method may involve having the patient wear a *jantra* or soaking the written formula in water and consuming it. This is symbolic of lasting protection. The belief that spirits or *bhūta*s cause disease and misfortunes is the basis of Teyyam in Kerala and Dakṣiṇa Kannaḍa's spirit devotion (*bhūtāradhanā*) is comparable to this kind of devotion and healing (Rao *et al.*, 2015).

Effectiveness of Indigenous Healing and Potential Harm

The effectiveness of indigenous healing practices is debatable. Some may regard these practices as beneficial in relieving distress symptoms through the placebo effect, particularly for disorders such as depression (Sarkar, 2014). The placebo effect is a phenomenon in which a fake treatment can imitate the action of a genuine, active treatment and improve a person's symptoms. Placebos have the greatest influence on subjective symptoms of sickness, such as pain, anguish, and discouragement, and are especially beneficial in anxiety and depressive disorders, as well as possession (Zartaloudi & Madianos, 2010). A placebo effect is a term used to describe positive outcomes that arise from the clinical encounter itself, including the therapeutic alliance and treatment ritual, as opposed to positive outcomes that are the result of particular or distinctive pharmacological, spiritual, religious, or physiological effects of interventions (Miller, Colloca & Kaptchuk, 2009).

For the last sixty years, the placebo effect has been a source of interest, frustration, and misunderstanding within biomedicine, even though scientific inquiry has intensified in the last ten years, with a special focus on neurological mechanisms (Miller, Colloca & Kaptchuk, 2009). The placebo effect is comparable to indigenous healing in mental health. Spirit rituals provide an opportunity for the patient to ventilate the unexpressed pain. The rhythmic dancing and the opportunity to cry and abuse is a platform for the patient to vent their pain or anger, and he becomes the symbol of unconditional positive regard for the patient. According to Sciberas and Fournier (2023), the patient is permitted to express his fears healthily throughout the healing process. Spirit dance ceremonies, where the ceremonies are predicated on the belief in the supernatural, are said to employ the same principles. This belief is also shared by those who seek service from healers. Spirit dance ceremonies are often performed in groups, including participants who are acquainted with the patient. The patient receives this therapy without shame, and the family takes on joint responsibility for solving the situation rather than blaming the patient. The public accepts both the healer's role as an agent of God and his healing abilities.

The patient's and the healer's dual faiths significantly impact how well the therapy works (Rao *et al.*, 2015). Healing is facilitated by the healers and patients working together in spirit dancing ceremonies. The patient receives ongoing assurances that the treatment will heal him during the administration of healing rituals; however, a suppressive aspect is prevalent, especially while treating psychosis. The sacramental components of sacrificial rites have been shown to have significant anxiety-reducing benefits (Saravanan *et al.*, 2007). The therapeutic process also assists the patient in expressing aggressiveness and some deviant behaviour (such as possession). They are temporarily freed from the responsibility for their actions. The patient receives emotional support throughout treatment, contributing to an increased sense of value and self-worth. The patient receives relief from guilt by attributing the cause to outside factors; as with other psychotherapies, the interaction between the healer and the patient is crucial to healing (Kleinman & Sung, 1979).

Conclusion

In India, spiritual and traditional healers have long provided mental health care for millennia. As a result, a large number of the population frequently visits indigenous healers before consulting medical professionals or psychiatrists. The fundamental tenet of indigenous healing is the belief in spiritual power. This idea is also shared by those who seek the services of healers. It won't be easy to influence people's beliefs about these practices. It has become a part of the social fabric. It is critical to comprehend the connection between indigenous healing and mental health since it permeates practically every element of modern life and is a fundamental and integral part of social and religious life. To address the demands of the public in terms of mental health, psychiatric social work intervention is also necessary to comprehend the effectiveness of healing in mental health issues. Educating healers in these areas would be very beneficial.

REFERENCES

Abdullah, T. & Brown, T.L. (2011). "Mental Illness Stigma and Ethnocultural Beliefs, Values, andNorms: An Integrative Review".

Clinical Psychology Review, *31*(6): 934-48. https://doi.org/10.1016/j.cpr.2011.05.003

Alarcón, R.D. (2009). "Culture, Cultural Factors andPsychiatric Diagnosis: Review and Projections". *World Psychiatry*, *8*(3): 131-139. https://doi.org/10.1002/j.2051-5545.2009.tb00233.x

Avasthi, A., Kate, N. & Grover, S. (2013). "Indianization of Psychiatry Utilizing Indian Mental Concepts". *Indian Journal of Psychiatry*, *55*(6): 136. https://doi.org/10.4103/0019-5545.105508

B.J., Hunter, D.E. & Whitten, P. (1977). "Encyclopedia of Anthropology". *RAIN*, (19), 11. https://doi.org/10.2307/3032170

Baniya, R. (2015). "Traditional Healing Practices in Rural Nepal". *Journal of Patan Academy of Health Sciences*, *1*(1): 52-53. https://doi.org/10.3126/jpahs.v1i1.13020

Bathla, M., Bathla, J., Kaloiya, G. & Chandna, S. (2011). "91 Seeking Help of Faith Healers in Modern Psychiatric Practice: Results of a 4 Years Study in Northern India". *Asian Journal of Psychiatry*, *4*: S52. https://doi.org/10.1016/s1876-2018(11)60199-8

Benedetti, F. (2020). "Mental and Behavioural Disorders". *Placebo Effects*, pp. 333-65. https://doi.org/10.1093/oso/9780198843177.003.0012

Better Mental Well-being: Practical Tips to Boost Brain Health For Healthier Living: Infographic [Chinese]. (2019). https://doi.org/10.26419/pia.00037.005

Castillo-Lorente, E., Rivera-Fernandez, R. & Vazquez-Mata, G. (1997). "Limitation of Therapeutic Activity in Elderly Critically Ill Patients". *Critical Care Medicine*, 25(10): 1643-48. https://doi.org/10.1097/00003246-199710000-00012

Chadda, R., Agarwal, V., Singh, M.C. & Raheja, D. (2001). "Help Seeking Behaviour of Psychiatric Patients Before Seeking Care at a Mental Hospital". *International Journal of Social Psychiatry*, *47*(4): 71-78. https://doi.org/10.1177/002076400104700406

Chakravarty, T. (2015). "Interface in Approaches to Mental Disorder in India: A Sociological Analysis". *Sociological Bulletin*, *64*(2): 197-218. https://doi.org/10.1177/0038022920150204

Corrigan, P.W. & Kleinlein, P. (2005). "The Impact of Mental Illness Stigma". On the Stigma of Mental Illness: Practical Strategies for Research and Social Change, pp. 11-44. https://doi.org/10.1037/10887-001

Dalal, A. (2010). "P02-338: Characteristics of Traditional Healing Practices and Its Implications for Modern Psychotherapies". *European Psychiatry*, *25*(S1): 1-1. https://doi.org/10.1016/s0924-9338(10)71037-3

Fabrega, H. & Nutini, H. (1993). "Witchcraft-explained Childhood Tragedies in Tlaxcala, and their Medical Sequelae". *Social Science and Medicine*, *36*(6): 793-805. https://doi.org/10.1016/0277-9536(93)90040-b

Farooqi, Y.N. (2006). "Traditional Healing Practices Sought by Muslim Psychiatric Patients in Lahore, Pakistan". *International Journal of Disability, Development and Education*, *53*(4): 401-15. https://doi.org/10.1080/10349120601008530

Hollenberg, D. & Torri, M.C. (2013). "Linking Complementary and Alternative Medicine, Traditional Medicine and Primary Health Care: The Role of Local Health Traditions in Promoting Health Security". *Primary Health Care and Complementary and Integrative Medicine*, pp. 93-114. https://doi.org/10.1142/9781848169784_0006

Kakar, S. (2003). "Psychoanalysis and Eastern Spiritual Healing Traditions". *Mysticism*, 109-24. https://doi.org/10.1163/9789004494725_006

Kapungwe, A., Cooper, S., Mayeya, J., Mwanza, J., Mwape, L., Sikwese, A. & Lund, C. (2011). "Attitudes of Primary Health Care Providers Towards People with Mental Illness: Evidence from two Districts in Zambia". *African Journal of Psychiatry*, *14*(4). https://doi.org/10.4314/ajpsy.v14i4.6

Kapur, R. (1979). "The Role of Traditional Healers in Mental Health Care in Rural India". *Social Science & Medicine. Part B: Medical Anthropology*, *13*(1): 27-31. https://doi.org/10.1016/0160-7987(79)90015-2

Kar, N. (2008). "Resort to Faith-healing Practices in the Pathway to Care for Mental Illness: A Study on Psychiatric Inpatients in Orissa". *Mental Health, Religion & Culture*, *11*(7): 720-40. https://doi.org/10.1080/13674670802018950

Kishore, J., Gupta, A., Jiloha, R. & Bantman, P. (2011). "Myths, Beliefs and Perceptions about Mental Disorders and Health-seeking Behaviour in Delhi, India". *Indian Journal of Psychiatry*, *53*(4): 324. https://doi.org/10.4103/0019-5545.91906

Kleinman, A. & Sung, L.H. (1979). "Why do Indigenous Practitioners Successfully Heal?". *Social Science & Medicine. Part B: Medical Anthropology*, *13*(1): 7-26. https://doi.org/10.1016/0160-7987(79)90014-0

Kua, E.H. (2019). "Culture and Mental Health Care in Asia-Pacific Rural Communities". *Mental Health and Illness Worldwide*, pp. 1-12. https://doi.org/10.1007/978-981-10-0751-4_33-1

Kuruppuarachchi, K.A. & Rajakaruna, R.R. (1999). "Psychiatry in Sri Lanka". *Psychiatric Bulletin*, *23*(11): 686-88. https://doi.org/10.1192/pb.23.11.686

Manjunatha, N., Jayasankar, P., Rao, G., Gururaj, G., Varghese, M. & Benegal, V. (2022). "Epidemiology of Common Mental Disorders: Results from 'National Mental Health Survey' of India, 2016'". *Indian Journal of Psychiatry*, *64*(1): 13. https://doi.org/10.4103/indianjpsychiatry.indianjpsychiatry_865_21

Marks, M.L. (2009). "Recovering from Economic Crisis: Preparing Employees for Opportunities and Challenges". *PsycEXTRA Dataset*. https://doi.org/10.1037/e626702009-001

Miller, F.G., Colloca, L. & Kaptchuk, T.J. (2009). "The Placebo Effect: Illness and Interpersonal Healing". *Perspectives in Biology and Medicine*, *52*(4): 518-39. https://doi.org/10.1353/pbm.0.0115

Moodley, R. & Stewart, S. (2010). "Integrating Traditional Healing Practices Into Counselling and Psychotherapy". *Counselling Psychology Quarterly*, *23*(3): 239-40. https://doi.org/10.1080/09515070.2010.505731

Moodley, R., Sutherland, P. & Oulanova, O. (2008). "Traditional Healing, the Body and Mind in Psychotherapy". *Counselling Psychology Quarterly*, *21*(2): 153-65. https://doi.org/10.1080/09515070802066870

Neumann, A.K., Bhatia, J.C, Andrews, S. & Murphy, A.K. (1967). "Role of the Indigenous Medicine Practitioner in two Areas of India—Report of a Study". *Social Science and Medicine* , *5*(2): 137-49. https://doi.org/10.1016/0037-7856(71)90094-1

Okasha, A., Karam, E. & Okasha, T. (2012). "Mental Health Services in the Arab World". *World Psychiatry*, *11*(1): 52-54. https://doi.org/10.1016/j.wpsyc.2012.01.008

Padmavati, R., Thara, R. & Corin, E. (2005). "A Qualitative Study of Religious Practices by Chronic Mentally Ill and their Caregivers in South India". *International Journal of Social Psychiatry*, *51*(2): 139-49. https://doi.org/10.1177/0020764005056761

Paranjpe, A.C. (2012). "Jyoti Anand: Healing Narratives of Women: A Psychological Perspective". *Psychological Studies*, *57*(3): 320-21. https://doi.org/10.1007/s12646-012-0156-8

Parks, F.M. (2008). "Psychotherapeutic Implications of Tibetan Folk-healing Practices". *PsycEXTRA Dataset*. https://doi.org/10.1037/e503242008-001

Poznyak, V. (2018). "World Health Organization Guidelines for the Treatment of Substance Use Disorders and Comorbid Conditions". *Revista Internacional de Investigación en Adicciones*, *4*(1): 1-3. https://doi.org/10.28931/riiad.2018.1.01

Raj, A., Saleem, T.K. & Vidyadharan, V. (2019). "Somatic Complaints and their Relationship with Depressive Symptoms among Adolescent

Girls: A Descriptive Study". *Kerala Journal of Psychiatry*, *31*(1). https://doi.org/10.30834/kjp.31.1.2019.152

Ram, D. (2017). "Explanatory Models and Medication Adherence in Patients with Depression in South India". *Journal of Clinical and Diagnostic Research*. https://doi.org/10.7860/jcdr/2017/23954.9170

Ranjan, J.K. & Asthana, H.S. (2017). "Prevalence of Mental Disorders in India and Other South Asian Countries". *Asian Journal of Epidemiology*, *10*(2): 45-53. https://doi.org/10.3923/aje.2017.45.53

Rao, A., Sibbritt, D., Phillips, J.L. & Hickman, L.D. (2015). "Prayer or Spiritual Healing as Adjuncts to Conventional Care: A Cross-sectional Analysis of Prevalence and Characteristics of Use Among Women". *BMJ Open*, *5*(6): e007345. https://doi.org/10.1136/bmjopen-2014-007345

S.R. (2018). "Traditional/Folk Practices of Kerala Case Studies: Part V: Healing art of Tribal Communities of Kerala". *Journal of Traditional and Folk Practices*, *5*(2). https://doi.org/10.25173/jtfp.2017.5.2.76

Saini, A. (2016). "Physicians of Colonial India (1757-1900)". *Journal of Family Medicine and Primary Care*, *5*(3): 528. https://doi.org/10.4103/2249-4863.197257

Saravanan, B., Jacob, K., Johnson, S., Prince, M., Bhugra, D. & David, A.S. (2007). "Belief Models in First Episode Schizophrenia in South India". *Social Psychiatry and Psychiatric Epidemiology*, *42*(6): 446-51. https://doi.org/10.1007/s00127-007-0186-z

Sarkar, S. (2014). "Ethical Issues Relating to Faith Healing Practices in South Asia: A Medical Perspective". *Journal of Clinical Research and Bioethics*, *5*(4). https://doi.org/10.4172/2155-9627.1000190

Sarkar, S. & Seshadri, H. (2015). "Dealing with Requests for Faith Healing Treatment". *Indian Journal of Medical Ethics*. https://doi.org/10.20529/ijme.2015.062

Sciberas, C. & Fournier, M.A. (2023). "Undefined Chottanikkara Healing Tradition: A Psychological Perspective". *Journal of Humanities and Social Science*, *22*(12): 61-64. https://doi.org/10.1177/19485506231191084

Srivastava, K., Chatterjee, K. & Bhat, P. (2016). "Mental Health Awareness: The Indian Scenario". *Industrial Psychiatry Journal*, *25*(2): 131. https://doi.org/10.4103/ipj.ipj_45_17

Subudhi, C. (2021). "Beliefs about Etiology, Help-seeking and Consequences of Mental Illness: A Study on Tribal Patients from a Psychiatric Setup" (Doctoral dissertation).

Subudhi, C., Biswal, R. & Acharya, S. (2017). "Healers and Healing Practices of Mental Illness in India: The Role of Proposed Eclectic

Healing Model". *Journal of Health Research and Reviews, 4*(3): 89. https://doi.org/10.4103/jhrr.jhrr_64_17

Subudhi, C., Biswal, R. & Meenakshi, J.R. (2020). "Healing Preferences among Tribal Patient with Mental Illness in India". *Journal of Neurosciences in Rural Practice, 11*(02): 361-62.

Subudhi, C., Biswal, R. & Pathak, A. (2024). "Pathways to Psychiatric Help among Tribal Patients with Mental Disorders in India". *Indian Journal of Psychiatric Nursing, 21*(1): 22-28.

Subudhi, C. & Biswal, R. (2021). "Perceived Beliefs about Etiology of Mental Illness among Tribal Patients in India". *National Journal of Professional Social Work*, pp. 3-11.

Tischendorf, A.K. (2009). "Traditional Healing Meeting Modern Health Care Policy". *Culturally Sensitive Health Care Practices for the Indigenous People of Norway and Hawaii: A Comparison* (Master's thesis). [Unpublished doctoral dissertation] (n.d.).

Trivedi, J. & Jilani, A. (2011). "Pathway of Psychiatric Care". *Indian Journal of Psychiatry, 53*(2): 97. https://doi.org/10.4103/0019-5545.82530

Turner, T. (1991). "Mental Illness: The Fundamental Facts. A Mental Health Foundation Report, 1990". The Mental Health Foundation, 8 Hallam Street, London W1N 6DH. *Psychiatric Bulletin, 15*(4): 251-52. https://doi.org/10.1192/pb.15.4.251

Viswanath, B. & Chaturvedi, S.K. (2012). "Cultural Aspects of Major Mental Disorders: A Critical Review from an Indian Perspective". *Indian Journal of Psychological Medicine, 34*(4): 306-312. https://doi.org/10.4103/0253-7176.108193

Yasmeen, A. (2016, December 2). "India Needs to Talk About Mental Illness". *The Hindu.* Retrieved http://www.thehindu.com/sci-tech/health/India. (n.d.). *The Hindu.*

Younis, M.S., Lafta, R.K. & Dhiaa, S. (2020). "Faith Healers are taking Over the Role of Psychiatrists in Iraq". *Qatar Medical Journal, 2019*(3). https://doi.org/10.5339/qmj.2019.13

Zartaloudi, A. & Madianos, M.G. (2010). "Mental Health Treatment Fearfulness and Help-seeking". *Issues in Mental Health Nursing, 31*(10): 662-69. https://doi.org/10.3109/01612840.2010.490929

12

Indigenous Approaches to Social Work Practice in India

Ghanshyam Choudhary and *Maya Kumari*

Introduction

Indigenous social work is a new and emerging field incorporating indigenous knowledge, traditions, and values into social work practice. It is a comprehensive approach that emphasizes the interdependence of all areas of life, including physical, emotional, mental, and spiritual dimensions (Hart, 2010). Indigenous social work recognizes the value of community, culture, and spirituality in the healing process. It recognizes colonialism's historical and current consequences while advocating for decolonization and self-determination. Indigenous social work practices often rely on indigenous traditions and ceremonies. Indigenous social workers frequently use storytelling, circle methods, and traditional healing practices. These approaches provide a culturally appropriate and effective way to address social difficulties in indigenous communities. Indigenous social work emphasizes the importance of relationships. This includes connections to family, community, the natural world, and the spiritual realm. These relationships are regarded as essential to the well-being of individuals and societies (Gray *et al.*, 2008).

India has a long history of social services, yet its unique professional social worker is not indigenous. The Tata Institute of Social Sciences in Bombay was founded in 1936, marking the start of professional social work education in India. The director was an American citizen, and they contributed to establishing other social work institutes. The foundation of social work education in India may have resulted from an elite group's ideas and principles, which influenced the American model of professional social work training. Indigenous social work in India promotes cultural awareness and respects community beliefs, rituals, and traditions. It incorporates active community participation in identifying, planning, and executing interventions. This method incorporates holistic methods encompassing spiritual, emotional, and physical well-being. It values traditional knowledge and wisdom while encouraging a balance of modern and traditional ways. It campaigns for the rights of indigenous groups, addresses social inequities, and promotes social equality (Ponnuswamy & Chechimada, 2018; George & Ramakrishnan, 2005).

Indigenous Social Work

The discourse of indigenous social work has been a source of much debate and research. Educators and practitioners have played critical roles in starting these talks. Initially, the debate on indigenous social work focused on social work methods in developing countries in Africa, Asia, and South America. The term "indigenization" was first used in the context of social work in 1971, during the United Nations' fifth international assessment of social work education. It was used to demonstrate the weakness of American social work theories when applied to societies outside of the United States. Recent debates have given insight into indigenous social work's historical and conceptual growth. The importance of indigenous viewpoints and approaches has grown, particularly considering globalization, modernization, and a variety of global difficulties such as socio-economic inequality, ecological concerns, climate change, security threats, and the COVID-19 pandemic (Majumdar *et al.*, 2023). As we manage these complicated concerns, it is critical to acknowledge the interdependence between indigenous and international social work. The profession addresses local and global issues while promoting fairness, social justice, and human rights. Efforts to indigenize and decolonize social work education and practice are crucial, emphasizing the significance of context and cultural relevance (Black Deer *et al.*, 2023).

The debate highlights Western conceptions' irrelevance in non-Western cultures, notably in Eastern countries, as well as a lack of consensus on the definition of indigenous social work. It underlines the need to understand indigenous social work as a concept and investigates its varied discourses worldwide. Decolonization and diversity of culture have emerged as essential components for advancing indigenous social work. By highlighting unique values like Ubuntu, ecological sustainability, conscientization of religious heritage, natural family networks, racism and privilege, self-reflection, critical consciousness frameworks, and spirituality, the concepts associated with culture are broadened (Jaswal *et al.*, 2023).

The field of social work has advanced and grown in terms of its characteristics, principles, and methods. It has experienced a paradigm shift in the last few decades in response to the shifting socio-economic, political, religious, and cultural contexts. It has done this by recognizing and incorporating voices from a broader range of caste, class, gender, ethnicity, culture, and religion categories and by incorporating values like interdependence and collectivism into its pre-existing set of values. However, these changes coincide with its changing character, which has become increasingly administrative. The profession more frequently focuses on creating and providing social work services according to Western paradigms

(Gray *et al.*, 2007). In recent years, broader arguments have questioned the relevance of the social work profession and how it was structured in Western society before being adopted and practised in Eastern and Asian countries. This has sparked an extensive argument among social work authors (Law and Lee, 2016). Gray and Fook (2004) also emphasize that while arguments and movements on numerous topics continue, social work authors have advocated for the dominance and irrelevance of Western influences on social work for the past three decades (Gray and Fook, 2004). The value conflicts between Western and Indian cultures are significant, especially in social work education. The goal is philanthropy and enablement, which cannot be solely based on science but must also consider cultural expectations and aspirations. To achieve this, the curriculum and social work theories must accommodate religion-based social service and the local context of culture. The social service tradition, based on *dharma*, volunteerism, and charity, must also be included (Dash *et al.*, 2020).

Foundation of Indigenous Social Work in India

Indian culture, which is profoundly founded on ancient wisdom and different traditions, has important implications for social work education. Incorporating philosophical concepts with social work practice in India results in a distinct framework that prioritizes cultural sensitivity, holistic well-being, and ethical engagement. This synthesis exemplifies the seamless integration of ancient values and contemporary social work ideas. Vedānta, Nyāya, Vaiśeṣika, Sāṁkhya, Yoga, and Mīmāṁsā are among the many schools of thought in Indian culture, each with its own unique perspective on reality, ethics, and the nature of existence (Bilimoria, 2008; Divatia, 1994). Vedānta with the concept of *dharma*: Vedānta, which originates from the Vedas, promotes the quest for knowledge and self-realization.

The concept of *dharma* is central to Vedāntic thought, including duty, morality, and moral law. *Dharma* helps people fulfil their social responsibilities and commitments to others, encouraging harmony and social cohesiveness (Bhaskarananda, 2002). Sāṁkhya philosophy asserts the presence of two vital entities: *Puruṣa* (consciousness) and *prakṛti* (nature). This dualistic perspective acknowledges the interplay of individual perception and the material universe. Sāṁkhya's philosophy influenced social work practice, which stresses self-awareness, personal change, and understanding one's connectivity with nature (Radhakrishnan, 1992). The *Yogasūtra* of Patañjali presents a methodical spiritual development and self-realization approach. The eight limbs of *yoga*, which include ethical principles (*yama*s and *niyama*s), *āsana*s (physical postures), and meditation, constitute a comprehensive framework for personal and social reform. Social work based on *yoga* encourages overall well-being, self-care, and mindfulness practices. Buddhism, founded by Gautama Buddha, aims to alleviate suffering through the Four Noble Truths: the fact of suffering, its origin, cessation, and the road to cessation. Buddhist philosophy emphasizes the importance of compassion, non-violence, and mindfulness. Buddhist-inspired social work stresses empathy, compassion, and social justice (Dalai Lama, 2001).

The Upaniṣads, *Bhagavad Gītā*, Jaina, and Buddhist teachings add to the philosophical landscape by explaining notions such as *dharma*, *karma*, *ahiṁsā*, and *mokṣa*. Indian culture's fundamental concept of *dharma* is consistent with social work's focus on moral obligation and accountability. Social workers find motivation in improving people's lives and communities to fulfil their *dharma* and serve the greater good (Mukherjee, 2014). *Karma* philosophy emphasizes the idea of cause and effect by emphatically emphasizing the personal choices people make and the results of those choices. Under the guidance of this notion, social workers endeavour to achieve social justice by resolving systemic problems, supporting oppressed communities, and promoting constructive transformation (Mukherjee, 2014). The quest for *mokṣa*, or freedom from the cycle of life and death, is consistent with social work's emphasis on supporting people to overcome obstacles while making their advancement. Social workers use education, advocacy, and assistance to empower and liberate people from social restrictions. *Ahiṁsā*, a vital attribute of Jainism and Mahatma Gandhi's ideology, is apparent in social work's determination to practice non-violence. Social workers support peaceful dispute resolution, fight against discrimination, and strive to create inclusive environments (George, 2017).

While the amalgamation of Indian culture and social work values is beneficial, it is not without impediments. Different conceptions of philosophical principles, potential conflicts with modern perspectives, and the requirement for cultural sensitivity are all present issues. On the other hand, embracing these challenges opens the door for discourse, cultural humility, and creative approaches that combine tradition with today's significance. Integrating Indian culture with social work yields a distinct paradigm that respects indigenous cultures while dealing with contemporary problems of society. By incorporating the ageless wisdom of Indian culture with social work ideas and methods, practitioners may plot the way for holistic well-being, ethical involvement, and the pursuit of social justice.

In ancient India, social justice and compassion were not merely concepts but fundamental components of cultural norms that influenced every facet of daily existence. These ideas relied heavily on *dharma*, a multifaceted phrase encompassing duty, morality, compassion, and social responsibility. The practice of *dharma* guides the interactions and decisions of people, groups, and authorities, impacting every aspect of society. Several organizations that promote and aid the impoverished were founded because of this commitment to *dharma*. Social justice and communal care

are mentioned in ancient Indian literature, such as the Vedas, *Manusmṛti*, and *Arthaśāstra*, illuminating the practices and ideals of the time. Kauṭilya's *Yogakṣema* (welfare state) concept influenced various aspects of human life, civilization, and culture. Despite being a modern concept, Kauṭilya's ideas on the welfare state were not widely accepted by foreign scholars; they believe that the welfare state is modern and has originated in the West. Kauṭilya advocated for a state where citizens' prosperity and welfare were prioritized in terms of material and moral aspects. He believed that the ruler should be happy in the happiness of the citizens and understand their welfare only in the welfare of the citizens. Kauṭilya prioritized the public's welfare in his administrative policies, ensuring inclusive development while pursuing public interest. He made several laws for the welfare of society, such as banning the sale and purchase of children as slaves and ensuring that employers could not force a female slave to become naked or harm her chastity. These views on child slavery and women's liberty are significant in the modern period, as every state now makes laws against child labour and protects women's liberty. Kauṭilya's welfare state focused on citizens' material and moral welfare, ensuring inclusive development and protection of women's rights (Choudhary, 2021).

Professional Social Work Values in Indian Context

The National Association of Social Workers (USA) Code of Ethics outlines the core values of the social work profession, which include service, social justice, dignity, the importance of human relationships, integrity, and competence. Social workers have embraced these values throughout its history, reflecting the unique purpose and perspective of the profession (NASW).

Indian culture and social work share similarities in their philosophy and traditions. Indian culture emphasizes service, compassion, and sacrifice for others, emphasizing the interconnectedness of one's welfare with others. The concepts of God, soul, and *māyā* provide the foundation for social justice, holding all living beings equal and rejecting discriminatory practices. Hindu philosophy also believes in self-actualization, with spiritual and religious activities assisting in achieving this goal. The concept of *dharma*, or social functioning, is closely linked to social functioning, with mental well-being being based on fulfiling one's role and achieving satisfaction. Understanding *dharma* can help social workers provide effective professional service. The relationship between a worker and a person needing professional help is crucial in social work practice. The principle of acceptance is the most basic and is compatible with Hindu belief in the divinity of man. This belief allows for a non-judgemental attitude towards even the worst criminals, as life's goal is to merge with God. The practice of *ahiṁsā* emphasizes an absence of hatred towards or blaming the person in need of rehabilitation or reform. The principle of controlled emotional involvement is also well-expressed in the *Gītā*. The power and authority inherent in the worker-client relationship are often criticized, as the client feels inadequate and looks upon the worker as an expert capable of helping them. Hindu scriptures maintain that the giver is not superior to the receiver, and the two are intrinsically equal. The dignity of human beings is a core value in social work, with the belief that one's identity is defined by its divinity. The concept of innate worth supports the principles of self-help and self-determination, and the worker primarily enables or facilitates the client's mobilization of their inner and external resources. The concept of reincarnation and the law of *karma* align with the professional assumption that each person is unique, regardless of their shared characteristics. The development of the professional self is the cornerstone of professional social work training, as the social worker learns to believe in certain assumptions, develop core values, and offer help without seeking to satisfy their clients (Sinha, 2003; Nadkarni, 2007; Kumar, 2010).

Indigenous Way of Social Work Practice in India

Cultural Competence

Cultural competence is a crucial aspect of social work practice in India, which involves understanding and responding to the unique combination of cultural variables and the full range of dimensions of diversity brought by professionals and clients. It involves congruent behaviours, attitudes, and policies that enable professionals to work effectively in cross-cultural situations. India's vast diversity in culture, religion, language, and ethnicity presents a significant challenge for social workers, who must be culturally competent to understand and respect the cultural contexts of their communities. Cultural factors play an overwhelming role in social work practice in India, and understanding different cultures, practices, symbols, and their meanings is crucial. Respecting and operating within the confines of a set culture is very important. Cultural competence should undergird a social worker's service/practice with clients as enshrined in the National Association of Social Workers Code of Ethics. Failure to execute cultural competency can be detrimental to delivering appropriate and effective services to clients. Promoting indigenous social work involves co-creating "cultural competence" as a skill and knowledge among social work educators and professional social workers (Attipoe, 2024).

Holistic Well-being

Holistic well-being is a comprehensive approach to health that considers every aspect of an individual and their interactions with the environment. In India, indigenous social work must address the distinct needs of indigenous communities, each with its own physical traits and cultural practices. This approach considers not only the individual's needs but also the requirements of their community and their relationship to the environment. Indigenous social work in India involves problems such as respecting multiple traditions and practices, but it also offers potential for peacebuilding and long-term sustenance. Incorporating holistic well-being into indigenous social work in India can result in more effective treatments and improved outcomes for individuals and communities. It enables social workers to address the entire range (Carpenter, 2023; Clark-Decès, 2017).

Community Engagement

Community engagement is a vital aspect of indigenous social work in India, requiring close collaboration with communities, recognizing their distinct cultural backgrounds, and addressing their needs. It encourages collaboration between social work agencies and communities, improving the psychosocial well-being of people and families while tackling socio-economic issues. Community engagement is significant in indigenous social work because it allows social workers to understand the unique difficulties encountered by indigenous communities and develop culturally relevant and effective treatments. However, it also poses problems, such as respecting different cultures and practices and negotiating the complexity of working in these communities. To summarize, community engagement is essential to indigenous social work in India, helping social workers better understand their communities and devise more effective solutions (Bhagwan, 2017; Gulalia & Subudhi, 2021).

Cultural Healing Practices

In India, cultural healing and indigenous social work are inextricably linked to the country's different tribal populations and are founded on a wealth of traditional knowledge. These techniques, which are sometimes described as unscientific or irrelevant, constitute an important component of the country's health-care system. However, they frequently struggle for formal legitimacy and lack effective mechanisms for recognition and integration. These healing traditions must be recognized and integrated, including measures for certification and documentation. The Tharu tribe (a tribe on the Indo-Nepal border), exemplifies how firmly ingrained these rituals are in cultural traditions. Their therapeutic techniques play an important role in preserving their cultural heritage. Cultural healing is a crucial component of health care in India, however there is a need for recognition, integration, and support to ensure their preservation and development (Reddy *et al.*, 2023).

Community Resilience

Resilience in indigenous social work in India is critical to understanding community resilience, particularly among those afflicted by historical injustice. Like the Adivasis of north-east India, these communities have exhibited exceptional perseverance in the face of colonial adversity. Their social work activities, which involve collaborating closely with the community to handle difficulties, promote peace, and secure future sustainability, are inextricably linked to their resiliency. Globally, there is a push for social work to discover ways to reconcile with indigenous peoples, which includes combining Western therapeutic techniques with traditional healing practices, encouraging communication among all age groups, and cultivating respect and goodwill across all races. Resilience is essential to indigenous social work in India, showcasing the communities' strength and adaptability in adversity. However, these practices must have greater acknowledgement and support to ensure their survival and development (Middelton-Moz, 2023; Carpenter, 2023).

Conclusion

Indigenous social work in India blends traditional wisdom, cultural heritage, and contemporary social work principles. It has evolved significantly from Western models to emphasize cultural sensitivity, community engagement, and holistic well-being. It promotes social justice, community resilience, and cultural healing while respecting indigenous traditions and values. The foundation of indigenous social work is built on ancient philosophical concepts like *dharma, karma, ahiṁsā*, and *mokṣa*, which have integrated with contemporary social work principles. Cultural competence is a cornerstone of indigenous social work practice, enabling social workers to respectfully navigate India's rich cultural tapestry.

However, challenges remain, such as formal recognition of traditional healing practices, greater acknowledgement of Indic knowledge systems, and promotion of cultural humility among social work professionals. Fostering dialogue, collaboration, and mutual respect between indigenous communities and social work practitioners is crucial to ensuring indigenous approaches remain central to social work practice in India.

REFERENCES

Attipoe, H. (2024). "Cultural Competency: A Cardinal Force in Social Work Practice and Service: A Cultural Practice Guide for Human Services and the Helping Professions". *International Journal of Social Work*, *11*(1), 28-43.

Bilimoria, P. (2008). *Sabdapramana: Word and Knowledge in Indian Culture*. Deakin University.

Bhagwan, R. (2017). "Community Engagement within a Social Work Programme in Rural India". *Social Work*, *53*(3): 315-29.

Bhaskarananda, S. (1994). *The Essentials of Indian Culture: A Comprehensive Overview of the World's Oldest Religion*. Viveka Press.

Black Deer, A.A., Bennett, B., Baines, D., Gates, T.G., Ortega, D., Ravulo, J. & Mabvurira, V. (2023). *Indigenization Discourse in Social Work: International Perspectives*. K. Majumdar, R. Baikady & D.S. Ashok Antony (Eds.). Springer International Publishing AG.

Carpenter, D. (2023). "Indigenous Practice of Social Work in Northeast India: Issues and Challenges". *Indigenization Discourse in Social Work: International Perspectives*, pp. 253-64.

Choudhary, A.S. (2021). *Welfare State in Kauṭilya's Arthashastra: An Analytical Study*.

Clark-Decṛs, I. & Smith, F.M. (2017). "Well-being in India: A Historical and Anthropological Report". *The Pursuit of Human Well-being: The Untold Global History*, pp. 83-107.

Coates, J. (2009). *Indigenous Social Work around the World: Towards Culturally Relevant Education and Practice* (M. Gray, Ed.) (1st edn.). Routledge.

Dash, B.M., Kumar, M., Singh, D.P. & Shukla, S. (Eds.). (2020). *Indian Social Work*. Routledge.

Divatia, S.C. (1994). *Idealistic Thought in Indian Culture: Rise and Growth from the Vedic Times to the Kevalādvaita Vedānta Up to Prakāśānanda of 16th Century, Including as Propounded in the Mahāyāna Buddhism*.

Feuerstein, G. (2003). *The Deeper Dimension of Yoga: Theory and Practice*. Shambhala Publications.

George, V.J. & Ramakrishnan, V. (2005). "Professional Social Work in India: Some Historical and Contemporary Perspectives". *Indian Journal of Social Work*, *66*(4): 486-501.

Gray, M., Coates, J. & Bird, M.Y. (Eds.). (2008). *Indigenous Social Work Around the World: Towards Culturally Relevant Education and Practice*. Ashgate Publishing Ltd.

Gray, M., Coates, J. & Hetherington, T. (2007). "Hearing Indigenous Voices in Mainstream Social Work". *Families in Society*, *88*(1): 55-66.

Gray, M. & Fook, J. (2004). "The Quest for a Universal Social Work: Some Issues and Implications". *Social Work Education*, *23*(5): 625-44.

Gulalia, P. & Subudhi, C. (2021). "Constructing Supervisory Practices and Knowledge for Social Work Education in India". *Journal of Social Work Education and Practice*, *6*(4): 20-34.

Hart, M.A. (2010). "Indigenous Worldviews, Knowledge, and Research: The Development of an Indigenous Research Paradigm". *Journal of Indigenous Social Development*, *1*(1A).

Hans, N. (2016). "Dilemmas of Social Work Education in India". *The Indian Journal of Social Work*, *28*(3): 269-84.

Jaswal, S. & Kshetrimayum, M. (2023). "A Review of Indigenous Social Work Around the World: Concepts, Debates and Challenges". *International Social Work*, *66*(5): 1369-82.

Kumar, M. (2010). "Hinduism and Social Work". *Origin and Development of Social Work in India*, 139.

Lama, D. (2001). *Ethics for the New Millennium*. Penguin.

Law, K.Y. & Lee, K.M. (2016). "Importing Western Values Versus Indigenization: Social Work Practice with Ethnic Minorities in Hong Kong". *International Social Work*, *59*(1): 60-72.

Majumdar, K., Baikady, R. & D'Souza, A.A. (2023). "Understanding Indigenous Social Work Education and Practice: Local and Global Debates". In *Indigenization Discourse in Social Work: International Perspectives* (pp. 1-14). Cham: Springer International Publishing.

Middelton-Moz, J., Mishna, F., Martell, R., Williams, C. & Zuberi, S. (2023). "Indigenous Trauma and Resilience: Pathways to 'Bridging the River' in Social Work Education". *Social Work Education*, *42*(7): 968-85.

Nadkarni, M.V. (2007). "Does Hinduism Lack Social Concern?". *Economic and Political Weekly*, pp. 1844-49.

Ponnuswamy, I. & Chechimada, A. (2018). "Theoretical and Conceptual Approaches to Social Work Practice". In *Social Work Education: Theory, Research, and Practice* (pp. 43-62). Springer.

Radhakrishnan, S. (1992). *Indian Philosophy*. Oxford University Press.

Reddy, S., Subedi, B. & Guite, N. (2023). "Introduction: Ethnomedicine and Tribal Healing Practices in India: Challenges and Possibilities of Recognition and Integration". *Ethnomedicine and Tribal Healing Practices in India: Challenges and Possibilities of Recognition and Integration*, pp. 1-31.

Sinha, R.C. (2003). "The Interface of Swadeshi Culture and Technological Society". *Indian Philosophical Quarterly*, *30*(1): 45-56.

13

Role of *Yoga* in Promotion of Mental Health

Rakesh Dwivedi, Ramesh Kumar Tripathi, Hareem Fatima Nomani, and *Anjali Mishra*

Introduction

Mental health is an integral and essential part of one's health. Mental wellness encompasses more than just mental disorders but also speaks about peace of mind. It is more than just disorders and disabilities. Mental health affects a person's living and working conditions; it also affects their ability to feel, think, and act positively and properly. To survive in this hectic and stressful environment, it is very much necessary for a person to take proper care of his or her mental health. Numerous mental health problems exist that people face nowadays such as: stress, anxiety, loss of peaceful mind, unfocused mind and what not. Survival is the first and foremost concern of every individual, and without positive mental health, proper and meaningful survival is impossible. There are several ways to treat mental health problems which include psychotherapy, counselling, medications, psychological evaluations, physical exams, and meditation and *yoga āsana*s. In this chapter, our focus is on *yoga āsana*s and how *yoga* benefits mental health.

The Sanskrit word *yuj*, which means "to join", "to yoke", and "to unite", is the source of the word *yoga*. According to Yogic teachings, practising *yoga* results in the unification of one's own inner awareness with what exists in the universe, signifying a complete balance among the mind and body and between man and nature. Upon reaching a level of liberation known as *mukti*, *nirvāṇa*, or *mokṣa*, an individual is said to be in *yoga* and referred to as a *yogī*. *Yoga*, therefore aims to achieve self-realization and the transcendence of all forms of suffering in order to reach "the state of liberation" (*mokṣa*) or "freedom" (*kaivalya*). *Yoga*'s origins can be found more than 5,000 years ago.

Four significant periods of creativity, practice, and evolution throughout the long and rich history of *yoga*:

(i) **Pre-Classical Yoga:** The roots of *yoga* can be found more than 5,000 years ago in the Indus-Sarasvatī culture of northern India. The oldest sacred writings, the *Ṛgveda*, are where the word *yoga* originally appeared. Through internalizing ceremonial sacrifice and teaching egotistical reduction via knowledge of oneself, behaviour, and wisdom, the *brahmaṇa*s and *ṛṣi*s developed *yoga* through the writings of the Upaniṣads.

(ii) **Classical Yoga:** *Yoga* existed in a pre-classical era that synthesized concepts, theories, and methods. The initial systematic teaching of *yoga*, the yogic *sūras* by Patañjali, defines the classical period. It covers the eight levels of enlightenment for *rāja-yoga*, or "classical *yoga*", and was written in the second century.

(iii) Post-classical Yoga: To revitalize the body and extend life, *yoga* masters created *tantra-yoga* centuries after Patañjali. They accepted the physical body as the means of enlightenment and rejected the antiquated Vedic doctrines. *Hatha*-*yoga*, or *yoga* in the West, is a result of this investigation into the relationship between the physical and spiritual realms.

(iv) Modern Period: *Yoga gurus* came to the West in the late 1800s and early 1900s, drawing interest and disciples. Attendees were spellbound by Swami Vivekananda talks at the 1893 Parliament of Religions in Chicago. Throughout the 1920s and 1930s, T. Kṛṣṇamacharya and Swami Sivananda propagated *hatha*-*yoga* throughout India.

Yoga is a group of physical, mental, and spiritual practices or disciplines that originated in ancient India, aimed at controlling (yoking) and stilling the mind, and recognizing the detached "witness-consciousness" as untouched by the activities of the mind (*citta*) and mundane suffering (*duḥkha*). The actual essence of *yoga* is to raise the life energy, also known as *kuṇḍalini*, at the base of the spine. It intends to do this through a series of physical and mental activities. The approaches consist of numerous *yoga* postures *āsanas* that attempt to maintain the body healthy on a physical level. Relaxation techniques called *prāṇāyāma* and meditation called *dhyāna* are used to discipline the mind. However, the ultimate objective of *yoga* is to assist the individual in transcending the self and achieving enlightenment. As the *Bhagavad Gītā* says,

> "A Person is said to have achieved *yoga*, the union with the self, when the perfectly disciplined minds gets freedom from all desires and become absorbed in the self alone".

Yoga is indeed a therapy that aids in the control of one's mind, body, and soul. It combines the abilities of the body and mind to reach a serene body and mind; it benefits in coping with stress and relaxation. It also helps improve flexibility, muscle strength, and overall physical tone. It stimulates your energy, vitality, and respiration. *Yoga* may appear as being nothing more than stretching, but it has a multitude of perks for our body in terms of how we feel, look, and move. *Yoga* is far more than just bending and twisting the body whilst holding the breath. It's a method for bringing people in a state where people can see and perceive the world as it is. The sensory body grows as you allow your energies to become exuberant and ecstatic. The unity that *yoga* develops allows you to feel the entire universe as a part of yourself, making everything one.

Sthiram sukham āsanam, said Patañjali, the originator of *yoga*. It means that your *āsana* is a position that appears to be sturdy and comfortable. You might even be surprised to learn that an *āsana* is only the first stage in the *yoga* practice. It's a technique that motivates you to work for the greater benefit. *Yoga* aims to achieve perfect harmony between your mind, body, and spirit.

Main goals of *yoga* in daily life (Yaduv, Sunil Kumar, 2015):

1. Physical Health
2. Mental Health
3. Social Health
4. Spiritual Health
5. Self-realization.

1. Physical Health: "*Yoga*'s relaxing methods can help with chronic pain, including headaches, carpal tunnel syndrome, arthritis, and lower back pain", says Dr Nevins. "The practice of *yoga* can also help you sleep better and reduce the risk of stroke." Additional health advantages of *yoga* include:

enhanced flexibility, muscular endurance and tone, improved respiration, energy, and vitality, maintaining a balanced metabolism, calorie restriction, improved cardio and circulatory health, and injury prevention.

2. **Mental Health:** *Yoga* not only helps individuals physically but also mentally. *Yoga* is the combination of exercise, meditation, and relaxation, which helps in dealing with anxiety, stress and depression as well. It also helps in dealing with Post-Traumatic Stress Disorder (PTSD). *Yoga* also boosts concentration power, focus and maintains good memory. *Yoga* is definitely a practice one should adopt to stay vital in body and mind if you want to preserve your brain healthy, well-oxygenated, and tranquil.
3. **Social Health:** *Yoga* has indeed been associated with reducing stress levels. It can really strengthen your ability to communicate and relate successfully with family, friends, and co-workers. *Yoga* lessons are a fantastic place to engage new individuals who share similar interests. *Yoga* has additionally been connected to improved mental wellness. Both can help individuals become socially effective in a variety of settings, including personal, professional, and community-based. *Yoga* practitioners often claim higher levels of happiness. Once you're happy, you have the immediate ability to make others happy. Happiness is the most contagious state imaginable!
4. **Spiritual Health:** Attendance in a *yoga* class alone does not provide evidence of mental growth and experience. Holistic practice must be a part of life. In the science of *yoga*, people are not expected to follow the methods and verify the results through their experience. By abandoning ancient wisdom and patience, everyone can have the same inner experience as a great sage. Complete liberation by achieving *yoga*. By indulging

in deep religious meditation, one can control the body *cakra*s, such as the heart, root, and throat *cakra*. People often experience gratitude, empathy, forgiveness, and the awareness of being part of something big. In fact, better health is just a by-product, not a spiritual goal. Another advantage is to let go and give in to God! For example, in *bālāsana*, our forehead is placed on the ground in awe of the Almighty. When we tune into that infinite energy, it reminds us that a higher force at work can provide us with everything we need. Through *yoga*, we can overcome the causes of pain and suffering.

5. **Self-realization:** *Ahiṁsā-paramo-dharmaḥ* is the highest human precept and the fundamental tenet of spiritual life. This precept embraces the non-violent principle in all aspects of thought, speech, emotion, and behaviour. Spiritual health can be attained via prayer, meditation, *mantra*s, optimistic thinking, and tolerance. People ought to be defenders, not destroyers. The capacities for giving, understanding, and forgiving are what truly define humanity. One of the main tenets of *yoga* is to safeguard life and honour the uniqueness and autonomy of all living things. By abiding by this rule, people become more tolerant, understanding, loving, helpful, and compassionate towards one another and all other people, countries, races, and religions (Yadav, *et al.*, 2015).

Alyson Ross and Sue Thomas conducted a study to investigate the advantages of *yoga* practice on people's physical and mental well-being. A cross-sectional design was employed in the study, and anonymous online questionnaires measuring fatigue, social support, and sleep disturbance were administered via PROMIS. The majority of *yoga* practitioners reported very good or outstanding general health; however, 60 per cent reported at least one chronic health problem. All of the participants felt that *yoga* enhanced their weight, vitality, happiness, and social interactions. The likelihood of thinking that *yoga* enhanced health increased with the amount of practice. The study came to the conclusion that *yoga* might be advantageous for a number of demographics, including older women and people with long-term medical issues.

According to a study done at the All India Institute of Medical Sciences in India, parents of children with retinoblastoma reported dramatically reduced psychological stress and enhanced quality of life after a 12-week *yoga*-based lifestyle intervention. The intervention comprised lectures, films, interactive sessions, breathing exercises, physical postures, meditation, relaxation techniques, and personalized counselling. Moreover, the study discovered decreased cortisol and IL-6 levels and a rise in brain-derived neurotrophic factor, dehydroepiandrosterone sulfate, and sirtuin-1. According to the study, parents of retinoblastoma patients may benefit from a *yoga*-based lifestyle intervention for stress management and coping mechanisms.

Gupta, Khare, Vempati, Sharma, and Bijlani's study looked at how *yoga*-based lifestyle interventions affected anxiety levels in people with and without illnesses. *Āsana*s, *prāṇāyāma*, relaxation methods, individualized guidance, group support, and talks on Yogic thought, prayer, handling stress, dietary habits, and illness awareness were all a part of the intervention. The individuals' anxiety scores—both trait and state anxiety—significantly decreased, according to the findings. Patients with cervical spondylitis, high blood pressure, being overweight and, coronary heart disease, and psychiatric illnesses showed a significant improvement in their anxiety levels.

The goal of a study by Karen Pilkington, Graham Kirkwood, Hagen Rampes, and Janet Richardson titled *Yoga for Depression: the Research Data* was to thoroughly examine the data supporting the usefulness of *yoga* in treating depression. Five randomized controlled studies were discovered, with differing levels of severity of the disease and using various forms of *yoga* therapies. All of the trials had positive results, but methodological information about attrition rates, compliance, and randomization techniques was absent. Despite the possible exception of exhaustion and dyspnoea in one research participant, no side effects were noted.

Sharma, Das, Mondal, Goswampi, and Gandhi's study examined how well *sahaja-yoga* treated depression. In this study, thirty individuals between the ages of eighteen and forty-five were split intc two groups: those who took traditional antidepressants and those who practised *sahaja-yoga*. For eight weeks, the patients received instruction in *sahaja-yoga* from a qualified *sahaja-yogī*. The patient's scores on the Hamilton Rating Scale for Anxiety and Depression indicated a notable enhancement following two months of treatment. Nonetheless, patients who received *sahaja-yoga* showed a noticeably more significant percentage improvement in their HAM-D and HAM-A scores.

After reviewing research papers, it was noted that *yoga* postures and doing *yoga* as a routine help maintain a person's physical health and play a very important role in keeping mental health in good condition. It was discovered that individuals who practised *yoga* noticed positive changes in their health, patients found themselves mentally healthy and they also agreed that *yoga* improved their energy, happiness and sleep cycle. Other studies have found that *yoga* enhanced psychological stress and quality of life. Improvement was also seen in anxiety scores, hypertension level and other psychiatric disorders.

This chapter focuses on the mental benefits of *yoga* and how it helps to relax the mind and soul. Which posture of *yoga* will improve mental health, the *yoga*'s curative effects on individuals with anxiousness, stress, and other mental illnesses, and improvement in the quality of life after *yoga* treatment?

Yoga Āsana for Mental Health

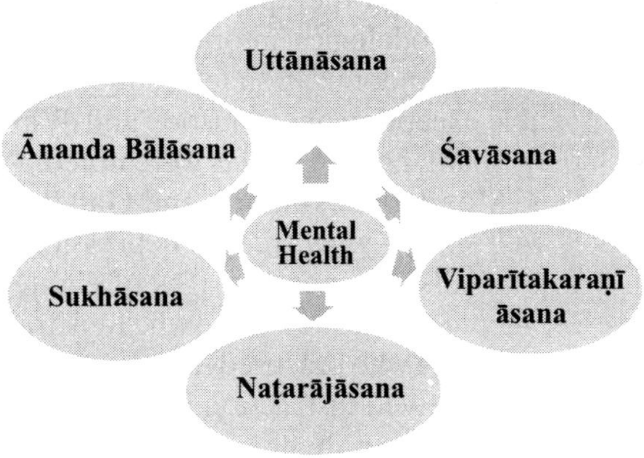

Uttānāsana

This is an intense forward stretch pose that works on the muscles of the entire back, improving strength and flexibility. The *uttānāsana* improves oxygen-rich blood flow to the brain as the head is positioned below the heart in this pose. Regular practice of *uttānāsana* relieves anxiety.

Śavāsana

This pose is used at the end of *yoga* routines and is excellent for meditation, boosting mental health, and relaxing the body.

Viparītakaraṇīsana

This inverted pose in one of the best *yoga āsanas* for improving blood circulation towards the head. It helps to calm anxiety, treat depression and insomnia besides regulating blood flow.

Naṭarājāsana

Doing this exercise regularly can make your core strong, improve body balance, increase flexibility, and overall physical strength. However, you must do this on an empty stomach or do this *yoga āsana* at least four hours post you meal. *Naṭarājāsana-yoga* is all about coordination and balance. It strengthens your shoulder, back, arms and legs strong. *Naṭarājāsana*-betters body balance and posture. Correcting posture, it makes the body less susceptible to aches and pain.*āsana* relaxes the mind, reduces stress and improves concentration.

Sukhāsana

Helps to improve concentration. Helps in reducing stress and anxiety. It has a relaxing effect on the mind and body which is helpful in reducing stress and anxiety. Improves focus and automatically makes you more attentive. Helps to improve one's sense of mind.

Ānanda Bālāsana

Practising *ānanda bālāsana* is a great way of destressing yourself. It helps in calming the mind and relieving anxiety and stress. This *āsana* is beneficial for people suffering from agitation, insomnia, or depression. Practising *ānanda bālāsana* is a great way of relieving fatigue and tiredness. It also releases tension from the lower back area which is a common source of discomfort for us due to our long hours sitting jobs or other activities. This *āsana* helps in lowering your heart rate and calming down both mind and body by releasing stress, anxiety, and depression. This pose is beneficial for people suffering from high blood pressure problems too. The Happy Baby Pose serves as a pick-me-up pose that energizes your body and increases blood circulation in the lower back region. It is also known to release tension from this area of your body which causes stress, anxiety, or fatigue.

How Yoga Improves Quality of Life

- Combining breathing and meditation in *yoga* might enhance one's mental health. "Regular *yoga* practice creates mental clarity and calmness; increases body awareness; relieves chronic stress patterns; relaxes the mind; centres attention; and sharpens concentration", says Dr Nevins.
- Regular *yoga* helps maintain good shape, strength, a healthy mind and a calm soul. It reduces stress and improves sleep quality. *Yoga* is powerful; anyone can practice anywhere, and doing it in the morning after a long sleep of 7-8 hours is very beneficial. At this point, mind is completely relaxed and reacts positively and effectively to movements.
- Incorporation of *yoga* into daily life helps to build better health, self-confidence, peace of mind, and a stress-free life. In fact, *yoga* is the most powerful armour for health and well-being in this mechanical world. Taking some *yoga āsana*s and postures everyday might have a significant impact.
- The tension is relieved and *yoga* reduces the physical effects of stress on the body. By promoting relaxation and deep breathing, *yoga* helps lower the levels of the stress hormone cortisol. Related benefits include lowering blood pressure and heart rate, improving digestion and strengthening the immune system, and alleviating symptoms such as anxiety, depression, malaise, asthma, and insomnia.
- People doing *yoga* will feel better on their body. *Yoga* can reduce pain. Anyone who practices *yoga* knows it, and in the studies, practising *yoga* posture (*āsana*) is used by people with symptoms such as cancer, multiple sclerosis, autoimmune diseases, and high blood pressure. It's been shown to reduce pain, arthritis and chronic pain. *Yoga* also helps improve body alignment,

which leads to better posture and helps alleviate back, neck, joint and muscle problems. When we feel better about our bodies, we can express ourselves more completely in our lives. The whole world celebrates with us when we are doing well! We tend to be more kind to others, serve our communities, and in return, good things happen.

- Those who do *yoga* are capable of concentrating greater on the present. *Yoga* helps us concentrate on the here-and-now moment and become more aware of our bodies and breath. When we direct our attention into each breath and each movement we deepen our concentration (*dhāraṇā*), improve our coordination and ability to balance, our reaction time and even our memory. When we become more present, we become more adaptable and less reactive. Living fully in the present moment is liberating and empowering. We strongly encourage you to unlock this powerful gift of the now, and immerse yourself in it.
- Even if you practice *yoga* only occasionally, one might still benefit if you find it very difficult to drop everything mentally while practising *yoga*. Imagine less stress, less fatigue, flexibility, mental and physical strength, optimal weight with improved posture and endurance, concentration, inner calm and transparency. What you dream of is what you can achieve.

Conclusion

To conclude, *yoga* can play a huge role in relaxing the mind and curing mental health issues. As we all know, *yoga* is one of the greatest and oldest treasures of Indian culture, and it has a lot of benefits and is a way to live life positively and actively. It has much to offer humankind for their existence and survival, including mental peace and solving mental health issues. People today are moving towards other medications and therapy for mental wellness issues. "*Yoga* is the process of eliminating pain from the body, mind, and the soul"—Amit Ray. This quotation is a firm reminder to every individual that among various treatment processes, *yoga* is one of the most excellent methods that one must adopt in their daily lifestyle; it will surely give positive results and changes in body, mind, and soul.

REFERENCES

Basavaraddi, Ishwar V. (2015). *Yoga: Its Origin, History and Development, Public Diplomacy.*

Bisht, S., Chawla, B., Tolahunase, M., Mishra, R., Dada, R. (2019). "Impact of *Yoga*-based Lifestyle Intervention on Psychological Stress and Quality of Life in the Parents of Children with Retinoblastoma". *Annals of Neurosciences*, *26*(2): 66-74. doi:10.5214/ans.0972.7531.260206

Bouya, Keikhaie, Hosseini & Keikhaie. (2021, March). "The Effect of *Yoga* on Uterine Artery Doppler Indices, Maternal and Fetal Complications in Pregnant Women: A Quasi-Experimental Study". *Journal of Āyurveda and Integrative Medicine*, *12*(1): 70-74. https://doi.org/10.1016/j.jaim.2020.07.003

Dalal (2022). "Quasi Experimental Study of Accessing the Effect of *Yoga* and Naturopath Panch Tatvas on Quality of Life and Mental Health". In *Shodhganga.*

Gupta, N., Khera, S., Vempati, R.P., Sharma, R. & Bijlani, R.L. (2006). "Effect of *Yoga*-based Lifestyle Intervention on State and Trait Anxiety". *Indian Journal of Physiology and Pharmacology*, *50*(1): 41-47.

https://breathenorfolk.com/blog/top-ten-ways-yoga-will-improve-life/

https://economictimes.indiatimes.com/news/how-to/yoga-poses-that-can-help-improve-your-mental-health/articleshow/86931591.cms?from=mdr

https://www.onlymyhealth.com/sukhāsana-health-benefits-and-right-way-to-do-the-yoga-pose-1630405332#:~:text=Benefits%20of%20Sukhāsana,-Sukhāsana%20is%20something&text=It%20has%20a%20relaxing%20effect,the%20spine%20and%20back%20muscles.

Importance and Benefits of Yoga, Dabur.

Knight, M., Pultinas, D., Collins, S. *et al.* (2014). "Teaching Mindfulness on an Inpatient Psychiatric Unit". *Mindfulness, 5*: 259-67. https://doi.org/10.1007/s12671-012-0175-5

Kṛṣṇamurthy (2022). "Effect of *Yoga* Therapy on Selected Clinical Physiological and Psychological Variables Among Lumbago Men". In *Shodhganga.*

Maintaining a Regular *Yoga* Practice can Provide Physical and Mental Health Benefits, American Osteopathic Association.

Medindia Content Team, *The Essence of Yoga.*

Mental Health Benefits, *Asutra* from https://asutra.com/blogs/asutra-life/top-5-yoga-mental-health-benefits

Physical, Mental and Spiritual Health benefits of *Yoga*, https://www.vibeindian.in/physical-mental-spiritual-health-benefits-yoga/

Pilkington, K., Kirkwood, G., Rampes, H. & Richardson, J. (2005). "*Yoga* for Depression: The Research Evidence". *Journal of Affective Disorders*, *89*(1-3): 13-24. https://doi.org/10.1016/j.jad.2005.08.013

Ross, A., Friedmann, E., Bevans, M. & Thomas, S. (2013). "National Survey of *Yoga* Practitioners: Mental and Physical Health Benefits". *Complementary Therapies in Medicine*, *21*(4): 313-23. https://doi.org/10.1016/j.ctim.2013.04.001

Sharma, V.K., Das, S., Mondal, S., Goswampi, U. & Gandhi, A. (2005). "Effect of Sahaj *Yoga* on Depressive Disorders". *Indian Journal of Physiology and Pharmacology*, *49*(4): 462-68.

Singh (2019). "Impact of Intervention Programme Upon Mental Health of Orphans". In *Shodhganga.*

Social Benefits of Practising *Yoga*, Meditation Daily from https://www.meditationdaily.com/social-benefits-practising-yoga/

Sukhdeo (2020). "Comparative Study of Yogic Exercise and Treadmill Exercise on Resting Heart Rate Variability and VO2 Max in Undergraduate Medical Student". In *Shodhganga.*

The Best Yoga Asanas for Mental Health by Kalwyna Rathod | 10 October 2019, FEMINA.

The Statesman, *Improve Your Quality of Life with Yoga*, Deepa Gupta, New Delhi, 20 June 2017.

Timothy Burgin, *History of Yoga*, *Yoga Basics.*

Yadav, Sunil Kumar, Ashwani Kumar, Anil Kumar, Vikas Kumar. (2015). *Importance of Yoga in Daily Life*, Research Scholar, Department of Physical Education, Banaras Hindu University.

14

Structure of Hindu Society

Its Contradictions and Dynamics

Manish Dwivedi

Introduction

Hinduism does not accord even to the Vedas the kind of absolute which Christianity and Islam accord to the Bible and the Quran respectively. It is essential to understand the significance of this remark to comprehend one more distinctive characteristic of Hinduism. The Sanskrit equivalent for a scripture's absolute, complete, unchallengeable final authority is *śabda-prāmāṇya*. It means that every word in the scripture is true and must be taken literally without an exception. That is the final authority; no other authority can be greater than that. According to Christian thinking, every word and statement in the Bible is true and it is the only and final truth; therefore, it cannot be challenged. Muslims hold the same view about Quran. They accept the principle of *śabda-prāmāṇya* with reference to their respective scriptures. In other words, they take words and sentences in their scriptures literally; they do not accept any other meaning of those words and statements except their literal meaning. Thus, the following statement from the Bible should be considered: "The Lord God then built up into a woman the rib that he had taken from the Man" (Genesis, 2: 22).

Here "rib" means "rib" and nothing else. Like this story of the creation of woman, there are in the Bible theories of the creation of the universe, of the place of the earth in it, the duties of the sun, the moon, stars and other heavenly bodies, the creation of man and other creatures. All these are, according to Christians, literally and finally true. But these came to be challenged after the Renaissance in Europe, which brought in its wake the spirit of free scientific inquiry into every phenomenon independently of the Bible. This changed the history of Europe by shaking the religious faith in Christianity to its foundation.

There are indications that the same history is likely to be repeated in the case of Islam. Winds of change have already started blowing in some Muslim countries. They have set aside the Shariat and enacted new laws which are in keeping with the spirit of modern times. They have given legal protection to women over and above the provisions of the Shariat.

Indian reformist Muslims are agitating against oral divorce by pronouncing *talaq* thrice. Why this has happened deserves to be understood in a book, but it does not tally with our actual experience, and we come to doubt its truth. If we can show, based on evidence, that it is false, we naturally cannot accept it. This is applicable also to the statements in the scriptures. Their authority is limited by the rule of common sense given above; it cannot be ultimate and unlimited. Great Hindu thinkers and philosophers had accepted this principle from time immemorial and made it an integral part of Hinduism. It would be more plausible to say that this principle was part and parcel of Hinduism from the very beginning; the great *ācārya* only vocalized it.

The first one of these quotations is taken from the *Abhinava-bhāratī*, the scholarly commentary of the great Ācārya Abhinavagupta on Bharata's *Nāṭyaśāstra,* an encyclopedic work on dramaturgy. It is not a religious work at all but a work on dramaturgy. But what the philosopher says in it is representative and therefore very important. In it Abhinavagupta says—What does it matter if it is so described in the *Rāmāyaṇa?* We are not afraid (to reject it) even if it is so described in the Veda? Here the expression so described is important. It means that which goes against our actual experience. This kind of statement cannot be binding on us even though it is scriptural statement. Even the scripture does not have the freedom to deny ground reality and make statements contrary to it, however great then it may be in eyes of the faithful.

The second quotation at the beginning is completely in line with the first one. It is taken from the erudite philosophical treatise *Sarvadarśana-saṁgraha* written by Vidyāraṇya Swāmī, the *Śaṅkarācārya* (highest pontiff) of the Śṛīṅgerī Pīṭha. This is the literal meaning of his words:

> "If the statements of *Vedānta* go against undeniable actual experience, they will *be* (*ridiculous and therefore unacceptable*) like "Stones float on water". More than a hundred scriptural assertions cannot establish as true what is contrary to experience as for instance, they cannot establish something as a pot when actually it is a piece of cloth."

This reminds me of one of the well-known words of Copernicus. The scriptures may maintain that the sun moves around the earth and a scientist under pressure from the church may recant and take back his theory as Copernicus did, but as he even asserted, the earth moves round the sun. No scriptural assertion can alter this fact of experience.

Acceptance of this principle naturally restricts the authority of scriptures and makes them open to impartial criticism. It becomes necessary in that case to examine which scriptural statements are contrary to actual experience and which are not in keeping with common good sense and logic. It is common to come across a single scripture statement that is mutually incompatible and contradictory. How to coordinate these is a big problem for interpreters. Great Hindu thinkers and philosophers had to face this difficulty quite often. Here are some examples.

The Pūrva-Mīmāṁsā school of Hindu philosophy maintains that the Vedic *mantra*s (verses) are meant to be used in different Vedic rituals and sacrifices. But it had to decide which verses were to be used in which ritual and which sacrifice. Further, it had to accept that certain portions in the Vedas are not meant for this purpose. It had to accept that these portions were less important and merely incidental and at the most recommendatory (*arthavāda*). This subject is not as simple as it appears from these casual remarks. It is an extremely complex subject; the Mīmāṁsā school of philosophy has an elaborate science of textual interpretation. However, all these exercises were developed and came to be seriously challenged by the Vedānta school of Hindu philosophy. It completely rejected the ritualistic approach of the Mīmāṁsā school and maintained that attainment of heaven through Vedic sacrifices and rituals was not the highest goal of life. The Vedānta school put all the stress on the philosophical cogitations of the Upaniṣads. But these are innumerable and diverse. It became necessary, therefore to coordinate all these into a philosophical system, since the direction of Upaniṣadic thinking was one and well-defined. The result of the efforts to build a philosophical system out of the Upaniṣadic cogitations was the *Brahmasūtra*, the basic treatise of the Vedānta philosophy ascribed to the Sage Bādarāyaṇa. The same is the story of the celebrated *Bhagavad Gītā*; it touches upon so many subjects in just 700 verses and its style is so terse that an interpreter finds it challenging to make the reader remember all these without losing any part and at the same time retain a consolidated view of the whole. It is customary, therefore, for commentators to summarize the topics covered in brief to facilitate the readers understanding. To confirm this fact, one must consult the famous Marathi commentary *Dnyāneśvarī* on the *Gitā*. The great poet-saint philosopher Dnyaneshwar has followed this practice in chapters 6 and 9 of his work.

Our discussion so far is enough to give some idea of Hinduism's approach to its most important scriptures. We have covered in this brief discussion the Vedas, including the Upaniṣads, the *Brahmasūtra* and the *Bhagavad Gītā*. These three are called *prsthāna-trayī* and are the bedrock of Hinduism.

Hinduism's views are welcome. It is because of this liberal and open approach, even to the most sacred basic scriptures, that Hinduism has developed so many schools of philosophy and so many sects, all existing peacefully together. The essential criterion of the acceptability of the scripture, according to Hindu tradition, as explained earlier, is that it must not be contrary to experience; in addition, it must also successfully stand other epistemological tests; they must not disprove it. Even the topics which are outside the scope of these tests must pass the tests of *alaukika jñāna.* It is only after passing these various stringent tests that the acceptability of the scripture is established. In short, Hinduism is not unquestioningly accepted as final and unchallengeable, even in its scriptures.

The Vedas' authority is to be considered in light of this discussion. The seeds of all the questions about Hinduism as a philosophical religion are in the Vedas, and these have been listed. The answers to these questions constitute the essence of Hinduism. We will study some of these answers in due course in this book. The authority of the Vedas as scriptures principally centres around these answers. As explained already, these are all outside the scope of science in its present state and its approach to its problems. Science has no answers to these questions. Other prevailing religions do have their answers, but how they suffer from serious flaws and are unsatisfactory has already been shown in this chapter. Hinduism surpasses other religions in its answers to these fundamental questions because it has explored all the possible answers, subjected them to a close critical examination, shown their shortcomings and then given its answers. Based on this thorough critical scrutiny, Hinduism has propounded its doctrines. But the seeds of all these are in the Vedas. It is the truth that gives the Vedas their great authority. Later, these very seeds in the Vedas developed into full-fledged and elaborate theories and doctrines of Hinduism. It is very significant that in the modern age of science, some of these seeds of thought and the theories developed by Hinduism are attracting advanced modern science. In brief, the authority of the Hindu scriptures is of this nature. In the following paragraphs, we shall examine this in a comparative light.

Some consideration of an incidental subject is essential in this context. With other prevailing religions in the world, it is mandatory to take scriptural statements as literally true; therefore, there is no scope to interpret them in any other way. For example, according to Islamic law, the evidence given in a law court by a man is more important than that given by a woman. This is because, according to the scriptural authority of the Quran, a man is superior to a woman; one man's testimony is more acceptable than two testimonies of two women. This is a fundamental principle of Islamic jurisprudence, and the Quran supports it. The basic question is as follows: Is it an experiential truth that every man is superior to every woman simply because he is a man? Is a woman prime minister's peon superior to her because he is a man? This is a case of discrimination based on sex.

Even more important from the legal point of view is the following question: What is more important in a legal case—the evidence or the sex of a witness? Common sense gives weight to the evidence and ignores the sex of the witness, which is irrelevant. But, Islamic jurisprudence takes an inflexible and literal view of the scriptural injunction and ignores common sense. In the background of this additional explanation, one is in a better position to understand the open, liberal, free, and logical approach of Hinduism to the authority of its scriptures. It always respects the undeniable truth of experience and common sense dictates.

We have already touched upon law-making and the administration of justice. No civilized life is possible without these. Religion has a great interest in it since one essential function of religion is to sustain society. Hinduism also gives it all due importance. It would be interesting to note in this connection that the well-known Sanskrit word *dharma* does not mean religion at all; it means law and jurisprudence; *dharma* as religion is a modern usage and is specific to modern Indian languages like Marathi, Hindi, Gujarati, etc. The function of *dharma* as law is to frame rules and regulations to guide and govern all kinds of transactions in society, as per the principles of justice and fair pray. It aims to bring stability, discipline and regularity to social life. It lays down the rules regarding the duties of individuals as citizens and their rights, the duties of the king and his rights, and the administration of justice in case of any dispute. This entire subject is the jurisdiction of the Smṛti literature of Hinduism. A large number of Smṛti treatises came to be written in this tradition. The most widely recognized among these works are the *Manusmṛti* and the *Yajñavalkyasmṛti.* All these are also scriptures, but they don't have absolute and final authority. The function of the Smṛtis is strictly mundane and practical as explained above. It is to regulate social life and control human dealings according to justice. However, social life and the nature of human dealings are based on the specifics of time and place. Naturally, the laws regulating them have to change to cope with the changes in circumstances. This is subject to change depending on the accepted view of Hindu jurisprudence. Its practice also completely adheres to this view. To substantiate this we shall take into consideration its thinking vis-à-vis the much-maligned but ever-changing caste system in Hindu society. Since this is a subject well within the jurisdiction of Smṛti literature, its relevance in the present context is self-evident. There is no mention of profession-based castes in the Veda. In the Puruṣasūkta of the *Ṛgveda* there is a description of the creation of the four *varṇa*s, namely brāhmaṇas, kṣatriyas, vaiśyas and *śūdras*, but it is metaphorical and not historical. The *Bhagavad Gītā* mentions that God created the four *varṇa*s on the basis of quality and duty (*guṇa* and *karma*). It does not say that birth is the determining factor of *varṇa*. But castes based on birth and profession were known to the *Mahābhārata*; *sūta* (carpenter) and *dhīvara* (fisherfolk) are mentioned in it as birth and profession-based castes. Karṇa, a warrior in the *Mahābhārata,* was *sūta*, whereas Matsyagandhā was a fisherwoman; several other such castes are mentioned in the *Mahābhārata*. Later, when *smṛti* literature came to be written, the caste system seemed to have stabilized. It has continued till the present time, offering an extremely intricate and complicated picture, and it has become a social and national problem of great magnitude. We shall deal with this problem in a separate chapter in due course. It must be borne in mind that the caste system in Hindu society has a very long history and nobody really knows how it originated. Various sociological theories of its nature and origin are mutually contradictory and serve only to disprove each other. What is certain is that the leaders of Hindu society in the past considered it to be good and useful. Its modern critics point out only its faults and disadvantages, but it must also have its own inherent strengths and advantages. Otherwise, it would never have survived so long. It is because of the inherent strength of the caste system that the Hindus could withstand the terrible onslaught of Islamic rule for well over 1,000 years. Even the lowest of the low castes remained loyal to their parent society and to their Hindu faith because of the tightly-knit caste system. And they remain so even today. The same is the story of the attempts to convert Hindus to Christianity. Despite the state patronage that Christian missionaries enjoyed during the British rule and the immense material resources of the church, evangelical missions had only marginal and negligible success. The credit here also goes to the tight caste organization.

However, the caste system must not be considered defensible now. Hindu social reformers are clear that it has outlived its purpose and is anachronistic. They point out that it does not keep up with the modern spirit of democracy and social equality. It is no longer the strength of Hindu society but its weakness; the sooner it is dispensed with, the better. In short, the new times need a new *smṛti*. In response to the emotional calls of social reformers, after Independence, the Government of India enacted innumerable social laws to remove caste discrimination and bring social justice to all.

Our discussion so far should enable the reader to understand the nature and scope of scriptural authority and its limitations in Hinduism. This is why Hinduism is an open, inclusive, growing, and developing system that has not stagnated. It is because of this that Hinduism is not averse to reforms. Not that reforms were not resisted; initially, they were vehemently resisted and reviled, but after much debate and discussion, Hindu society slowly but surely absorbed them. One example is the status of women in society. It is not the contention here that all women enjoy their rightful equal legal status in Hindu society; the overall situation is far from satisfactory and new social problems like female infanticide and phoeticide have recently cropped up. But still, there is a great change even then in the status of women. The *purdāh* system, which confined women to a merely domestic existence behind the veil, has, to a large extent vanished. There is no opposition to equal education for girls. There is no opposition to women entering any profession of their choice. Many women occupy high offices and top positions throughout the country's length and breadth, and this number is steadily increasing.

There is a strong legislative example to corroborate the point that Hindus are not opposed to social reforms. When the Government of India introduced a strongly pro-reform

Hindu Code Bill in 1950, there was stiff resistance from the conservative sections of the society. Later, the same Bill was passed as the Hindu Succession Act, Hindu Marriage Act, and other related laws. In the meantime, the government held extensive debates with the people opposing these measures and convinced them of the following two things: (1) It updated the existing Hindu law to keep with the needs of modern times, and (2) it only implemented several provisions in the Smṛtis that had remained neglected in the existing Hindu law.

It would be wrong to suppose that the Smṛtis do not contain anything of permanent value because new Smṛtis are warranted by changing times. These treatises are replete with guides for human beings on the path of virtue and a good life. All these are of everlasting value. The wisdom that can Hindu social life has remained remarkably stable for centuries and has undergone several transformations. It has seen many reforms and has lived with them. Hindu family life is remarkably strong, and Hindu marriage is exceptionally stable. Not that there are no exceptions, but they are few and go to prove the rule.

The credit for all this goes to the Hindu scriptures, which carefully created the typical Hindu ethos over thousands of years. Both kinds of Hindu scriptures, namely, Śrutis (i.e., the Vedas) and Smṛtis, support this view. They have kept Hinduism from being narrowly dogmatic and stagnant. The Smṛtis are principally responsible for keeping Hinduism away from becoming a creed centred around the life-work of a single person. They are chiefly responsible for making it an ethical way of life. They have made it dynamic and progressive.

REFERENCES

Chaturvedi, T.N. (2010). *Manusamriti*. Diamond Pocket Books (P) Ltd.

Eggeling, J. (Trans.), (n.d.). *Gopatha Brahmana*, Kessinger Publishing.

Griffith, R.T.H. (Trans.), (n.d.). *Rigveda*. Forgotten Books.

Pandey, K.C. (Trans.), (n.d.). *Abhinav Bharati*, Eastern Book Linkers.

Radhakrishnan, S. (Trans.), (n.d.). *Bhagavad Gītā*, Harper Collins Publishers.

______, (n.d.). *Mundaka Upaniṣad*. Harper Collins Publishers.

______, (n.d.). *Isavasya Upaniṣad*, Oxford University Press.

Radhakrishnan, S. & C.A. Moore, (Trans.) (n.d.). *Upaniṣads,* Princeton University Press.

Rāya, P. & Ganguli, K.M. (1893). *The Mahabharata of Krishna-Dwaipayana Vyasa Translated Into English Prose: Anushasana Parva* Vol. 9, Bhārata Press.

Swami Tapasyananda, (Trans.), (n.d.) *Sivamahimna Stotra*, Sri Ramakrishna Math.

The Holy Quran (n.d.). King Fahd Complex for the Printing of the Holy Quran.

15

Cultural Integration and Social Transformation

Exploring the Indianized Social Work Approaches to Public Health

Suraqua Fahad

Introduction

In the realm of public health, integrating cultural perspectives and indigenous knowledge systems has gained increasing recognition for addressing the diverse health challenges communities face. This acknowledgement stems from the understanding that cultural beliefs, practices, and traditions are pivotal in shaping health behaviours and attitudes. In the Indian context, where diversity thrives across various dimensions, including culture, religion, language, and socio-economic status, incorporating Indianized approaches to public health holds significant promise for advancing health equity and promoting social transformation.

Indianized approaches to public health are rooted in the rich philosophical traditions that have evolved over centuries within the Indian subcontinent. These traditions encompass a holistic understanding of health and well-being, emphasizing the interconnectedness of the body, mind, and spirit (Jasemi, Valizadeh, Zamanzadeh & Keogh, 2017). For instance, Ayurveda, an ancient Indian system of medicine, promotes harmony between the mind, body, and spirit through practices such as *yoga* and meditation to enhance overall health and vitality. Such integrative approaches underscore the enduring legacy of Indian philosophical wisdom in shaping public health paradigms, fostering comprehensive wellness that transcends mere physical health. Central to ancient medication perspective are concepts such as *dharma, karma*, and Ayurveda, which underscore the importance of balance, harmony, and alignment with natural laws in achieving optimal health outcomes. Moreover, these philosophical foundations emphasize the interplay between individual health and the broader social, cultural, and environmental contexts in which people live.

Against this backdrop, this chapter endeavours to thoroughly investigate the philosophical underpinnings of Indianized approaches to public health. It explores how integrating cultural elements can contribute to societal transformation and enhance health outcomes. By scrutinizing the intersectionality of culture, philosophy, and public health practice, the study aims to elucidate the fundamental principles that underlie Indianized approaches and their potential implications for addressing contemporary health challenges. Through a comprehensive analysis of pertinent literature, case studies, and empirical evidence, the research endeavours to illuminate the significance of cultural integration in shaping public health policies, programmes, and interventions within the Indian context.

Objectives

The primary objectives of this chapter are twofold (as mentioned in Table 15.1): first, to provide a comprehensive overview of the philosophical underpinnings of Indianized approaches to public health, elucidating key concepts and principles derived from Indian philosophical traditions; and second, to explore the implications of cultural integration for addressing health disparities, promoting community well-being, and fostering social change. This chapter seeks to contribute to a deeper understanding of Indianized approaches' role in advancing health equity and social justice in India and beyond by critically examining the intersections between culture, philosophy, and public health.

Table 15.1: Objectives with their Description

Objective	**Description**
Overview of Philosophical Underpinnings	Provide a comprehensive exploration of the foundational concepts and principles rooted in Indian philosophical traditions that inform Indianized social work approaches to public health.
Implications of Cultural Integration	Investigate how integrating cultural perspectives influences the effectiveness of public health interventions, addresses health disparities, promotes community well-being, and facilitates social change.
Contribution to Understanding	Critically analyse the intersections between culture, philosophy, and public health to contribute to a deeper understanding of the role of Indianized social work approaches in advancing health equity and social justice.

Philosophical Underpinnings of Indianization

Indian philosophical traditions have long served as the bedrock of indigenous approaches to health and well-being, shaping how individuals perceive and engage with health. Rooted in ancient texts such as the Vedas, Upaniṣads, and the *Bhagavad Gītā*, these traditions offer profound insights into the interconnectedness of human existence, nature, and the cosmos (Srivastava, 2010) as mentioned in Table 15.2.

Table 15.2: Perspectives on Interconnectedness in Ancient Indian Texts

Text	Perspective on Interconnectedness
Vedas	Emphasize the harmony between humans, nature, and the cosmos.
Upaniṣads	Explore the concept of *Brahman*, the ultimate reality that underlies the universe, emphasizing unity and oneness.
Bhagavad Gītā	Discuss the interconnectedness of the self (*ātman*) with the universal consciousness (*Brahman*), promoting harmony and balance.

The notion of *dharma* is central to these philosophical frameworks, which encapsulates the moral and ethical principles governing human conduct and social order. *Dharma* emphasizes the importance of living in harmony with one's duty, righteousness, and cosmic law, all of which are integral to the pursuit of holistic health (Sagaram & Kaipa, 2020).

Karma is another fundamental concept that informs Indianized approaches to health, which underscores the principle of cause and effect and the cyclical nature of existence (Kalra, Ved & Baruah, 2017). According to this world view, individuals are believed to reap the consequences of their actions, both in this life and in subsequent incarnations. *Karma* thus influences health beliefs and practices by emphasizing the role of personal responsibility, moral conduct, and the cultivation of positive virtues in maintaining physical, mental, and spiritual well-being.

In addition to *dharma* and *karma,* Ayurveda is one of the cornerstones of Indian philosophy and medicine, offering a holistic framework for understanding health and disease. Ayurveda, which translates to "the science of life", emphasizes the balance and harmony of bodily energies (*doṣa*s), the importance of proper diet and lifestyle, and the use of natural remedies to promote health and prevent illness (Behere, Das, Yadav & Behere, 2013; Ravishankar & Shukla, 2007). Grounded in the concept of *prakṛti* (individual constitution) and the interconnectedness of mind, body, and spirit (Shilpa & Venkatesha Murthy, 2011), Ayurveda provides a comprehensive understanding of health that extends beyond the mere absence of disease.

These philosophical concepts deeply influence health beliefs and practices in Indian society, shaping individuals' attitudes toward health, illness, and healing. They inform traditional healing systems such as Ayurveda, *yoga*, and naturopathy, which emphasize the importance of holistic interventions that address the root causes of disease and promote overall well-being. Moreover, they underscore the interconnectedness of individual health with broader social, cultural, and environmental factors, highlighting the need for a multifaceted approach to public health that honours indigenous knowledge and values (as reflected in Table 15.3).

Table 15.3: Traditional Healing System and Holistic Health Approaches

Traditional Healing System	Example in Indian Context
Ayurveda	Ayurveda, an ancient Indian system of medicine, emphasizes the balance of bodily humours (*doṣa*s) and advocates for lifestyle modifications, dietary changes, and herbal remedies to prevent and treat diseases. For example, Ayurvedic treatments often include the use of medicinal plants like *neem*, turmeric, and *aśvagandhā* (Behere, Das, Yadav & Behere, 2013).
Yoga	*Yoga*, originating from ancient Indian philosophy, encompasses physical postures, breathing exercises, and meditation techniques aimed at promoting physical, mental, and spiritual well-being. Practices such as *prāṇāyāma* (breath control) and *āsana*s (*yoga* poses) are believed to enhance overall health by improving circulation, reducing stress, and fostering inner harmony (Jasemi, Valizadeh, Zamanzadeh & Keogh, 2017).

(*Contd.*)

Traditional Healing System	Example in Indian Context
Naturopathy	Naturopathy, influenced by traditional Indian healing practices, emphasizes natural therapies and lifestyle modifications to support the body's inherent ability to heal itself. Modalities such as hydrotherapy, dietary counselling, and detoxification techniques are commonly used in naturopathic treatments to address various health concerns while promoting overall wellness (Myers & Vigar, 2019).
Interconnectedness	Traditional healing systems in India recognize the interconnectedness of individual health with broader social, cultural, and environmental factors. For instance, Ayurveda considers dietary habits, seasonal changes, and mental well-being as integral aspects of holistic health, highlighting the interconnected nature of human health with the surrounding environment and societal influences. Similarly, *yoga* philosophy emphasizes the unity of mind, body, and spirit, emphasizing the interconnectedness of individual well-being with the universal consciousness.

Sociocultural Integration in Public Health

Sociocultural integration plays a pivotal role in influencing health behaviours and attitudes within communities, thereby significantly impacting public health outcomes. In India, for instance, the preference for traditional healing practices reflects deeply ingrained cultural values related to holistic well-being and harmony with nature. Also, it contributes to the broader sociocultural identity of the population (Panda & Subudhi, 2020).

Moreover, case studies abound in the Indian context, demonstrating the profound impact of cultural integration on public health initiatives. For instance, community-driven interventions that leverage local customs and traditions have successfully addressed health disparities. One such example is the use of community-based rituals or festivals to disseminate health information and promote preventive measures against diseases like malaria or tuberculosis (Chavez-Rimache, Ugarte-Gil & Brunette, 2023). By embedding health messages within cultural practices, these initiatives enhance awareness and foster community participation and ownership of health programmes.

Impact of Cultural Integration on Public Health Initiatives: Case Studies

Case Study 1: Swachh Bharat Mission (SBM)

The SBM launched by the Indian government in 2014 aimed to achieve universal sanitation coverage and eliminate open defecation nationwide (Behera, Pradhan, Behera, Jena & Satpathy, 2021). Recognizing the sociocultural significance of cleanliness and hygiene in Indian society, the SBM integrated cultural elements into its messaging and interventions. For example, the campaign utilized traditional cultural symbols like the broom (representing cleanliness) and the lotus (symbolizing purity) to resonate with local communities. Moreover, community-led initiatives such as "cleanliness drives" during religious festivals like Dīwālī and Gaṇeś Caturthī encouraged active participation and ownership of sanitation efforts. By leveraging cultural norms and practices, the SBM succeeded in mobilizing widespread support and achieving significant progress in improving sanitation infrastructure and behaviour change.

Case Study 2: Pulse Polio Immunization Campaign

The Pulse Polio Immunization Campaign in India exemplifies the successful integration of cultural practices into public health initiatives. The campaign adopted culturally sensitive approaches tailored to local contexts to address cultural beliefs and misconceptions surrounding vaccination. For instance, health workers engaged with community leaders, religious institutions, and traditional healers to dispel myths and build trust in vaccination (Coates, Waisbord, Awale, Solomon & Dey, 2013). Additionally, the campaign strategically leveraged cultural events and gatherings, such as religious festivals and community fairs, to conduct vaccination drives. These efforts increased vaccine acceptance and fostered a sense of community ownership and participation in immunization efforts. As a result, India achieved remarkable success in eradicating polio and maintaining its polio-free status through sustained cultural integration in public health programmes (Coates, Waisbord, Awale, Solomon & Dey, 2013).

Case Study 3: National Rural Health Mission (NRHM)

The NRHM, launched in 2005, aimed to improve access to quality health-care services in rural India (Nandan, 2010). One of the key strategies of NRHM was the deployment of Accredited Social Health Activists (ASHAs) who served as community health workers (Nandan, 2010). Recognizing the importance of cultural competence in health-care delivery, ASHAs were selected from the local community and received training in culturally sensitive communication and practices. They played a crucial role in bridging the gap between formal health-care systems and rural communities by addressing cultural barriers and promoting preventive health-care practices rooted in local traditions. Through their culturally tailored interventions, ASHAs contributed significantly to the success of NRHM in improving maternal and child health outcomes and reducing morbidity and mortality rates in rural India (Nandan, 2010).

However, despite the evident benefits, integrating cultural perspectives into public health programmes poses several challenges.

Challenges and Opportunities

One significant obstacle in India is the clash between traditional beliefs and modern medical practices, often leading to scepticism or resistance towards Western interventions. For example, Kasthuri's (2018) research reflects that the use of vaccines in certain rural communities may be met with distrust due to misconceptions rooted in traditional healing practices or religious beliefs. Community engagement and education become essential in such cases to dispel myths and promote vaccine acceptance.

Additionally, ensuring cultural sensitivity and relevance in health communication materials and interventions is crucial in the Indian context. For instance, when designing public health campaigns, considerations must be made regarding linguistic diversity to ensure messages are effectively understood across different regions and languages. Moreover, religious and socio-economic factors play a significant role in shaping health behaviours and attitudes. Failure to address these nuances may lead to ineffective or counterproductive outcomes in public health initiatives. For example, a health promotion campaign that overlooks religious customs or socio-economic disparities may fail to resonate with the target audience, resulting in limited impact or unintended consequences. Therefore, public health programmes must incorporate cultural competence and tailor interventions to the diverse sociocultural landscape of India.

However, acknowledging cultural diversity as a strength rather than a barrier offers substantial opportunities for advancing public health agendas in India. For instance, in the State of Kerala, initiatives to combat malnutrition have incorporated traditional dietary practices such as the inclusion of millets and locally grown vegetables in government-sponsored nutrition programmes (Jaleel, Arlappa,

Ramakrishna, Sunu, Jayalakshmi, Neeraja, Narasimhulu, Kumar & Kumar, 2023; Subudhi *et al.*, 2024). By aligning with cultural preferences and dietary habits, these programmes have witnessed increased acceptance and participation among the local population, improving health outcomes.

Furthermore, partnerships with local community leaders, traditional healers, and cultural influencers have proven instrumental in designing and implementing effective health interventions. For instance, in Rajasthan, community health workers collaborate with village elders and religious leaders to promote maternal and child health practices during religious festivals and community gatherings (Snodgrass, Most, Upadhyay, Gold, Hinton, Lang, Sosis, Shidhaye & Xygalatas, 2017). This collaborative approach enhances the cultural relevance of health messages and fosters trust and engagement within the community. Ultimately, sociocultural integration serves as a cornerstone of public health strategies to achieve equitable health outcomes for all segments of society.

Social Transformation through Indianized Social Work Approaches

The pursuit of social transformation through Indianized social work approaches involves deeply exploring how Indian philosophical principles intersect with contemporary social change efforts. Drawing upon ancient Indian wisdom rooted in philosophies like Vedānta, Buddhism, and Jainism, practitioners of Indianized social work seek to integrate these principles into their strategies for addressing societal challenges (as mentioned in Table 15.4). For instance, the concept of *ahiṁsā* (non-violence) from Jainism inspires initiatives promoting peace-building and conflict resolution, while the 'principle of *dharma*' (duty/righteousness) guides efforts to uphold social justice and human rights (Gandhi, 1969; Jain, 2007; Sharma, 2014).

Table 15.4: Strategies for Indianized Social Work Rooted in Ancient Indian Wisdom

Ancient Indian Wisdom	Strategies for Indianized Social Work
Vedānta	It incorporates principles of Vedānta, which emphasize self-realization (*ātman*) and interconnectedness (*Brahman*), into community empowerment programmes. This involves fostering a sense of inner fulfilment and recognizing the inherent unity among individuals and communities, leading to collective action for social change.
Buddhism	They are applying Buddhist principles such as mindfulness and compassion in social work interventions. By cultivating awareness of the present moment and fostering empathy towards others, practitioners can facilitate conflict resolution, promote mental well-being, and build inclusive communities based on mutual respect and understanding.
Jainism	It is integrating Jaina's teachings of non-violence (*ahiṁsā*) and ethical conduct (*dharma*) into advocacy efforts for social justice and human rights. This includes promoting peaceful means of protest, advocating for the rights of marginalized communities, and upholding principles of fairness and equality in policymaking and social reforms.

Moreover, Indianized social work emphasizes community empowerment and participatory approaches as central tenets of its practice. By actively involving community members in decision-making processes and programme implementation, practitioners aim to cultivate a sense of ownership and agency among those affected by social issues.

Case studies serve as compelling illustrations of successful social transformation achieved through Indianized social work approaches. For instance, the Self-Employed Women's Association (SEWA) in India has empowered millions of women in the informal sector by providing access to financial services, skills training, and advocacy for labour rights (Datta, 2003). Similarly, initiatives like the Community-Led Total Sanitation (CLTS) approach have led to significant improvements in sanitation practices and hygiene behaviours in rural communities, driven by grassroots mobilization and collective action (Lawrence, Yeboah-Antwi, Biemba, Ram, Osbert, Sabin & Hamer, 2016).

The exploration of social transformation through Indianized social work approaches underscores the importance of integrating indigenous wisdom and community-driven strategies into efforts to address social inequalities and promote sustainable development. By embracing philosophical principles rooted in Indian heritage and adopting participatory approaches that empower communities, social work practitioners can catalyze positive change and foster inclusive societies where all individuals can thrive.

Implication of Public Health Practices

Indianized social work approaches hold significant implications for public health policy and practice, particularly in the Indian context. One implication is the recognition of the interconnectedness of health with broader sociocultural and environmental factors. For example, the concept of *dharma* emphasizes the importance of living in harmony with one's duty and righteousness. When applied to public health practice, this principle underscores the need for interventions that address individual health behaviours and social determinants such as poverty, education, and gender inequality. For instance, initiatives promoting education and economic empowerment among marginalized communities align with the principles of *dharma*, as they contribute to social justice and human rights.

Moreover, Indianized social work approaches emphasize community empowerment and participatory approaches in public health interventions. Instead of adopting top-down approaches, practitioners engage with communities to co-create culturally appropriate and sustainable solutions. For instance, initiatives that involve local community leaders, traditional healers, and cultural influencers in decision-making processes can enhance the acceptability and effectiveness of public health programmes (as mentioned in Table 15.5). This participatory approach fosters ownership and accountability among community members, leading to greater engagement and adherence to health recommendations.

Table 15.5: Community Engagement in Public Health Initiatives

Example	Description
Village Health Committee	In rural India, a Village Health Committee comprising local community members, including elders, women representatives, and traditional healers, collaborate with health-care providers to identify health priorities and develop culturally appropriate interventions (Karuga, Kok, Mbindyo, Hilverda, Otiso, Kavoo, Broerse & Dieleman, 2019). The committee ensures that health programmes address community needs and concerns through regular meetings and discussions, leading to improved health-care access and outcomes.
Traditional Healers' Involvement	In tribal communities, traditional healers play a significant role in health-care delivery. Public health programmes engage with these healers to integrate traditional healing practices with modern health-care approaches. According to Allen, Hatala, Ijaz, Courchene, and Bushie (2020), the integration of indigenous knowledge and practices, including herbal remedies and spiritual healing rituals, into health interventions foster community trust and acceptance. This approach leads to improved health-seeking behaviour and outcomes among the population.

(*Contd.*)

Example	Description
Cultural Influencers' Participation	Public health campaigns leverage the influence of cultural icons, religious leaders, and local celebrities to promote health messages and behaviour change. For example, during vaccination drives, Bollywood actors or sports personalities may endorse immunization to encourage vaccine uptake among the population. This collaborative effort enhances the reach and impact of health initiatives by leveraging existing social networks and channels of communication.
Women's Self-Help Groups (SHGs) Engagement	Women's SHGs, prevalent in many Indian communities, serve as platforms for collective action and empowerment. Public health programmes partner with these groups to address maternal and child health issues, nutrition, and sanitation. Through capacity-building workshops and community-led initiatives, women gain knowledge and skills to improve health practices within their families and communities, contributing to positive health outcomes and community well-being.

Incorporating cultural integration into public health programmes from social work perspectives requires a nuanced understanding of ethical and practical considerations. For example, practitioners must navigate complex sociocultural dynamics and community power structures to ensure that interventions are respectful and inclusive. Additionally, they must address cultural competence and sensitivity issues among health-care providers to avoid perpetuating stereotypes or biases. By integrating cultural perspectives into public health policies and practices, Indianized social work approaches can potentially promote health equity and social justice in diverse communities across India.

Challenges and Future Directions

Integrating Indianized social work approaches into public health represents a promising avenue for addressing the complex health challenges Indian communities face. Looking ahead, there is a need for continued reflection on the potential trajectory of these approaches and their implications for public health policy and practice. While significant progress has been made in recognizing the value of cultural integration, key challenges and barriers remain that must be addressed.

One such challenge is navigating the tension between traditional and Western medical paradigms. Despite growing recognition of the importance of indigenous knowledge and practices, there is still a tendency to prioritize Western biomedical approaches in public health programmes (Horrill, McMillan, Schultz & Thompson, 2018). This can hinder efforts to integrate cultural perspectives fully and may perpetuate disparities in health outcomes among different population groups.

Additionally, the lack of standardized frameworks for incorporating cultural integration into public health practice poses a significant obstacle (Handtke, Schilgen & Mṭsko, 2019). While there is widespread acknowledgement of the importance of cultural sensitivity, there is often a lack of guidance on how to translate this concept into actionable strategies effectively. This highlights the need for further research and collaboration to develop culturally competent approaches that can be tailored to the diverse needs of Indian communities.

Furthermore, ongoing efforts are needed to address structural barriers to cultural integration, including issues related to funding (for instance, a community health project in rural India faces challenges in securing funds for implementing traditional healing practices alongside modern medical interventions), policy support (for example, despite the effectiveness of traditional herbal remedies, there are no policies mandating their inclusion in government health-care programmes, limiting their accessibility to the population), and institutional resistance (for example, health-care institutions in urban areas show reluctance to collaborate with traditional healers, hindering efforts to integrate indigenous knowledge into public health initiatives). Without adequate resources and support from policymakers and health-care institutions, initiatives promoting cultural integration may struggle to achieve meaningful impact.

Despite these challenges, there are opportunities for future research and action in this area. By fostering interdisciplinary collaborations between social workers, public health professionals, policymakers, and community stakeholders, it is possible to develop innovative approaches that leverage the strengths of Indian cultural traditions while addressing contemporary health issues (as mentioned in Table 15.6).

Table 15.6: Future Initiatives to Address Public Health Issues

Future Direction	**Plan of Action**
Interdisciplinary Collaboration	A research project brings together social workers, public health professionals, and community leaders to develop culturally sensitive mental health interventions for tribal communities in India.
Community Engagement and Participatory Approaches	A public health initiative in an urban slum involves community members in designing and implementing sanitation programmes, leading to increased hygiene practices and reduced disease burden.
Leveraging Cultural Traditions for Contemporary Health Challenges	A community-based organization in rural India integrates *yoga* and Ayurveda practices into diabetes prevention programmes, resulting in improved health outcomes among participants.

Moreover, by prioritizing community engagement and participatory approaches, public health programmes can empower communities to take ownership of their health and well-being, leading to more sustainable and equitable outcomes.

Conclusion

This chapter has explored the philosophical foundations of Indianized approaches to public health, highlighting concepts such as *dharma*, *karma*, and Ayurveda, which underpin holistic health practices in India. It has discussed the implications of cultural integration for addressing health disparities, promoting community well-being, and fostering social change. Case studies and examples from the Indian context have illustrated the profound impact of cultural integration on public health initiatives, demonstrating the success of community-driven interventions and the importance of leveraging indigenous knowledge systems. Additionally, the chapter has identified challenges and opportunities in incorporating cultural perspectives into public health programmes, emphasizing the need for interdisciplinary collaboration, community engagement, and participatory approaches.

Cultural integration is crucial in addressing public health challenges, particularly in diverse and heterogeneous societies like India. Public health programmes can enhance their relevance, acceptability, and effectiveness among target populations by recognizing and respecting cultural beliefs, practices, and traditions. Moreover, cultural integration fosters a sense of community ownership and empowerment, leading to more sustainable and equitable health outcomes. By incorporating Indian philosophical principles and indigenous knowledge systems, public health initiatives can better address the interconnected nature of health and well-being, thereby promoting holistic health and social transformation.

Moving forward, there is a pressing need for further exploration and adoption of Indianized approaches to public health. This requires continued research, collaboration, and innovation to develop culturally sensitive and contextually appropriate interventions. Policymakers, health-care providers, social workers, and community leaders must work together to overcome structural barriers to cultural integration and promote incorporating Indian cultural traditions into public health policies and programmes. By embracing Indianized approaches, we can harness the rich diversity of India's cultural heritage to address contemporary health challenges and advance health equity and social justice for all segments of society.

REFERENCES

Allen, L., Hatala, A., Ijaz, S., Courchene, E.D. & Bushie, E.B. (2020). "Indigenous-led Health Care Partnerships in Canada". *CMAJ: Canadian Medical Association Journal = journal de l'Association medicale canadienne*, *192*(9): E208-E216. https://doi.org/10.1503/cmaj.190728

Behere, P.B., Das, A., Yadav, R. & Behere, A.P. (2013). "Ayurvedic Concepts Related to Psychotherapy". *Indian Journal of Psychiatry*, *55*(Suppl 2): S310-S314. https://doi.org/10.4103/0019-5545.105556

Behera, M.R., Pradhan, H.S., Behera, D., Jena, D. & Satpathy, S.K. (2021). "Achievements and Challenges of India's Sanitation Campaign Under Clean India Mission: A Commentary". *Journal of Education and Health Promotion*, *10*: 350. https://doi.org/10.4103/jehp.jehp_1658_20

Chavez-Rimache, L., Ugarte-Gil, C. & Brunette, M.J. (2023). "The Community as an Active Part in the Implementation of Interventions for the Prevention and Control of Tuberculosis: A Scoping Review". *medRxiv: The Preprint Server For Health Sciences*, 2023.01.10.22283706. https://doi.org/10.1101/2023.01.10.22283706

Coates, E.A., Waisbord, S., Awale, J., Solomon, R. & Dey, R. (2013). "Successful Polio Eradication in Uttar Pradesh, India: the Pivotal Contribution of the Social Mobilization Network, an NGO/UNICEF Collaboration". *Global Health, Science and Practice*, *1*(1): 68-83. https://doi.org/10.9745/GHSP-D-12-00018

Datta, R. (2003). "From Development to Empowerment: The Self-Employed Women's Association in India". *International Journal of Politics, Culture, and Society*, *16*(3): 351-68. http://www.jstor.org/stable/20020171

Gandhi, M.K. (1969). *The Moral and Political Writings of Mahatma Gandhi*, 2. Oxford, UK: Oxford University Press.

Handtke, O., Schilgen, B. & Mṭsko, M. (2019). "Culturally Competent Healthcare: A Scoping Review of Strategies Implemented in Healthcare Organizations and a Model of Culturally Competent Healthcare Provision". *PloS one*, *14*(7): e0219971. https://doi.org/10.1371/journal.pone.0219971

Horrill, T., McMillan, D.E., Schultz, A.S.H. & Thompson, G. (2018). "Understanding Access to Healthcare among Indigenous Peoples: A Comparative Analysis of Biomedical and Postcolonial Perspectives". *Nursing Inquiry*, *25*(3), e12237. https://doi.org/10.1111/nin.12237

Jaleel, A., Arlappa, N., Ramakrishna, K.S., Sunu, P.V., Jayalakshmi, G., Neeraja, G., Narasimhulu, D., Kumar, T.S. & Kumar, S.B. (2023). "Examining the Triple Burden of Malnutrition: Insights from a Community-based Comprehensive Nutrition Survey among Indigenous Tribal Children (0-19 years) in the Western Ghats Hills of India". *Nutrients*, *15*(18): 3995. https://doi.org/10.3390/nu15183995

Jasemi, M., Valizadeh, L., Zamanzadeh, V. & Keogh, B. (2017). "A Concept Analysis of Holistic Care by Hybrid Model". *Indian Journal of Palliative Care*, *23*(1): 71-80. https://doi.org/10.4103/0973-1075.197960

Jain, L. (2007). *The Essence of Jainism*. New Delhi: Concept Publishing Company (Pvt.) Ltd.

Kalra, S., Ved, J. & Baruah, M.P. (2017). "Diabetes Destiny in Our Hands: Achieving Metabolic Karma". *Indian Journal of Endocrinology and Metabolism*, *21*(3): 482-83. https://doi.org/10.4103/ijem.IJEM_571_16

Karuga, R.N., Kok, M., Mbindyo, P., Hilverda, F., Otiso, L., Kavoo, D., Broerse, J. & Dieleman, M. (2019). "It's like these CHCs don't Exist, are they Featured Anywhere?: Social Network Analysis of Community Health Committees in a Rural and Urban Setting in Kenya". *PloS one*, *14*(8): e0220836. https://doi.org/10.1371/journal.pone.0220836

Kasthuri A. (2018). "Challenges to Healthcare in India: the Five A's". *Indian Journal of Community Medicine: Official Publication of Indian Association of Preventive & Social Medicine*, *43*(3): 141-43. https://doi.org/10.4103/ijcm.IJCM_194_18

Lawrence, J.J., Yeboah-Antwi, K., Biemba, G., Ram, P.K., Osbert, N., Sabin, L.L. & Hamer, D.H. (2016). "Beliefs, Behaviours, and Perceptions of Community-led Total Sanitation and Their Relation to Improved Sanitation in Rural Zambia". *The American Journal of Tropical Medicine and Hygiene*, *94*(3): 553-62. https://doi.org/10.4269/ajtmh.15-0335

Myers, S.P. & Vigar, V. (2019). "The State of the Evidence for Whole-System, Multi-Modality Naturopathic Medicine: A Systematic Scoping Review". *Journal of Alternative and Complementary Medicine 25*(2): 141-68. https://doi.org/10.1089/acm.2018.0340

Nandan, D. (2010). "National Rural Health Mission: Turning into Reality". *Indian Journal of Community Medicine: Official Publication of Indian Association of Preventive and Social Medicine*, *35*(4): 453-54. https://doi.org/10.4103/0970-0218.74338

Panda, P.K. & Subudhi, C. (2020). "Pattern and Determinants of Maternal and Child Healthcare Services among Tribals: With a Special Reference to Tribal Regions of Odisha". *Journal of Development Policy and Practice*, *5*(2): 167-83.

Ravishankar, B. & Shukla, V.J. (2007). "Indian Systems of Medicine: A Brief Profile". *African Journal ofTraditional, Complementary, and Alternative Medicines: AJTCAM*, *4*(3): 319-37. https://doi.org/10.4314/ajtcam.v4i3.31226

Sagaram, M. & Kaipa, P. (2020). "Practical Wisdom in Sanatana Dharma". In: Schwartz, B., Bernacchio, C., González-Cantón, C., Robson, A. (eds.) *Handbook of Practical Wisdom in Business and Management*. International Handbooks in Business Ethics. Springer, Cham. https://doi.org/10.1007/978-3-030-00140-7_22-1

Sharma, A. (2014). *Indian Social Problems*. New Delhi, India: Atlantic Publishers & Distributors.

Shilpa, S. & Venkatesha Murthy, C.G. (2011). "Understanding Personality from Ayurvedic Perspective for Psychological Assessment: A Case". *Ayu*, *32*(1): 12-19. https://doi.org/10.4103/0974-8520.85716

Snodgrass, J.G., Most, D.E., Upadhyay, C., Gold, A.G., Hinton, D., Lang, M., Sosis, R., Shidhaye, R. & Xygalatas, D. (2017). "Religious Ritual is Good Medicine for Indigenous Indian Conservation Refugees: Implications for Global Mental Health". *Current Anthropology*, *58*(2): 257-84. https://www.jstor.org/stable/26544331

Srivastava K. (2010). "Human Nature: Indian Perspective Revisited". *Industrial Psychiatry Journal*, *19*(2): 77-81. https://doi.org/10.4103/0972-6748.90335

Subudhi, C., Biswal, R. & Pathak, A. (2024). "Pathways to Psychiatric Help among Tribal Patients with Mental Disorders in India". *Indian Journal of Psychiatric Nursing*, *21*(1): 22-28.

16

Tagore and Community Development

An Indigenous Approach to Social Work Practice

Saro Jos and *Prasanta Kumar Ghosh*

A Poet's Indigenous Pursuit for Evolutionary Change

The argument that social work needs to be indigenized is decades old. It is argued that social work methods to curriculum, practised anywhere other than the West, are referred to, even though the argument and debates followed is subtle. One of the observations underlines this argument is Kendall (1986), who states that "the models of social work education that have emerged in the developing countries seem to be imported from Western social work". Kendall adds again,

> "particularly in Asia, the efforts towards indigenization of the curriculum to increase their relevance to the local situation seem to move rather slowly. Equally important is the slow process of indigenization of the body of knowledge in these

> countries which is the key to the indigenization of social work equation and practice".

But then the indigenization of a profession like social work, which is as old as human civilization, deserves more open-mindedness and patience to delve in. It is customary to date back the baptism of professional social work to the year 1936, when the first school of social work was constituted in Bombay by Sir Dorabji Tata followed by other schools in different parts of India.

But those who have taken time to read and grasp the rich history and philosophy of this country would know that social work practice has been an underlying current of this land's evolution as a country even when the inspiration for those "voluntary efforts" have been varied, scaling from religious, humanitarian, rational to secular. This rooted indigenous base reveals itself as a counter narrative to Kendall's observation that generalizes social work practice as transplanted. As P. D. Kulkarni observes, professional social work in India was like forming crystals in an already saturated chemical solution.

A batch of indigenous forerunners to this formation included individuals, societies, and organizations that received the light of social welfare and developmental pursuance. But then, what would a poet, a multifaceted genius like an artist, have anything to do with a discipline like social work is an important question. It is in the answering of this pondering question that the numerous stories, essays, letters, and speeches given by one single man in a sleepy town of Bengal amidst canopies of trees lead to a social work practice of its own that has whole of its heart and soul seated in the need to do something for another in pain. In English we say empathy, but for a poet, it is seeing the reflection of his own pain of agony in another human. That is why it must have been a pursuit of healing oneself by healing the immediate community of his own by their own means that drove a poet like Tagore to become a humanist without his expertise.

As a young man meant to manage estates of his familial property, the young poet was thrown into the expanse of a rural gloss of Bengal in the 1890s. But the initial charm of flawless nature, lush trees, and rhyming rivers soon drowned its way to the silent cries of pain that were etched in the skin and hearts of the people in the villages. They were fighting never-ending poverty and life-eating diseases in the backdrop of the brutal effect of British imperialism. The influence of this raw reality of loss and complexities is reflected in the fifty-nine short stories he wrote in the 1890s. It did not end there as a literary inspiration but found its way to a national programme of "constructive *swadeśī*" in 1903-08 and a tangible 15-point village reconstruction charter (1906) in Pabṇa (Bangladesh). Tracing Tagorean epistemology and finding a shape in these two phases could culminate like a finale in his third phase of rural reconstruction in Sriniketan, where this myriad mind wanted to experiment or rather fight his best at last through the medium of an idea amidst a decaying community. He kept affirming his position only as a facilitator and would aid the community members in healing themselves from within.

"We are beginning to discover that our problem is world-wide, and no one people of the earth can work out its salvation by detaching itself from others. As part of their life-long correspondences, we shall be saved together or drawn together into destruction", wrote Rabindranath Tagore to C.F. Andrews in 1921. The internationalism of thought and rationale of it paved the way to constructive thoughts and action, were the pillars of poet's approach to social work and community development. Rabindranath Tagore and his beginnings of engagement with immediate society around him were thus the vastness of nature and poetry. It is subtly revealed in the lines he wrote in the *Gitanjali* (Song Offerings), where he writes, "my heart can never find its way to where thou keepest company with the companionless among the poorest, the lowliest and the lost". The enormous exposure of his youth in Indian villages had sculpted his idea of development. He was clear that these poverty-stricken villages were saved through knowledge conjoined with cooperative spirit and relentless encouragement for self help and mutual help.

Thus, based on these ideas, his community development work took its form. Even before Kenyan soil rose up for community development initiatives in 1930s, Tagore had began his journey of experimenting for the betterment of marginalized populations in the rural Bengal. The establishment of two of his educational trinity, Brahmacharya Ashram, Visva-Bharati and Sriniketan in 1901, 1921 and 1922 respectively, is proof of that. The thought of community development was in fact not at all new in India because of this humanist who had fixed his mind to it during the *swadeśī* days which materialized as Sriniketan experiment through humble demonstrations and word of mouth. He perceived Sriniketan, the Institute of Rural Reconstruction as a symbol of true *swarāj*, for his people. It worked as a beacon of hope for a new way of living with dignity, a world of its own where everyone had an opportunity to thrive through self-respect and self-help. Tagore's work had many of its roots grounded in how the indigenous ways rural folk made their life. His time as a manager of his ancestral property, he remained exposed to the lives of villagers beyond the glossy serenity. He realized the veil of wide plains, flowing rivers was actually hiding the slow deaths of its people drown in poverty and illnesses. Tagore has spoken of how this meeting with reality paved the way for its better destiny.

> "...I continually endeavoured to find out how villagers' minds could be aroused, so that they could accept the responsibility for their own lives. If we merely offer them help from outside, it would be harmful to them. How could they themselves be stirred to life?"

His approach to rural problems was built upon two ideals of self-reliance and independence. Even before the concept of "exit strategy" was coined in a social work curriculum, he cracked the crux of any community development programme:

its people's felt needs and their ability to trust themselves for fulfilling it. Other than these two principles, the third principle of Sriniketan was possibly, "If we want to serve, we must learn (all the time)". This can be one of the first implicit outlines of how a social worker should work for a society.

The Potisar Initiative for Rural Reconstruction

The idea of rural reconstruction found its metal from Tagore's observations as the landlord in three districts (now in Bangladesh). *Potisar* was such block where he persuaded peasants in his estate to organize themselves into welfare community known as Hitaishi Sabha, covering 125 villages with a population of around 70,000. The idea was to encourage the community to raise its funds to solve the problems. Tagore estate contributed the fund gap at times in order to keep up the momentum. This idea of a *sabhā* found its way to maintain a resource of their own and through this community effort they continued to maintain their own schools, hospitals and other centres of community welfare. The observation that helped Tagore mould his rural reconstruction idea was that villagers did all the work necessary to sustain the *sabhā* and its activities. It was a living example of a community healing itself. The workers were from the village. They were aware of what was the ailment by which the community was affected. Thus, finding a cure became a community's shared goal to be achieved. Principles of self-help shaped the seed of empowerment from within and it was the enlightenment Tagore searched for his future programme encompassing more villages which turned out to be the Sriniketan experiment.

Sriniketan: Tagore's Experiment on Sustainable Social Developmental Model

In a letter to C.F. Andrews (1921) he wrote, "Foresight is a gift I wholly lack", then he continues to playfully admit his fear of losing freedom to be foolish and irresponsible citing his decision to take charge of his new university, Visva-Bharati, which later truly became an abode where the world meets in a single nest. This man who introspect his foresightedness, was the architect of his brainchild, Sriniketan experiment, which encompassed villages with multiple challenges at hand. Sriniketan was a pit stop of decay and death when he first stepped into its arena. A breeding nestle with populations of Hindus, Muslims and aboriginals (Santals), helplessly accepting their fate of despair. In early 1920s, Bengal suffered a severe Malaria epidemic resulting in 7,30,000 deaths in 1921 alone. The villagers, unknown to the new phenomena of an epidemic were struggling to understand it. Thus in 1922, Sriniketan Experiment was officially an Institute of Rural Reconstruction. Under its wings, a demonstration farm, poultry unit, outdoor clinic, a department of cottage industries and village school began reaching out to nearby communities. The idea was to keep the institute as an agency where villagers could come and discuss their problems, and as a laboratory for humans, this institute tested and updated the problems with available resources. The workers were from the village and lived among the community's people. The work of Sriniketan began with Tagore's tie up with Surul Samiti (association) which later became Surul village welfare department. This gradually developed into its other branches such as craft school (Silpa-Bhavan), village economics and Sikha-Satra—another school for the children of the nearby communities with focus on skill development. One of the innovating initiatives was *calantika granthāghāra* or mobile library that carried 200 books on cycles and other available vehicles to nook and corners of villages, targeting women who were not allowed to step out of their homes. One of the major aims of this experiment was to unleash the inner energy latent in the villages and reconnect urban Bengali middle class to rural roots and responsibilities.

Leonard Elmhirst, who joined Tagore for this experiment to resurrect a village, had a work with threefold specific tasks. The first was to conduct a general survey on the socio-economic and scientific layers of the given population, followed by helping the community come out of their ignorance and deal with the disease, which led to a strong public relation. Tagore, in his "life work" was a man of moments. He would deal with what is immediately challenging him with the possible resources available. That is how he came up with, a solution that was multi-folded. A rural reconstruction institute that had its roots in the community and branches with laboratories for better farming aids. Elmhirst in his retrospection about this institute, remembers that the most important and sole aim of the institute was to retard the decay of the countryside and put an end to this process of race suicide. In every juncture where the institute detoured to scientific explorations for its curiosity, Tagore unabashedly intervened to remind that science should be the servant of man not master. For the challenge of bridging the gap between the village community and the institute, his guidance was to change the lens of approaching the community from despair to respect which can result in removing fears of suspicion from their mind. This standpoint of the poet unquestionably works as a practical example of what it means by evolutionary change. in the realm of social work practice, professionals are mostly handling scenarios packed with long-term problems that can only be dealt with curing the root cause in a process of intentional slowness that results in an evolutionary change. This clarity of his thought was why Tagore emphasized initiating his experiment religiously within the framework of two or three villages. He wanted to observe the community's patterns and responses in each step of this experiment and give the phenomena its own time to correct itself.

Over the months of the institute's work, it formed itself into a unit or hub of knowledge necessary for transitioning itself to Tagore's vision of "life in its completeness". Elmhirst through his work guided the institute to extensive activities and projects like road repairs, construction of drains, mosquito-ridden ponds being filled up, cleaning of tanks, quantities of quinine distribution and spraying of kerosene in mosquito breeding areas. The five B's (better soil, better cultivation, better health, better education, and better recreation) were also taken care of. Experiments on paddy, sugar cane and cotton were carried out. Parallel activities like training artisans from the villages, health cooperatives, improvement of seeds, introduction of new breeds of cattle, strengthening of village councils, and an active village scout movement were also conducted and monitored.

Sriniketan experiment was in a way, a two-sided sword. When one part of it kept cutting off the deadly ignorance with spontaneous actions to deal with what was immediate, the other part enlarged its intervention to education. Tagore, in an 1910 essay titled "Tapovan", introduced a new idea called *bodher sādhanā* (education of feeling). It distinguishes itself from the education of senses and intellect. He states,

> "realization of man's bond of union with universe through spirit, through the soul and through deeper initiation of feeling. He visualized education system of India to attain the characteristic truth of her civilization pursued through centuries by her prophets, thinkers, saints and that truth is not commercialism, imperialism or nationalism; that truth is universalism".

This philosophy led Sriniketan to be fortitude of knowledge, as indigenous as it could be. He structured the institute so that the problems of the village and the fields became the topic of study, continuing discussions of the classroom for its experimental pursuits. This facilitated a platform to put students into practical experience in cultivation, dairy, animal husbandry, poultry keeping, carpentry, practical sanitation work, weaving, tannery, etc., leading to a strong collaborative spirit and act of service. The institute gave prime importance to its educational endeavours to be the catalyst of training students to due sense of their own intrinsic worth through its elementary instruction in science.

Tagore's Interpretation of Community Organization Method

It would be interesting to highlight the initiatives carried out under his work as a humanist with the lens of modern "community organization method" practised in the professional social work. As one of the pioneer professional social worker Murray G. Ross defines,

> "Community organization as a process by which a community identifies its needs or objectives, gives priority to them and develops the confidence and will to work at them, find resources (internal and external) to deal with them, and in doing so, extends and develops cooperative and collaborative attitudes and practices in the community".

In detailed study, that is exactly Tagore practised within the communities of rural Bengal in the 1900s. His role was well defined as a mediator and facilitator leaving the democratic decisiveness and implementation to the community itself. He was a pure social worker in that sense as he started building a network of workers from community for its self-sustenance. Rural organizations like health cooperatives, credit cooperatives, farmer's cooperatives, etc. He wanted to remind the community about their strengths and ability to sustain them. The entire process of any community organization that is, identifying problem areas, analysing causes of problems, formulating a plan, developing a strategy, mobilizing necessary resources and encouraging interrelationships, were carried out by the identified community leaders from the villages under the guidance of the rural reconstruction institute.

He coined designations like "grāma kārmic" (village workers) responsible for a village's social, economic, and cultural improvement. They were assigned to keep a check of ongoing practices and other workings of a village in order to intervene efficiently at times. The young generations are the future leaders of any community. It is with this thought that he came with the idea of a village scout movement for young boys and girls, named as *bratī bālaka/bālikās*' (*bratī* means devoted boys and girls scouts) where they dedicated a part of their time for the village community and exposed themselves to an opportunity to develop spirit of service. They were taught about health, hygiene and citizenship instilling the future idea of becoming a responsible countryman.

In a community's health-related aspect, Tagore was exposed to villages during British regime where no context of health service was available. He initiated health cooperatives where cluster of villages coming together in 1932 forming and norming the operative principles. It was followed in 180 communities where each family had a meagre yearly subscription amount to fund for a doctor, pharmacist and cleaner. Even though it was phased out in 1980s as government authorities began health services, this thought of a community coming together for its own well-being was a milestone. The word well-being was also an important contribution of his philosophy. In most of his writings, the concept of *ānanda* (bliss) is evident. His adherence to a process of making a human being amidst its natural surroundings where life has its deep rooted relationship with its entire ecology was fuelled by this component of blissful joy. That is why he became the first to start environmental education in the country, where students were taught under the *chatim* trees and immersed in a lyrical embrace of nature. His reverence for the nature's healing power has incomparable tie ups to the indigenous wisdom worldwide where Nature is Divine itself. He was keen to encourage preserving and circulating folk stories with indigenous elements for imparting value-based lessons on life and living to his students. Here, ecological perspectives which is one of thirst area of social work found place much before the concept adopted in social work.

Relevance of Tagorean Epistemology in the Twenty-first Century

In one of his essays on spiritual union, Tagore sketched some qualities of a social work (Joseph, Sherry & Ghosh, 2002). He writes,

> "To be united with Him, we have to divest to our work of selfishness and become *viśva karma*, the world worker, who works for all. I do not mean for a countless number of individuals. All work that is good, however small in extent is universal in character. Such work makes for the realization of *viśva karma*. In order to be one with Mahatma, 'the great soul', one must cultivate the greatness of soul, which identifies itself with soul of all people and thereby with that of one's own".

In deeper understanding of these lines, it is understood that for him, service to another human being was service to the Divine itself. His social work philosophy is born from the thought of enabling oneself to be selfless and emancipate one's own soul to a higher divinity or sacredness of being. Tagorean epistemology of social work is one that has its own philosophical roots that find its branches grown like a huge banyan tree of light that reach even the farthest one. The relevance of this perspective for that instance has to be studied from varying aspects of it. The remains of his work that still flows as an undercurrent in Santiniketan is of all shades. The university he envisioned continues to adopt nearby villages as part of its academic curriculum for working in the community with the community. The long tradition of rural immersion pedagogy continue to be practised in the university. In fact, Visva-Bharati is one of the very few universities that have its campus set in a completely rural setting of an indigenous community, where the students and the community are in a continued dialogue of change. It is to be noted that, the philosophy of Tagore to blend a human's spiritual seeking and realization with his or her altruistic human needs for the weary around is still prevalent in many of the initiatives that have been active in and around Sriniketan. The idea remains like a stalwart lighthouse guiding the lost.

In a conversation with Tagore's elder brother, Satyendranath's great-grandson Supriyo Tagore, who served as the Principal of Patha Bhavana, the school Tagore started in 1901, the relevance of Tagore's centuries old idea. He says with an affirmation of surety that Tagore's vision is relevant now, more than ever in a society where selfishness and competitive spirit drive a man's actions in life. He continues,

> "Tagore's entire work had three elements: nature, man, and the divine. These three were constantly interlinked and complemented in order to bring out the work that the world witnessed as Tagore's life work. His decision to introduce his idea of social work in a small community where everyone kept a one-to-one relationship was inspired by the goal of unraveling the cooperative spirit and cohesiveness."

And this philosophy has inspired many to find their own path to the service of others. Even Leonard Elmhirst, who had to leave Sriniketan in 1925 due to ill health, established Dartington Hall at Devon, UK, as a replica of Tagore's Sriniketan experiment. Like many others in the journey, he was deeply moved and emotionally invested in Tagore's philosophy. It is evident to note that, in a culture of instant gratification where humans becoming merely records or numbers, his idea to nurture a person in his/her completeness and bridging each of such individuals for creating a feeling of comradeship among the community is a key to sustainability.

Conclusion

The objective with which Rabindranath founded Sriniketan was to

> "Bring back life in its completeness into the villages, making the rural folk self-reliant, self-respectful, acquainted with the cultural tradition of their own country and competent to make efficient use of the modern resources for their social, cultural and intellectual improvement."

This indicates how indigenous approaches were important to Tagore in rebuilding the social and cultural tradition of the country's villagers. He was convinced that the indigenous model of development was as sustainable as it did in the ancient and medieval periods in India. The social service and social work was in-built in Indian social system. However, due to change in the modern era's social systems, we must reshape and rebuild the rural social and economic institutions like cooperatives and community-based organizations that benefit the rural mass.

He valued human dignity and worth as most important and crucial for the achievement of goals through community development initiatives at different levels. This furthered the way to invent and utilize local resources from and within the community. He never wanted to impose anything on the people of the community even though the people often misunderstood while implementing the projects.

He was very much scientific in his approaches to social development. The communities adopted for intervention were surveyed and studied to assess the needs of the communities in association with inhabitants to ensure the intervention needed will be sustainable development with the beneficiary's ownership. He invited specialists to plan and intervene in the targeted communities, which is most scientific in nature, as is the case with social work interventions today.

He relied more on the strength of the people and the community as a whole and worked for building resilient community for successful and sustainable social development. He believed in building community-based organizations for community development that paved the way for multiplying benefit to the people who make and maintain the organizations. The community-based organizations are built on democratic principles and the benefits comes back to the people who are the stakeholders of the organization.

Most organizations, e.g., cooperatives, were built on a macro level consisting of a cluster of communities that corroborates with the community organization and community development practices in social work today. He relied on the strength-based social development approaches adopted in social work practice much later. Partially, India's government adopted this community development model while experimentally launching the community development blocks in 1952 and roping in the whole of rural India in the following years, considering its ecological and rural perspectives of community development.

REFERENCES

Arthur, Geddes (1937). "The Population of Bengal, Its Distribution and Changes: A Contribution to Geographical Method". *The Geographical Journal*, *89*(4): 345.

Dutta, Kṛṣṇa and Andrew, Robinson (1991). *Selected Letters of Rabindranath Tagore*, p. xxiv.

Ecological Approach http://ecologicaltheory.tripod.com/accessed on 3 May 2019.

Gandhi, M.K., in his essay, "A Great Sentinel", *Young India*, 13 October, 1921.

Gupta, Uma Das (2004), *Preface in Rabindranath Tagore: A Biography*, New Delhi: Oxford University Press, pp. 9-11 (p. IX).

Gupta Uma Das (1978). "Rabindranath Tagore on Rural Reconstruction: the Sriniketan Programme, 1921-41". *Indian Historical Review,* 354-78 (p. 364).

Kulkarni, P. D. (1993). "The Indigenous Base of Social Work Profession in India". *Indian Journal of Social Work, 54*: 555-65.

Libois, Joelle, Bhattacharya, Kumkum, Ghosh, Prasanta Kumar (2022). *Tagore and Social Work: A Universal Inspiration*, Concept Publishing Company (Pvt.) Ltd. New Delhi. ISBN-13:978-93-5439-087-6.

Pal, Tapas (May 2015). *People's Educational Council of Rabindranath Tagore: A Model of Distance Education*, European Academic Research, *3*(2).

Radice, William (1994). *Introduction to Rabindranath Tagore: Selected Short Stories*, Penguin Publishers, London, pp. 1-28.

Roy, J. (2015). "Re-Visiting Tagore's Thoughts on Economic and Rural Development". *International Multidisciplinary Research Journal*, 4(II).

Sen, P.C. (1961), *Rabindranather Sikshachinta*, Kolkata: General Printers and Publishers Pvt. Ltd.

Sen, Sudhir (1943). *Tagore on Rural Reconstruction*, Visva-Bharati.

Sinha, Dikshit (2010). *Rabindranather Pallypunarghatham Prayas*, Pashchimbanga Bangla Academy, Calcutta.

Tagore, Rabindranath "Society and State (Swadeshi Samaj)". In *Towards Universal Man,* pp. 49-66.

Tagore, Rabindranath (1910). *Gītānjali*, Visva-Bharati.

Tagore, Rabindranath (1921). *Letters to a Friend,* London: George Allen & Unwin, 1931 [1928]), pp. 155-7 (p. 156).

Tagore, Rabindranath (1958). *On the Edges of Time*, Orient Longmans, Bombay, p. 31.

Tagore, Rabindranath (1961). "City and Village". In *Towards Universal Man*, London: Asia Publishing House.

17

Concept of Welfare State

Perspectives from Kauṭilya's *Arthaśāstra*

Braja S. Mishra

Introduction

After scanning a number of pieces of literature, it can be concluded that there is no unanimity in Western literature on the genesis of the welfare state. However, it is described as the embryonic version of the welfare state in Germany with Chancellor Bismarck's social insurance laws in the 1880s. After about a decade, governments in Denmark, New Zealand, and Australia started schemes like old-age pensions. Similarly, in the early twentieth-century liberal governments in Britain introduced workmen's compensation, old age pensions, labour exchanges, and a system of National Insurance for sickness, invalidity, and unemployment for industrial workers (Garland, 2016). Subsequently, in the 1930s, President Roosevelt established the American welfare state through the "New Deal" legislation. The idea of welfare states subsequently expanded to other developed nations and developing nations like India.

In majority of the literature, the welfare state is described as an outcome of the period immediately following the end of the Second World War. Introduction of "social insurance" is an widely used indicator of beginning the concept of welfare state. The idea of "social insurance" was recognized as provisions to mitigate the issues like incapacity to earn a living through contingencies such as old age, sickness or unemployment of workers in an industrialized society (Flora and Heidenheimer, 1981; Flora, 1987). A careful scanning of historical evidence on cross-national experiences show that present-day OECD (Organization of Economic Cooperation and Development) countries like Belgium, Netherlands, France, Italy, Germany, Ireland, UK, Denmark, Norway, Sweden, Finland, Austria, Switzerland, Australia, New Zealand, Canada, and USA started their social insurance programmes varying between 1871-1930 (Flora and Heidenheimer, 1981). It covered industrial accidents, health, pension, unemployment and family allowances. Nevertheless, the purpose of this chapter is not to look at the literature of West on the genesis of welfare state, but to look at the knowledge of ancient India, where the idea and practice of "welfare state" flourished once upon a time.

Interestingly, by design the larger part of the world has been ignorant that the idea of welfare state was conceived even around 2500 years ago in Bhārata (India) during Maurya Empire of Candragupta Maurya during 320 BCE to 298 BCE and the main architect of the welfare state was none other than Cāṇakya (Kauṭilya), a brilliant teacher, author, strategist, philosopher, economist, jurist, and royal advisor in those times. The description of "welfare state" is clear and loud in the *Arthaśāstra*, the masterpiece produced by Kauṭilya. It is said, both Kauṭilya and *Arthaśāstra* is either highly misunderstood or least understood in India, let alone outside India. There could be a very few scholars of ancient Indian history who were aware of the range and depth of the *Arthaśāstra*, which is considered to be a pioneering work on statecraft in all its aspects. The original book was written in Sanskrit, and it also talks about palm leaves. A copy of the *Arthaśāstra* in Sanskrit, written on palm leaves, was presented by a Tamil brāhmaṇa from Tanjore to the Mysore Oriental Library headed by Benjamin Lewis. In 1909, the librarian Shri Shamashastry transcribed the *Arthaśāstra* into fresh palm leaves and published it in English (Temple Purohit, n.d). There is also information available that in 1923-24 two German Indologists and Sanskrit scholars namely Julius Jolly and Richard Schmidt of University of Wurzburg and Muenster University respectively published an edition of *Arthaśāstra* which was based on Malayalam manuscript in the Baverian State Library of Munich, Germany (Temple Purohit, n.d). It is also said, some fragmented parts of *Arthaśāstra* written in Devanāgarī script were discovered in a Jain Library in Patan of Gujarat during 1950s. In 1960, Sanskrit professor R.P. Kangle attempted to publish interpretations of *Arthaśāstra* in Sanskrit and English. Based on the work of Shamashastry and Kangle, L.N. Rangarajan, a former Indian Foreign Service Officer and a contributor of knowledge in the sphere of political economy, made an attempt to edit and rearrange interpretations of *Arthaśāstra* in the form of a book published (as a Penguin Classics) by Penguin in 1992. The author primarily referred to the book published by Rangarajan as there were challenges on the author"s part to have access to some credible literature available on *Arthaśāstra*. Hence, the number of references is very limited.

In *Arthaśāstra*, the state is represented by king, hence the word "king" is used instead of the "state" at most of the places. Some key ideas and interpretations of a "welfare state" as described in *Arthaśāstra* have been articulated in this chapter as following.

The Idea of Welfare State

The *Arthaśāstra* describes welfare as not just an abstract

concept but realistic practices. "In the happiness of his (king's) subjects lies his own happiness." Though it sounds metaphorical, but this was the underlying value of the concept of welfare. It gives prime importance to the maintenance of social order, providing supporting ecosystem for increasing economic activity, protection of livelihood, protection of the weaker sections of the population, prevention of harassment of the subjects, consumer protection and even welfare of slaves and prisoners. However, two glaring exemptions from the ambit of welfare were found to be education and health care. Possibly because promoting education was the responsibility of the community, with little or no intervention of the state, while health care was part of the every household as a way of life, without any institutional health-care system as we see in the modern times.

Ensuring welfare of the people was considered to be king's *dharma* (duty). According to *Arthaśāstra*, an ideal king is one who has the highest qualities of leadership, intellect, energy and personal attributes (6.1.2-6)* and behaves like a sage monarch, a *rājarṣi.* A *rājarṣi* promotes *yogakṣema* of the people—the word, *yogakṣema*, is a compound word made up of *yoga*, thy means the successful accomplishment of an objective and *kṣema*, means celebrating the same peacefully (1.7.1). Thus, the welfare of the people is given utmost importance and is always celebrated with knowledge, self-control, and observance of *dharma.* A king's duty is to obey his own *rājadharma* and ensure that his subjects obey their respective *dharma*. It further says "when *adharma* overwhelms *dharma*, the king himself will be destroyed" (3.16.42). This was a sort of moral code of conduct for the king and his subjects to maintain justice, peace, and tranquillity in the society, which is the basic premise of a welfare state. It is the duty (*dharma*) of the king become just, impartial and lenient in protecting his subjects (8.2.12; 3.10.46; 1.19.33-34; 3.1.41; 3.20.24).

*6.1.2-6 implies—Book 6, Chapter 1, verse number 2 to 6. These are quoted by Rangarajan from the original book of Kangle's *The Kauṭilya Arthaśāstra*, published by the University of Bombay in 1969.

General Economic Welfare

The king has a responsibility in enhancing the economy of the state by enhancing livelihoods of the citizens. *Arthaśāstra* talks about diversified livelihoods of the households (as risk mitigation mechanism) so that they are capable of absorbing the shocks and risk due to natural calamities like flood, drought, crop failure, etc. It further says that king is primarily responsible for providing financial education to the citizens, so that they manage their economy efficiently, prudently and profitably. Savings were always emphasized as a household risk mitigation and social security measure (1.19.35-36). To provide a favourable economic ecosystem, the king was advised to develop and maintain good infrastructures like good roads, seamless waterways, irrigation canals, ports, setting up market yards, warehouses in different remote parts of the country, opening domestic and foreign trade routes, preserving and harvesting natural resources like the river and other water bodies like pond, lake, and reservoirs, forests, wetlands in a sustainable manner to enhance their productivity (2.1.19-20).

Farmers were under the obligation to cultivate their land. It was a punishable offence for a farmer, or a tenant, not to cultivate or abandon his land at the time of sowing/ transplanting season. A farmer could not escape cultivating because he had enough to eat. The idea was to encourage able bodied people to work instead of sitting idle. Kauṭilya was a strong proponent for hard work, which could bring prosperity to the household as well the nation (3.10.8). On his advice, the king conveyed this message to all his subjects in a reinforcing manner. From recent history we can draw an analogy to it on the rapid growth of Japan, just by virtue of the hard work done by the people for not only rebuilding the devastated Japan in Second World War but also make Japan the most progressive country in the world.

However, there were exceptions based on the disadvantaged status of some subjects. The state had to provide social protection to the disadvantaged section of population such as aged, the sick and the handicapped. As a matter of special consideration, compulsory livelihood activities were exempted for ascetics such as monks and nuns, hermits, *vānaprastha*s, *brāhmaṇas* in their *āśrama*s and mendicants. Besides, during natural calamities, king was responsible for providing all types of protection to the affected people, including emergency feeding (2.15.22-23). In the modern parlance we call it disaster management and risk reduction (DRR) with support from the state.

> A king becomes more powerful when his subjects become economically prosperous across the state. Kauṭilya was a strong proponent of an old saying "poverty anywhere is a threat to prosperity everywhere". Though it has been a popular statement from the 1944 International Labour Organization (ILO) Declaration of Philadelphia, this concept was well articulated in *Arthaśāstra*—creating a supportive ecosystem for economic prosperity of subject is the prime responsibility of the king.

Labour Welfare (Including Child Labour, Women Labour and Small/Marginal Producers)

Traditionally skilled people like self-employed/wage employed, such as weavers, washermen, dyers, tailors, goldsmiths, silversmiths, and blacksmiths, were paid at higher rate according to the work done by them (4.1.10-12, 22, 25, 32-35, 40, 42). This implies that labour classification did exist based on the level of the skill, which can be analogized in today's classification like highly-skilled, skilled, semi-skilled, unskilled workers.

Child labour in all forms were prohibited, except when children (above the age of eight years) extended their support in lighter household work (3.13.1-2, 4). Of course, the age bar was kept too low during that period and is now 18 years old. In the event a child became an orphan due to death of both the parents, the property of minor child was to be held in a community-based trust and looked after by the village elders (2.1.27). Similarly children of destitute women were given special care by the community. In the modern parlance we describe it as community-based rehabilitation (CBR).

Women's welfare in term protection of women workers from exploitation and protection of prostitutes against exploitation and physical injury was part of the governance system (2.27. 13-18, 23). Childless single women were being provided social protection in terms of food and social security. Even a prostitute has dignity and no one can have sex with her against her will (4.13.38-39).

The principles of fair trading were emphasized where even the economically marginalized people would get an opportunity to trade their products without any barrier, intimidation or exploitation. A principle of local economy-based livelihood promotion was always emphasized than importing goods and services. Thus, economic interest of marginal farmers and local artisans was protected, while regulating the trade and commerce (2.16.4).

Consumer Welfare (including Welfare of the Entrepreneurs)

The phenomena like consumer protection and welfare is also described in *Arthaśāstra*, where the rules regarding the protection of the welfare of the consumer by control over merchants and weights and measures were clearly laid down. There were rules to deal with cheating to the public by traders, artisans and craftsmen. Even the physicians were also obligated to protect the patients' lives. They were under the mandate to inform the authorities before undertaking any treatment that might be dangerous to the patient's life. If, as a result of the treatment, the patient dies or is physically deformed, the physician used to be punished (4.1.56-57).

Protecting the interest of partners/members of an enterprise or cooperative was clearly laid down so that no partner/member would feel s/he was being exploited or cheated at any point of time. The agreement was being made just and transparent. Partners/members in an enterprise/cooperative would divide the profits among themselves either equally or by prior agreement [over unequal shares] (3.14.18). Once the work has been undertaken, no partner shall refuse to do his share of the work, except on the grounds of illness. Abandoning the partnership halfway was a punishable offence (3.14.23-24).

Welfare of the Prisoners

The welfare of prisoners was safeguarded by having separate prisons for men and women, providing halls, drinking and bathing facility, toilets, keeping the prisons clean, tidy and free of fire hazards and poisonous insects, etc. Protecting the rights of prisoners in respect of getting timely food, a reasonable place to sleep, open spaces for doing physical exercises and putting restrictions on prison warders from harassing or torturing the prisoners were ensured under strict monitoring. Dealing with women prisoners by male warders was also strictly regulated, prescribing severe punishments for rape of women prisoners. The prisoners used to be released on parole periodically. They also were getting released by general and special amnesties (3.1.38, 41-42; 3.20.24).

Animal Welfare (including Conservation of Nature and Biodiversity)

Conserving biodiversity and welfare of all animals (wild as well as domestic) is also clearly reflected in *Arthaśāstra*. There used to be regulations for the protection of wildlife and system of punishment for cruelty to animals. The system of declaring some forests as reserve forests and sanctuary (with clear guidelines on restrictions of anthropogenic activities) for the welfare of the wild animals, with clear declaration of special protection of endangered animals and birds (2.2.4). Poaching wild animals used to be dealt with severe punishments. Even modern nations have failed to do this to the desired extent! The responsibility of protecting the forest, sanctuary and the wild animals was entrusted to the village headmen of the neighbourhood villages. In the modern parlance we can compare it with joint forest management where the neighbouring community is involved in protection of forest resources and wildlife along with harvesting certain forest resources for their livelihoods.

For domestic animals, the system of rationing animal feed, especially during crises like drought and flood, is well described. Earmarking exclusive grazing land for domestic animals was also there. Veterinary care used to be provided for domestic animals. Old, infirmed and unproductive domestic animals used to be given special humane care as a moral responsibility of the household, community and the state (king). State used to make feed rationing for these vulnerable animals, which even modern states have not been able to do! In slaughtering the animals there used to be strict regulations like prohibiting slaughter of female and young animals and castration of males, etc. (13.5.12-13) to maintain their population balance.

There was a proper plan to protect and harness from common property resources like water bodies, forest conservation, river embankments for agriculture, livestock, forest, and fishery-based livelihoods. Farmers were made to contribute their labour for conservation of natural resources if they wanted to get the benefit. This not only enhanced the farmers' stake but also encouraged creating wealth out of available natural resource base. Sustainable use of natural resource system for sustainable livelihood was always been emphasized, which has been the focus of current development narratives.

Minimum Support Price

There used to be a system almost akin to minimum support

price being provided to the farmers by the government on certain agri-produces. When there used to be an excess supply of a commodities because of bumper production, there was a system of procuring the commodities by the state for building up buffer stock by paying a price higher than the market price. When the market price reaches the support level, farmer had the privilege to change the price, according to the situation. As a matter of fact, in present times, we are struggling to address the distressed sale of farmers' produces.

Good Governance

There is no disagreement on the theory that good governance contributes immensely to the welfare of the underprivileged and development of all. Putting efficient, qualified and responsive ministers and officials was considered to be the key conditions to good governance, which has been categorically described in *Arthaśāstra*. Officials at *janapada* (*maṇḍala* or block) and below were considered to be the most critical interfaces between the state and the subjects. Since they are the frontline officials and responsible for delivery of services and support being rendered by the state, their responsiveness makes governance more effective and efficient (1.11.19-20).

There was severe and proportionate (commensurate with gravity of the offence) punishment system for inefficient, errant or dishonest officials. Even common subjects had the privilege to lodge complaint against them at appropriate levels of the government (2.9.20-27).

Maintaining just law and order also strengthens governance. Therefore, responsive law and order contributes to smooth functioning of socio-economic activities of the state and therefore a prerequisite for any welfare state to thrive. In case of any unrest or conflicts between groups or communities, there used to be provisions to deal with them with strict law enforcement by imposing curfew during nighttime. There were provisions of relaxation in curfew for essential services like midwifes attending a delivery, doctors attending to illness, those who are obliged to do so due to a death in the family, those who go with a lamp in their hand for some urgent work, visitors to the city officials for official purposes, those summoned by a trumpet-call, fire-fighters and those having a valid pass (2.36.34, 36, 38-39).

Conclusion

It is said the epicentre of the Indus Valley Civilization (*c*.7000-*c*.600 BCE) was in India and it was among the greatest of the ancient world, covering more territory than either Egypt or Mesopotamia and producing an equally vibrant and progressive culture. Some great religions (or faith systems) like Sanātana Dharma (popularly known as Hinduism), Jainism, Buddhism, and Sikhism flourished in India largely without coercion, prosecution, and violent methods. A philosophical school of thought like "Cārvāka" also took birth in this country around 600 BCE, influencing scientific thoughts and inquiry development. In ancient Bhārata, people experienced many aspects of today's modern life, including the flush toilet, drainage and sewer systems, public pools, mathematics, veterinary science, plastic surgery, board games, *yoga* and meditation, and many more (*World History*, n.d). The concept, ideas and application of "welfare state" described in Kauṭilya's *Arthaśāstra* is a classic example in this direction. If the scholars give systematic efforts along with continuous support from the state, the production of the Indian knowledge system shall certainly take a leap forward.

Compared to the literature developed in the Western world, ours is limited for various reasons—which was largely because of the destructions of our knowledge system by the invaders over thousands of years and partly because of our ignorance and negligence of preserving the same. Hence, to have a credible literature and research we have very few citations, unlike the ones being produced in Western world.

REFERENCES

Britannica (n.d). https://www.britannica.com/money/welfare-state accessed on 10 March, 2024.

Flora, Peter (Ed.)(1987). *Growth to Limits: The Western European Welfare States since World War II.* Walter de Gruyter, Berlin.

Flora, Peter & Heidenheimer, Arnold, J. (1981). *The Development of Welfare States in Europe and America.* Transaction Books in New Brunswick, New Jersey, pp. 415-45.

Garland, David (2016). *The Welfare State: A Very Short Introduction*, Oxford; online edn., Oxford Academic.

Rangarajan, L.N. (1992). *Kauṭilya: The Arthashastra.* Penguin Books.

Temple Purohit (n.d). https://www.templepurohit.com/arthasastra (accessed on 5 March 2024).

World History (n.d). https://www.worldhistory.org/india (accessed on 20 March 2024).

SECTION THREE
Indian Spiritualism, Philosophy and Social Work

18

Indian Social Work Practices

A Harmonious Blend with *Bhagavad Gītā* in Counselling and Casework

Mukshita Dhrangadharia and *Anamika Christi*

Introduction

Indian social work is indistinguishably linked to our country's unique drapery of cultural and ethical diversity. In this regard, the ageless wisdom contained in the *Bhagavad Gītā* strongly resonates with the principles and methods applied in social work. Essentially, this chapter aims to close the gap between traditional and modern applications of knowledge by recognizing the *Bhagavad Gītā*'s offerings within the framework of contemporary social work. Our goal is to elucidate the transformational potential of this amalgamation and improve the effectiveness and depth of social work interventions by plowing meticulously. This study attempts to provide new ideas and views that help improve social work practitioners' practice by carefully examining how *Gītā*'s principles meet with real-world counselling and casework contexts.

In addition, this chapter aims to thoroughly grasp how social workers may use the ideas expressed in the *Bhagavad Gītā* as a beacon of guidance. The *Gītā*'s focus on responsibility, kindness, and selfless service strikes a deep chord with social work's ethical underpinnings and provides an enduring framework that may guide and inspire modern practice. This chapter highlights the *Gītā*'s timeless wisdom and how it might integrate and develop more sensitive, successful, and culturally appropriate social work therapies. By writing this chapter, the authors seek to pave the way for a more holistic and revolutionary approach to social work. Eventually, it will improve the well-being of individuals and communities by fusing traditional knowledge with contemporary methods.

Ethical Foundations: *Dharma* in Counselling

The *Bhagavad Gītā* makes oneself acquainted with the idea of *dharma*. It guides us through the difficulties and ambiguities of life, much like a compass (*Bhagavad Gītā* 2.31). Imagine yourself offering advice as a caseworker to someone challenged with choosing between convenience and righteousness, similar to Arjuna on the battlefield. The *Gītā* inspires us to hold our moral principles even in difficult situations. The offerings inspire us to choose what is right.

The working professionals frequently feel like they are experiencing on Arjuna's hardships. They face moral puzzles daily, but by abiding by their *dharma* (principles), they can make decisions that sustain integrity and trust. It's like having a compass that guides the sailor with their counselling techniques and allows them to cross rivers gracefully and honestly.

Responsiveness and Holistic Well-being

The *Bhagavad Gītā*'s teachings apply to the core of casework because it emphasizes the practitioner's disassociation from the decisions about the clients' issues/problems (*Bhagavad Gītā* 2.47). This very idea assists social workers in counselling and through which they inspire clients in their self-discovery while keeping an objective viewpoint on outcomes. Allowing clients to make their own decisions regarding how to proceed further in their lives for the problems is a therapeutic approach that aligns with *Gītā*'s advice on detachment. Social workers adopt this detached perspective from the *Bhagavad Gītā* in order to give clients the space they need to examine their stories and come to well-informed conclusions.

Cultural Sensitivity and Inclusivity

The culturally sensitive approach in casework and counselling plays a significant role in the field of social work. Social workers are encouraged by the universal principles of the *Gītā* to utilize the same. The *Gītā* promotes varied viewpoints as Arjuna struggles with his identity and responsibilities (*Bhagavad Gītā* 4.13). In social work, this translates to appreciating clients' cultural diversity and implementing cultural competency into practice. Social workers respect differences and establish rapport and trust—two crucial components of successful counselling.

Self-awareness and Self-transcendence

The *Gītā*'s emphasis on self-awareness perfectly matches the therapeutic objective of encouraging resilience and personal growth. The journey of Arjuna shows how people fight to find their identity and meaning in life (*Bhagavad Gītā* 2.14). Inspired by the *Bhagavad Gītā*, social workers assist individuals to find their deepest selves. This process of becoming conscious of oneself turns into a tool that transforms people, develops them into stronger beings, and allows them the capacity to pass through their past difficulties gracefully.

Guidance in Ethical Dilemmas

Arjuna is confronted with ethical dilemmas on the battlefield, so the *Bhagavad Gītā* offers advice on navigating competing principles (2.14). The *Gītā*'s wisdom inspires social workers who deal with complex ethical issues in their profession. To make sound decisions, one must look inside oneself and discover a deeper orientation. When social workers adopt the guidelines laid out in the *Bhagavad Gītā*, they can deal with moral problems in a way that gives rational meaning. To understand the ethical dilemmas, one needs to have clarity towards oneself and become self-aware. Therefore, self-awareness plays a crucial role while dealing with the ethical dilemmas that Arjuna faced.

Therapeutic Role as a Facilitator

The *Gītā* portrays Kṛṣṇa as Arjuna's guide and companion, capturing the essence of the therapeutic connection. Social workers take on the role of facilitators in counselling and casework, walking alongside clients as they travel. The *Gītā*'s focus on providing constructive instruction aligns with the therapeutic objective of cultivating a cooperative and empowered dynamic. Social workers establish a secure environment for clients to explore and develop by exhibiting empathy and compassion.

Promoting Individual Ownership and Self-efficacy

The *Bhagavad Gītā*'s strong emphasis lies in accepting ownership for one's actions/conduct (*Bhagavad Gītā* 3.35). Social case work imitates the same by urging clients to accept responsibility for their choices and behaviours. The clients can be guided in developing self-efficacy and confidence in themselves and their capacity to impact their own lives by encouraging personal responsibility. By doing so, clients are encouraged to participate actively in their healing and progress. This method may induce more sustainable results.

Origination of Concept of Balance in Daily Routine

According to *Bhagavad Gītā* 6.16-17, the *Gītā* underscores the value of living an equilibrium state of life, balancing social, professional, and personal lives. With this comprehensive approach, clients may attain a sense of balance and well-being and are protected from becoming overpowered by any one aspect of their lives. Another social work theory, "person-in-environment", also discusses a person's balance with their environment. Apart from that, to avoid exhaustion and stay productive, social workers could also practice keeping balance in their personal lives.

Improving Sensitivity and Empathy with the Tool of Self-reflection

The *Bhagavad Gītā* 6.5 promotes introspection and a knowledge of one's inner self. This idea can help social workers to become more compassionate and empathetic. Social workers who habitually practice self-reflection could relate to their clients. The underlying reason is that, due to self-reflections, social workers develop a deeper understanding of their own prejudices and feelings. This therapeutic approach strengthens the relationship by fostering a more meaningful support system and as a result, builds a stronger connection with clients.

उद्धरेदात्मनात्मानं नात्मानमवसादयेत् ।
आत्मैव ह्यात्मनो बन्धुरात्मैव रिपुरात्मनः ।।

—*Gītā* 6.5

Recognizing Impermanence to Promote Resilience

An important lesson that the *Bhagavad Gītā* leaves us with is "the transience/uncertainty of life's circumstances" (*Bhagavad Gītā* 2.27). Being a social worker, clients can be guided with apprehending and accepting the uncertain nature of their present difficulties. The idea of "uncertainty of life" changes clients' perception of their lives. Their lives can become more resilient and optimistic about their future by accepting the concept of "impermanence". This knowledge may be especially helpful in guiding clients through life changes and crises. The same will foster mental and emotional stability among clients.

मात्रास्पर्शास्तु कौन्तेय शीतोष्णसुखदुःखदा।
आगमापायिनोऽनित्यास्तांस्तितिक्षस्व भारत।।

—*Gītā* 2.14

Using a Client-centred Method

Kṛṣṇa stresses comprehending and attending to the requirements and circumstances of each individual in his advice to Arjuna (*Bhagavad Gītā*, 3.21). One of the values of social work is that every individual is unique. Therefore, sometimes, problems of a similar nature could also impact differently to different individuals. Social workers must adopt a client-centred approach by concentrating on each client's particular needs and circumstances. Using a customized approach will improve the results by ensuring that treatments are successful and pertinent. Social workers may create a conducive atmosphere that will be helpful to the clients. It is undeniable that each client as an individual is distinct in terms of their experiences and strengths.

Incorporating Mindfulness Techniques

The *Bhagavad Gītā* 6.10 illustrates the value of mindfulness and living in the present. Social workers may endorse mindfulness exercises like meditation and deep breathing for their clients. They can emphasize on making it a part of their daily lives because consistency is the key to any mindfulness practice. With these techniques, clients may learn how to restrict/channelize their emotions, focus on the better version of themselves, and manage stress effectively.

Earning the Trust of the Clients through Persistent Support

The emphasis of the *Bhagavad Gītā* 2.5 is on constancy and dependability. The method of social casework promotes trust with clients by rendering faithful and consistent assistance to them. Social workers are required to create a safe space where clients feel comfortable talking about and exploring their problems. The role of social caseworkers becomes crucial here; they must always be trustworthy and there for their clients. The "trust" works as a foundation in social casework and creates an effective/purposeful relationship with the client.

Conclusion

This chapter tries to shed light on the connection between Indian social work and the timeless wisdom of the *Bhagavad Gītā*. The text of the *Bhagavad Gītā* helps discover an enormous trove of information that can change how social workers approach clients regarding counselling. As we all confront difficult decisions in our daily lives, social workers do as well. The *Bhagavad Gītā* gives us the tremendous principle of doing the right thing even when it's complicated. It's like having a moral compass that always directs us to what's fair and just.

Then, there's the idea of not being overly concerned with the repercussions of our actions. Every action has some reactions. The teachings of the *Bhagavad Gītā* suggest that it should be like when we put all our efforts into achieving something, but we are acceptable even if things don't go exactly as planned. Professional social workers can also benefit significantly from this, as they can aid their clients without becoming agitated if their achievements/ambitions/goals don't go as planned. One should not forget to respect everyone's heritage and culture. The *Bhagavad Gītā* urges us to comprehend others' perspectives in the same way we want them to understand ours. The field of social work teaches the same ethical considerations and encourages them to adhere to their everyday practice. The field emphasizes recognizing people's uniqueness while making them feel heard and respected.

Another important lesson from the *Bhagavad Gītā* is understanding ourselves and learning from our experiences. Just as we learn from our errors and become stronger, social workers assist individuals in learning about themselves and being better prepared to face life's problems. Social work also doesn't foster to make clients depend on themselves. When making tough choices, the *Gītā* has some incredible advice to offer. It's like having a friend to lean on when making difficult decisions. Social workers can think about right and wrong, just like Arjuna did on that battlefield, and find the best path forward.

Additionally, social workers are like guides, believing and adhering to the motto of helping people to help themselves. And making them sail through tough times. They listen, support, and encourage, just like Kṛṣṇa did for Arjuna. It's about being there for someone when they need it most, guiding them with kindness and understanding.

Moreover, the goals and values of social work align very well with the teachings of the *Bhagavad Gītā*. The goal is higher: "Because God is seated in everyone, everyone deserves to be treated with respect & dignity". The vision that "everyone is the form of God" emerges at the pinnacle of *yoga*. The Vedic writings repeatedly assert that the universe is a manifestation of God. *īśāvāsyam idam sarvaṁ yat kiñca jagatyaṁ jagat* (*Īśopaniṣad* 1) [v2] "The Supreme Being, who resides within the universe, is manifested throughout it in all living things and non-living entities." Thus, when social workers incorporate these ancient principles into their work, they are not just performing their job but making a genuine impact in people's lives. Caseworkers would be able to improve their skills, become more caring, and feel more connected to the clients they are treating. Therefore, social work is about making the world better and more conducive. As we conclude this exploration, it's clear that integrating *Bhagavad Gītā*'s principles into social work practices offers a timeless and profound framework for guiding our actions and interactions. It's a reminder that in our quest to help others, we can draw wisdom from ancient texts and timeless truths, enriching both our professional practice and our personal lives.

REFERENCES

Bhagavad Gita (n.d.). Retrieved from Sacred Texts Archive: https://www.sacred-texts.com/hin/mbs/mbs06047.htm

Bhagavad Gita (n.d.). Retrieved from Vedanta Press: https://www.vedanta.com/store/bhagavad-gita/

Davis, J.M. (Ed.). (2019). *The Bhagavad Gita: A New Translation.* Shambhala Publications.

Dash, B. (2012). *Professional Social Work in India: Contexts and Opportunities.* PHI Learning Private Limited.

Easwaran, E. (2007). *The Bhagavad Gita* (2nd edn.). Nilgiri Press.

Feuerstein, G. (2011). *The Bhagavad Gita: A New Translation.* Shambhala Publications.

Graham, A.C. (1981). *The Bhagavad Gita: A Translation.* Oxford University Press.

Miller, B.S. (2016). *The Bhagavad Gita: Krishna's Counsel in Time of War.* Columbia University Press.

Nimmagadda, J. & Cowger, C.D. (1999). "Cross-cultural Practice: Social Worker Ingenuity in the Indigenization of Practice Knowledge". *International Social Work*, *42*(3): 261-76.

Radhakrishnan, S. (Ed.). (1992). *The Bhagavad Gita.* Harper Collins.

Reddy, M.S. (2012). "Psychotherapy-insights from *Bhagavad Gita*". *Indian Journal of Psychological Medicine*, *34*(1): 100-104.

Sargeant, W. (2009). *The Bhagavad Gita: Twenty-fifth Anniversary Edition.* State University of New York Press.

Swami Sivananda (n.d.). *The Bhagavad Gita.* Retrieved from Divine Life Society: https://www.dlshq.org/download/bgita.pdf

Swami Vivekananda (n.d.). *The Bhagavad Gita.* Retrieved from Divine Life Society: https://www.dlshq.org/download/bgita.pdf

Thompson, G. (2014). *The Bhagavad Gita: A New Translation.* North Point Press.

Unknown (n.d.). *The Bhagavad Gita: Chapter 2, Verse 14.* Retrieved from *Bhagavad Gita* Online: https://www.bhagavad-gita.org/Gita/verse-02-14.html

Unknown (n.d.). *The Bhagavad Gita: Chapter 2, Verse 31.* Retrieved from *Bhagavad Gita* Online: https://www.bhagavad-gita.org/Gita/verse-02-31.html

Unknown (n.d.). *The Bhagavad Gita: Chapter 2, Verse 47.* Retrieved from *Bhagavad Gita* Online: https://www.bhagavad-gita.org/Gita/verse-02-47.html

Unknown (n.d.). *The Bhagavad Gita: Chapter 4, Verse 13.* Retrieved from *Bhagavad Gita* Online: https://www.bhagavad-gita.org/Gita/verse-04-13.html

[Please note that some references may be listed as "Unknown" as they are from online translations or versions where individual authors or translators are not specified.]

19

Holistic Preventive Health

A Social Work Perception of Transformational and Transactional Leadership by Bhagavān Mahāvīra, Gautama Buddha, and Mahatma Gandhi in India

K. Balasubramanian

Introduction

India, being a highly populated country, has been successfully progressing in its growth at all levels, mainly in terms of economic and health developments over the recent decades. Bold policies and guidelines on advanced technologies in diagnosis, upgraded treatment, and strong public health actions are in place. Nevertheless, communicable and non-communicable diseases, maternal and child health, mental health, and malnutrition are the major challenges in India (Shoba Suri, 2023), in addition to population, poverty, and pollution. India has to fight the highest burden of Tuberculosis, HIV, and Malaria and non-communicable diseases like heart and respiratory diseases, diabetes, and cancer, which lead to 63 per cent of deaths (Indrani Gupta, 2019). Mental health is still one of the least priorities in India, and around 5 per cent of the population suffers from stress, anxiety, and depression

(Narain, 2016). Emergency pandemics and epidemics are regular threats to the globe and India needs to invest on a large scale based on its population. Unequal access to health, affordability, health care spending, shortage of trained health-care professionals, and lack of health insurance (Sanjay, 2023), patients' out-of-pocket expenditure, adequate budget, public health policies, medical research, and proactive care are still serious threats to the national health reforms. One-third of the country's health budget goes for non-communicable diseases and injuries (Indrani Gupta, 2019), which could be effectively reduced by changing the lifestyle and behaviour of the recent technology friend community. The recent COVID pandemic has changed the individual lifestyle of preventive care. India was the first country to adopt the National Action Plan towards the WHO Global Action Plan for the Prevention and Control of Non-communicable Diseases (2013-20). National Program for Prevention and Control included other major risk factors of alcohol, tobacco, physical inactivity, and unhealthy diet and expanded across the districts of the country. In August 2021, the Government of Tamil Nadu launched the "Medicine at People's Doorstep" (Makkalai Thedi Maruthuvam—MTM) scheme, which includes screening and medications for non-communicable diseases in the community.

Indian social reforms, the social and economic changes, and the freedom movement also taught physical, emotional, and spiritual well-being by bringing changes in lifestyle and diet, leading to preventive health. Bhagavān Mahāvīra, Gautama Buddha, and Mahatma Gandhi are some of the foremost reformers in all aspects of human well-being. Bhagavān Mahāvīra's healthy living is a soul-oriented philosophy of human life's physical, mental, and spiritual well-being. The ways of supervising one's health including, being concerned, and encouraging, are the key parts of the eightfold path of Buddha.Mahatma Gandhi's nature cure *āśrama*—the concept of village sanitation and his eleven vows evidenced health and well-being. Social work principles and approaches are very much connected with the philosophy of these reformers on preventive health approach. Social work practice is about the humanitarian approach towards social treatment and psychological education in response to people's needs and its methods that contribute significantly to public health preventive care, which is essential in the current scenario. This chapter discusses the social reformers' contribution to preventive health on social work perception and its urgent transformation to the current and future of India with social work.

Profound Teachings of Lord Mahāvīra on Overall Health (599 BCE to 527 BCE)

"State of physical, mental, and spiritual well-being."

Lord Mahāvīra was born in 599 BCE in Bihar, India. He was the last, 24th *tirthaṅkara* and is considered the founder of Jainism who renounced his princely life at the age of 30 in pursuit of spiritual enlightenment after spending twelve and half years in deep silence and intensive meditation to eliminate the pain, sorrow, and suffering of the worldly life. He advised us to treat joy and suffering equally, and the right conduct, faith, and knowledge are essential principles. He believed that materialistic attractions and belongings lead to greed, hampering spiritual progress, material elements transform, and spiritual elements evolve forever in the world. Violent thoughts, deeds, anger, hatred, greed, and other vices are deep-rooted causes of self-centred results in the accumulation of *karma*. The soul is bound by *karma* and liberation is attainable by overcoming passions with *kārmic* forces towards attaining infinite greatness and transforming towards *Paramātmā*, the pure soul of knowledge, power and happiness. He advocated right faith, right knowledge, and right conduct, and respect to every form of life (Upadhyaya, 2016). Non-violence, truth, and compassion are the three key essences of his teaching in the soul-oriented Jaina philosophy (Wikipedia, 2023). Non-injury, truthfulness, non-stealing, chastity, and non-attachment are his five vows toward the supreme goal of life to attain salvation. Eating harmful food, oversleeping, sleeping very late in the night, obstructing urine and bowel movements, and uncontrolled sensual desires are the major challenges for health. Eating food, use of the body, use of sense, breathing, use of language, and mindset are the key factors for health (Amanda Keton, 2021). The right nutritious food improves all physical, emotional, and spiritual health. Control of the tongue leads to control of all senses, mainly food and speech. No harming or annoying other living beings, fasting for long periods, travelling barefoot throughout the lifetime, and being calm and peaceful mind are his ways of living to teach us about health. Overall, teaching reflects a positive attitude, universal compassion, freedom, spiritual joy, and internal beauty and harmony of the soul. Disease and cures belong to physical, mental, and spiritual well-being and are finally linked with happiness.

Profound Teachings of Lord Buddha on Health (563 to 483 BCE)

> "I teach suffering, its origin, cessation, and path."
>
> —Lord Buddha

Lord Buddha, an Indian spiritual traditional leader in the sixth century BCE, Prince Siddhārtha, realized the truth that birth, aging, and death are unavoidable in the universe. He learned about medicine, nature, and the cure of diseases from a young age. His medical philosophy was that true health depends on a healthy body, a compassionate heart, and a clear mind, which leads to the nature of the problems and helps resolve them. He stressed that greed, anger, and ignorance were the three reasons for the activation of psychological diseases. The levels of happiness, anger, anxiety, a ruminating mind, sadness, fear, and shock were the six internal elements, and coldness, summer heat, dryness, heat, dampness, and wind were the seven external elements as the root causes for illness in the Buddha's medical theories since it affects the five major organs namely, heart, liver, lungs, spleen, and kidneys by unbalancing earth, water, fire, and wind. Overeating, long sitting without movement, sadness, fatigue, anger, excessive sexual desire, postponing urination and excrement, and suppressing gas were the major behavioural causes of the illness (Zalta & Uri, 2023). He firmly believed that both bodies and minds are interdependent. An unhealthy mindset leads to physical disease and greed, anger, and ignorance were the three baskets for the diseases which he promoted through *dharma* to heal the illness. He practised and devoted medication as medicine for all ailments of life towards spiritual guidance to ensure overall well-being, which deals with the root cause of the problem, whereas Western medicine deals with physical symptoms and temporary relief. Even today, in the technology era, we seek a physician's care for a physical ailment without identifying the root cause of the problem and understanding human life. Practices of impurity, kindness, the true nature of all things, and the cultivation of wisdom were the key medications everyone should use to heal mind and body diseases. Discovering the origin of the illness, understanding the illness, prescribing the appropriate medication to cure the illness, and completely curing the illness in a manner that prevents it from reoccurring were the four major stages of any ailment in Buddha's medical practices (Asayo Horibe and Toshu Neatrour, 2003). Balance diet, rest, and awareness of the natural processes and the body were the four key elements of wellness. Most importantly, the health-care providers or doctors should have basic skills of kindness and compassion, which is the core of any medication. Buddha involved caretakers like family members, nurses, neighbours, and friends to support the patients. He encouraged caretakers to support the patients to ensure that they are reaching the right health-care providers, support their needs and help them to routine their regular work, spend time and understand their feelings with compassion, provides a balanced diet, and finally support them to take care of their body and mind. He also offered advice to patients on the selection of food choices, intervals of food, periodical follow-up with the doctors, and being optimistic to help themselves for early recovery. Lord Buddha's health practices are linked with spirituality, and he taught the Four Noble Truths of suffering, its origin, the cessation path of suffering, and the ways to relieve all the suffering of life (Kalra, Gagan Priya, 2018). He said that illness is the outcome of *karma*, the law of cause and effect. His "eightfold right" of understanding, thought, speech, conduct livelihood, efforts mindfulness, and meditation leads to holistic overall health. Finally, Buddha's health is all about meditation, prayer, psychotherapy, and healing (Zalta & Nodelman, 2023).

Preventive Health Reforms by Mahatma Gandhi (1869-1848)

> "India does not need imported drugs from the West when she has an inexhaustible stock of a variety of drugs grown in the villages themselves. But more than drugs they have to teach the people the right mode of living." (*Harijan*, 15.6.1947: 1845)

Mahatma Gandhi, the ever-global inspirational leader of non-violence and the father of the nation, a well-known social reformer of India, has also significantly contributed to preventive health in his way of life. He professed that "prevention is better than cure". Personal hygiene, palatal self-control, vegetarianism- cum-balanced diet and regular physical activity were his practices for the prevention of illnesses (Gandhiji, 1949). He believed that the use of earth, air, sunlight, water, and diet were the solution for any type of diseases to overcome, as well as preventive care. He started practising herbal medicine when he was suffering from digestive complaints in South Africa. He walked 18 km every day for nearly 40 years. Even though fasting was one of his political strategies, it was also his health reform. *Return to Nature* book helped him to understand the importance of drugless preventive therapy instead of depending on medicine. He strongly practised nature's cure and *yoga* as his health care and promoted the concept along with his freedom struggles. He established Nisargopchar, Nature Cure Ashram at Uruli Kanchan, Pune, in March 1946 and promoted village sanitation and healthy living along with his disciples, which was useful for all sectors of society without any discrimination through his *Grām Swarāj*. He conceptualized the moral of self-reliance on health care, encompassing community participation towards rural development of a sustainable preventive health approach (Komarraju Satyalakshmi, 2019). His well-known eleven vows, namely non-violence, truth, control over palate (taste), celibacy, physical work, non-stealing, non-possession, fearlessness, removal of caste barrier, equality in religion, *swadeśī* or self-reliance led healthy environment for mental well-being. Gandhiji believed that self-health reliance is the key to achieving self-reliance.

Social Work and Public Health

Social work is a welfare activity based on humanitarian philosophy, scientific knowledge, and technical skills for helping individuals, groups, or communities live rich and full lives (ICSW, 1957). The aim of social work, as generally understood, is to remove social injustice, relieve distress, prevent suffering, and assist the weaker members of society to rehabilitate themselves and their families and, in short, fight the five giant evils of physical want, disease, ignorance, squalor and idleness (Kher, 1947). Social work is help rendered to any person or group who has any disability, mental, physical, emotional or moral, so that the individual or group is being helped to enable the individual and society. Social work is merely a pathological practice that deals with the sufferings of individuals, groups, or communities (Moorthy & Rao, 1970).

Public health is an effort to help a group or community of people prevent disease, improve overall health, and live longer. It is a combination of science and art of preventing diseases, prolonging life, and promoting health and efficiency through organized community effort, where social work philosophy is one of the core components. Health promotion, prevention, and rehabilitation are key elements in public health and social work. Public health and social work are the two perspectives for a common mission of community well-being.

> "Social work and public health are inseparable, and no artificial boundaries can separate them. Social work is interwoven in the whole fabric of the public health movement and has directly influenced it at every point." (Hopkins, 1926)

Public health and social work have their roots in the early twentieth century. Efforts to improve sanitation and lower the risk of disease outbreaks led to the first public health programmes, immunizations, and directing trauma and disaster responses following First and Second World War. The relationship between the two fields was developed by (Richmond, 1917) on social diagnosis (Perlman, 1957), social casework on problem-solving approach (Rapoport, 1961). Prevention for social work, and the recent American Academy of Social Work and Social Welfare (2021), where social work focuses on society's overall well-being through its techniques and skills. Public health social work is based on an epidemiologic approach to preventing, addressing, and solving social health problems, originated in the early twentieth century, drawing upon both social work and public health theories, frameworks, research, and practice (Betty, 2008). The public health social work field has been evolving as an interdisciplinary field in the twenty-first century.

Rationale of Social Work and Holistic Health Prevention from the Reforms of India

The core objective of social work deals with solving the psycho-social and adjustment issues, strengthening harmonious social relations and values, creating opportunities for individual and community development, fulfilling the needs of love, care, and affection, and finally, creating self-sufficiency and a satisfying life of every human being and his social environment.

Restoration of social functioning, provision of resources, and prevention of social dysfunction are the three major areas of social work function. Physical and psychological health protection and rehabilitation are provided in the curative function of social work. Individual reforms, social relationships, family workplace community welfare, and social reforms like beggary are delivered through corrective functions. Disease prevention and social legislation are delivered through preventive functions. Socio-economic development activities and community development are the developmental functions of social work (Mishra, 1994). It is all about shifting from a *status quo* service-oriented approach to a change-oriented development approach.

Social casework deals with the individual relationship and its social environment. Group work deals with the individuals in a social group and supports opportunities and growth, and community organization supports the community's needs. The objectives, functions, and methods of social work are precisely reflected in the reformer's philosophy of wellness and harmony, where the reformers lived as an example and brought changes in every individual, family, and community. Finally, it can be grown as a universal practice.

Social work is an integral component of health care. Social workers are part of the integral settings across the health care continuum to provide services to individuals and families throughout their lifespan and address the range of physical, psycho-social, and economic issues affecting the individual's and community's well-being. Clinical social work is a speciality practice area of social work that focuses on the assessment, diagnosis, treatment, and prevention of mental illness, as well as emotional and other behavioural disturbances (Thomas, 2010).

Social workers are critical in advocating for policies that reduce health inequalities and improve access to health care, especially for vulnerable populations, by promoting specialized services and ensuring quality assurance. Over the years, social workers have been contributing to overall health, mainly in aging, clinical work, long-term care, oncology, substance abuse, depression, and maternal health. Health education and promotion, social determinants of health, advocacy, stigma reduction equity, collaboration, health risk management, and disaster-based health programmes were some of the significant roles of social workers in public health prevention in the new era.

The ethics and principles of the Indian social reforms and social work objectives are well interconnected. Lord Mahāvīra's three key elements, Lord Buddha's eightfold right, and Gandhiji's eleven vows and their way of living and reforms on social and health development were well demonstrated with the objectives and approach of social work.

Conclusion

Recently, developments in technology and employment opportunities have minimized physical exercise, balanced diet, and emotional and spiritual wellness among the community, especially among the youth, which leads to a high volume of non-communicable diseases in the country. India has had rich health and well-being for centuries through its social reformers. Bhagavān Mahāvīra, Gautama Buddha, and Mahatma Gandhi were the key preventive health and harmony revolutionaries. Regular physical exercise, a balanced diet, and psychological and spiritual well-being of the reformers' core teachings need to be transformed and translated by the social workers towards the national public health problem by positioning social workers on a large scale in the public health sector towards preventive health care catalyst is the urgent need of the hour. It will reduce around 30 per cent of the country's preventive health budget and support emergencies like youth employment, elderly, and disability needs in the community.

REFERENCES

American Academy of Social Work and Social Welfare (2021). "Grand Challenges for Social Work". Retrieved from https://grandchallengesforsocialwork.org/

Arihant Bhagwant (2021). *Health: The Jaina Perspective.* https://jainstudy.wordpress.com/2021/02/16/health-the-jaina-perspective/

Asayo Horibe, Toshu Neatrour (2003). *Buddhist: Metropolitan Chicago Health-care Council.* https://www.advocatehealth.com/assets/documents/faith/cgbuddhist.pdf

Gandhi, M. (1949). *Diet and Diet Reform.* In: Bharatan Kumarappa, editor. 1st edition. Ahmedabad: Navajivan Publishing House [Google Scholar].

Gidey, Gebrezgi, Taju, Sadik, Hagos, Ato Seifu (2005). *The Introduction to Public Health*, Mekelle University in collaboration with the Ethiopia Public Health Training Initiative, the Ethiopia Ministry of Health, and the Ethiopia Ministry of Education.

Giri, Swami Nirmalananda (2019). *Buddha's Eightfold Path: A Yogi's Pratical Analysis, Light of the Spirit Monastery,* https://ocoy.org/buddhas-eightfold-path/

Gupta, S., Shenoy, V.P., Bairy, I., Srinivasa, H. & Mukhopadhyay, C. (2011). "Diabetes Mellitus and HIV as Co-morbidities in Tuberculosis Patients of Rural South India". *Journal of Infection and Public Health*, 4(3): 140-44. https://doi.org/10.1016/j.jiph.2011.03.005

Hopkins, H.L. (1926). "The Place of Social Work in Public Health". Paper presented at: National Conference of Social Work, Cleveland, OH.

Jain, Aashi (2021). *Reconciling Illness through Devotion: The Medicalization of Modern Jain Faith Healing Practice Through Bhaktāmara Stotra*, Miami.

Kalra, Sanjay, Gagan Priya (2018). "Lessons for the Health-care Practitioner from Buddhism". *Indian J Endocrinol Metab*,*22*(6): 812-17. doi: 10.4103/ijem.IJEM_286_17

Keton, Amanda (2021). *Ethics of Jainism*, Wikepedia. Org, https://en.wikipedia.org/wiki/Ethics_of_Jainism

Komarraju, Satyalakshmi (2019). "Mahatma Gandhi and Nature Cure". *Indian J Med Res.*, S69-S71. doi: 10.4103/0971-5916.251660.

Lambert K. Engelbrecht (1999). *Introduction to Social Work*, Lanzo, Cape Town, ISBN 0 620 235675

Misra, P.D. (1994). *Social Work: Philosophy and Methods.* Inter-India Publications, New Delhi.

Narain, Jai Prakash (2019). "Mahatma Gandhi and Nature Cure". *Indian J Med Res.149*(Suppl 1): S69-S71.doi: 10.4103/0971-5916.251660

Narain, J.P. (2016). "Public Health Challenges in India: Seizing the opportunities". *Indian J Community Med.41*(2): 85-88.doi: 10.4103/0970-0218.177507.

Narain, J.P., Kumar, R. (2015). "Non-Communicable Diseases: Health Burden, Economic Impact and Strategic Priorities". *Chronic Non-communicable Diseases: The Health Challenge of 21st Century.* Delhi: Jaypee Brothers Medical Publishers, pp. 1-18[Google Scholar].

Nisal, Ravindra Vasant (2012). "Gandhian Approach towards Health", https://www.mkgandhi.org/articles/gandhian_approach_towards_health.htm

Perlman, H.H. (1957). *Social Casework: A Problem-solving Approach.* University of Chicago Press.

Press Information Bureau (2023). Ministry of Finance, Government of India, *Economic Survey, 2022-23*, Highlights, New Delhi.

Richmond, M.E. (1917). *Social Diagnosis.* Russell, Sage Foundation.

Samini Robit, Pragya (2015). *Health and Happiness in Jainism.* https://www.herenow4u.net/index.php?id=102511

Sanjay, Shashank (2023). *Public Expenditure on Non-Communicable Diseases & Injuries in India: A Budget-based Analysis*, doi: 10.1371/journal.pone.0222086

The University of Liverpool (2022). *Tackling Public Health Issues: Concepts and Evidence*, Online courses. https://www.futurelearn.com/info/courses/tackling-public-health-issues-concepts-and-evidence/0/steps/305348

Thomas, Gracious (2010). *Origin and Development of Social Work in India.* School of Social Work Indira Gandhi National Open University New Delhi.

Upadhyaya, Amar (2016). *The Distilled Essence of Non-Violence.* Print Masters F-45, Okhla Industrial Area Phase I, New Delhi, https://jainsindia.org/pdf/Distilled%20Essence.pdf

Wikepedia Foundation.org, (2023). *Ahiṁsā in Jainism*, https://en.wikipedia.org/wiki/Ahiṁsā_in_Jainism

World Health Organization (1946). *The International Health Conference Constitution*, New York. https://apps.who.int/gb/bd/

World Health Organization (2005). *Fifty-Eighth World Health Assembly Geneva*. document WHA58/2005/REC/2, https://apps.who.int/gb/ebwha/pdf_files/REC1/english/A58_2005_REC1-en.pdf.

Zalta, Edward N. & Nodelman, Uri (eds.) (2023), "Buddha", *The Stanford Encyclopedia of Philosophy*. URL = <https://plato.stanford.edu/archives/spr2023/entries/buddha/>.

20

Relevance of Buddha's Philosophy in Social Casework

Nikita Singh, Anjali Mishra, and *Nimisha Singh*

Introduction

India's social work history is a long-standing phenomenon. Even though social work was founded and recognized by Western nations, the roots of the field may be traced deep in Indian history. The world philosophies of secularism, humanism, protestantism, rationalism, welfare, liberalism, democracy, and utilitarianism may all be seen as providing ideal ground for the development of social work. The origins of *dharma* in India are where the idea of well-being originated. Human civilization has a long history of suffering and self-interest, so mutual aid was necessary to keep humanity safe. The history is filled with the actions of foreign conquerors, invaders, kings, queens, landowners, and under the diarchy system, as well as the 1935 constitutional change that brought in a new period of publicly elected provincial administration. The social work profession was born from social services, charitable reform, and welfare philosophies. The field of social work has come a long way from welfare to development and empowerment, and now it places a strong focus on defending and advancing individuals' rights. Buddhism is a convenient faith. It holds that although our world is filled with pain, it can rise beyond it. One may argue that the main focus of Buddhism is how to end this suffering. The concept of social work principles in terms of Buddhism becomes significant in this situation. Before discussing Buddhism and social work, it might be beneficial to understand the Buddha's perspectives on several matters closely related to social work. In recent decades, Buddhists have been re-evaluating their religion's teachings in order to develop a foundation for social action against issues such as racism, exploitation, war, commercialism, and environmental degradation. Buddhism is essentially a volitional endeavour to ensure the well-being of others. The Indian culture and Buddhist system are the sources of the social work ideology. In the early Buddhist tradition, social work is, therefore, a psycho-ethical idea that was started to bring about perfect harmony for all living things in society, along with a pleasant mixing and balance of material and spiritual accomplishments. The Buddha's conception of social order and the social labour principle are closely related. He imagined a societal structure and an order in which there is a base of pure love and affection, or *bhūmi*, that is widespread waves of compassion, joy, peace, and harmony that all people feel. This was called *bhrama-vihāra* by Buddha. Regarding the education and training of social workers, it should be mentioned that as monastic establishments grew, each *vihāra*—which housed a sizeable population of monastic residents—became an educational hub. Buddhism and social work beliefs both help people realize their obligations to society, the family, and themselves. Social workers are advised by Buddhism and social work ideals to prioritize their own well-being, as well as that of their families and the community they live in while carrying out their professional responsibilities. Both impart to the populace the values of deference to and reverence for elders and superiors, reverence and respect for all religions, honouring and respecting all individuals regardless of caste, creed, or gender, and regard for women in general. Social work literature has highlighted the therapeutic connection as a critical component of effective therapy in recent years. The practitioner and the client are viewed as ideally interacting with and being moved by one another under the relationality focus. Comparing this technique to the previous "blank slate", detached method, it is significantly more intricate. It has been said that approaching the therapeutic relationship is an art that requires both training and intuition (Coltart, 2000). The specifics of that dance and how it inevitably varies with every client necessitate a continuous exercise of competence and openness. Taking into account translation—the process by which social workers utilize their spiritual practices to inform their interactions with clients—is one method to support and direct such a practice. It has been said that approaching the therapeutic relationship is an art that requires both training and intuition (Coltart, 2000). Themes of compassion, connection, and transcending oneself are prevalent in spirituality and religion; these ideas may and do inform therapeutic involvement. The earliest branch of Buddhism, which is based on the teachings of the Pāli canon, incorporates a pragmatic approach to suffering that social workers may use to show up to and hold space for their clients consciously and presently.

The basis of Buddhist philosophy is the ongoing practice of the Four Noble Truths: The First Noble Truth, the truth of suffering (*dukkha*) acknowledges the inevitable presence of suffering in human life; the Second Noble Truth, the truth of the cause of suffering (*samudaya*) explores the cause of suffering as originating from desire; the Third Noble Truth, the truth of cessation of sufferings (*nirodha*) describes the end of suffering as enlightenment, or the ceasing of desire; and the Fourth Noble Truth, the truth of the path leading to the cessation of sufferings (*mārga*), describes the path toward the end of suffering through the Noble Eightfold Path.

The Truth of Suffering (Dukkha): The First Noble Truth explains that suffering exists in human existence and that having a body entails experiencing disease, pain, and death. As a result, the Buddha advocates for accepting that suffering is inevitable. This reality is "not falsely lulling you into living a fool's paradise, nor does it frighten and agonize you with ... imaginary fears and sins", according to Wapola Rahula (1967: 17). Social workers may adopt this philosophy by acknowledging and embracing the client's or patient's presenting pain and misery. In fact, the first step in every therapeutic interaction is to accept the client and their discomfort, according to Berlin (2005). "A relational feeling that sensitizes us to their distress and ultimately brings us to action" is how Berlin characterizes acceptance (p. 483). Before and during the engagement, social workers who embrace their clients' sufferings become more sensitive to it and recognize our shared humanity in it. The social caseworker defines accepting the client for who they are in life. The values that guide how a caseworker views and interacts with a client, taking into account both his strengths and weaknesses. His amiable and disagreeable traits, optimistic and pessimistic outlook, and creative and destructive traits without bias. When a client behaves differently than what is acceptable, the employee shouldn't feel antagonistic towards them. Acceptance serves as a therapeutic strategy to assist the social worker in understanding the client for who he truly is, increasing the casework's effectiveness. The acceptance principles are very crucial. Social casework professionals frequently come into contact with people or families who are suffering from a variety of conditions, including mental illness, addiction, abuse, poverty, and relationship troubles. Social workers recognize and are aware of their client's pain, much as the First Noble Truth acknowledges suffering in life. According to the first noble truth, life is full of hardships. Everything that is born of connection seems to be accompanied by pain: birth, old age, illness, death, sadness, grief, desire, and despair.

In other words, life's most basic conditions seemed to be full of misery. Similarly, social casework respects the pain that people and families go through, regardless of whether societal norms, personal struggles, institutionalized injustices, etc. bring it on. Incorporate Buddhist teachings on impermanence (*aniccā*) and non-attachment (*anattā*) into social casework treatments to support clients in exploring their expectations and attachments and to assist them in letting go of hard beliefs and attachments fuel their suffering. Encourage a positive outlook on uncertainty and change.

The Truth of the Cause of Suffering (Samudaya): The Buddha states that ignorance and desire are the root causes of suffering in the Second Noble Truth.

> "Craving for sensual pleasures, craving for existence, and craving for extermination is what causes renewed existence, accompanied by delight and lust, seeking delight here and there." (Boddhi, 2005: 76)

A tangible, knowledgeable, distinct, definite, and masterful concept of oneself over one's person and surroundings can be expressed in a variety of ways (Rahula, 1967: 30). Mary Ellen Kondrat's (1999) conception of the critically reflexive practitioner is similar. The self is viewed as a process, an ongoing, fluid construction whose identity is inextricably linked to social context and interpersonal interactions, according to Kondrat, who draws inspiration from critical theory. Social workers are urged to understand themselves as "co-constructed by individual consciousness in interaction with the social and physical environment and mediated through language and culture". Dialoguing with others' interpretations of oneself helps define one's own self-construct, at least in part (Kondrat, 1999: 459). It teaches about the root causes of suffering—ignorance, attachment, and desire. In social casework, professionals also seek to determine the root reasons for their clients' problems. Examining prior traumas, cultural influences, familial dynamics, or individual beliefs and actions that exacerbate their problems might all be part of this. According to Buddhist philosophy, attachment is the cause of suffering, and attachment is defined as (*tṛṣṇā*) lust, thirst, longing, or clinging. Self-reliance is important, and both Buddhism and social casework stress this, but they may approach it differently. In Buddhism, the ideas of personal accountability and self-improvement are intimately related to the concept of self-reliance. The Buddha taught that people may change their thoughts and end their suffering by working for it. This entails developing traits like compassion, wisdom, and awareness, which help people deal with life's obstacles more resiliently and clearly. Buddhism strongly focuses on self-reliance, which encourages followers to take charge of their spiritual development and rely on their inner resources rather than looking to others for approval or redemption. In social casework, clients frequently view self-reliance as a primary objective. Social caseworkers assist people and families dealing with a range of issues, including homelessness, poverty, and mental illness. Their goal is to provide their clients with the tools they need to overcome these obstacles and lead better lives. As part of this empowerment process, clients are frequently assisted in recognizing their assets and talents, learning how to solve problems, and connecting with local resources and support systems. Social caseworkers empower their clients to take charge of their situation and develop more independence and self-sufficiency by encouraging self-reliance. Self-reliance is not the same as isolation or self-sufficiency in the sense of being totally independent of other people in Buddhism or social casework. Rather, it is about realizing one's own agency and growth potential, as well as the interconnection of all creatures and the significance of cooperation and mutual support in the pursuit of both individual and group well-being. Working with customers may withstand "not knowing" if one can accept that they are flexible, conditioned creatures. As a result, one develops a keen curiosity for and regard for the client's vulnerable, evolving self. Christopher Bollas, a psychoanalytic therapist, explored this technique in detail in 1987. According to him, a practitioner "discovers who I am, even if this 'who' is a composite of the patient's mother, father, and former child self" (p. 277) when working with a client. The analyst serves as an object formed by the unresolved relationships of the client via the therapeutic interaction. In order to engage in that adaptable, co-created role, the practitioner must be able and willing to develop their own identity in this way. Thus, in Buddhist thinking, the Second Noble Truth serves as a reminder to avoid the temptation to be fixed, safe, and stagnant in one's social work practice. Instead, social workers should acknowledge and honour the porousness and history of both the practitioner and the client to provide a holding space for healing and not knowing and understanding our subjectivity in a new, relational, and co-constructed light.

The Truth of Cessation of Suffering (Nirodha): The Third Noble Truth discusses enlightenment as the end of suffering. The Buddha was motivated to achieve the embodied cessation of craving, desire, and attachment upon attaining enlightenment. According to Epstein (1995), the enlightened Buddha "[discovered] that which had been present all the time" rather than "enter some new territory". The Buddha had become aware of the reality of the illusory self, the self that yearns to validate its identity via heedless effort and consumerism constantly. The self is wrongly attached to that which appears to be safe or satisfying, which feeds the yearning and keeps the self-trapped in the circle of suffering. This is in line with the objective of social casework, which is to assist clients in finding solutions to their issues. This might entail offering assistance, counselling, empowerment, education, or pushing for a systemic end to ignorance. In an effort to lessen or end suffering, they also look for solutions to their issues, whether via activism, treatment, the supply of resources, or empowerment. Suffering may be put an end to, which is the third noble truth about suffering. The condition of existence known as *nirvāṇa* is one in which all attachment and suffering may be eradicated in this present life. The Buddha clarified that labour (*rāga, dveṣa,* and *moha*) devoid of attachment, anger, and infatuation does not lead to servitude.

The Truth of the Path Leading to the Cessation of Suffering (Mārga): The eightfold route—right vision, right thought, right speech, right action, right livelihood, right effort, right mindfulness, and right concentration—describes the behavioural, meditative, and wisdom practices and the road towards, besides, and amid moments of *nirvāṇa* or enlightenment that the Fourth Noble Truth describes. Such a balance is essential to social work clinical procedures, and it is well-known from Winnicott's (1991) concept of a "potential space" in the therapeutic relationship—one that establishes a balance that is "neither in behaviour nor in contemplation, but somewhere else" (p.105)—through relationships. It entails assisting individuals in acquiring abilities including self-awareness, problem-solving, communication, and coping mechanisms. The client can progressively overcome their pain and attain higher well-being by following this route. In Buddhism and social casework, empathy for others is highly valued. Compassion and empathy are basic characteristics in Buddhism. The Buddha himself stressed the value of developing loving-kindness (*mettā*) and compassion (*karuṇā*) for all living things. It entails assisting individuals in acquiring abilities, including self-awareness, problem-solving, communication, and coping mechanisms. The client can progressively overcome their pain and attain higher. In order to respond with compassion and a desire to lessen the suffering of others, practitioners are urged to cultivate empathy by learning about their struggles and suffering. This empathy, which recognizes the universality of suffering and the Buddhist concept of interconnectedness, extends beyond humans to all sentient beings. Similarly, empathy is a fundamental principle in social casework. Caseworkers receive training on listening intently to their clients, comprehending their viewpoints and experiences, and reacting to them in a sympathetic and understanding way. Empathy is not just a passive sentiment but also a driving factor behind action in both Buddhism and social casework. It encourages people to connect with one another, provide a hand and support, and strive towards building a more just and caring society. Practitioners of both religions may enhance their relationships with others and promote the well-being and pleasure of all creatures by developing empathy.

Conclusion

Known by many as "the great physician", Buddha sought to recognize, understand, and put an end to human suffering just like any other therapist would. Therapists do have common objectives as well. The Four Noble Truths are a diagnostic framework that explains suffering and its resolution. The First Noble Truth describes the ailment, the Second offers the cause, the Third offers a prognosis, and the Fourth provides a treatment. Over the years, millions of individuals have benefited from his innovative treatment approaches. Today's Western culture is aware of Buddhism's psychological core. The teachings of the Buddha are the source of many psychotherapy models used in the West. Buddha accepted everyone who approached him with compassion and without passing judgement. He relieved uncomfortable and painful feelings while assisting others in gaining understanding and promoting their progress. He uses amazing therapeutic techniques that are always applicable. Effective social work practice requires the compassion of the social worker. Social workers and Buddhists have sympathized with individuals. Social workers and Buddhists are kind people; they will identify and experience the suffering of the tragic or disturbed. They both value independence, the worth of every person, and the development of an atmosphere of fairness, collaboration, equality, and openness. The Buddha's teachings are applied practically in social casework to alleviate suffering. Social workers exemplify the values of compassion, understanding, and empowerment found in the Four Noble Truths by acknowledging the existence of suffering, comprehending its origins, striving to end it, and assisting people on a road to transformation. They incorporate Buddhist compassion and wisdom into their work, providing clients with all-encompassing assistance in meeting their social, spiritual, and personal requirements. This method promotes increased resilience, inner calm, and well-being for both clients and practitioners.

REFERENCES

Anderson, C.S. (1999). *Theravāda Buddhist Canon* (Pain and Its Ending, the Four Noble Truth). Richmond: Curzon.

Anālayo, Bh. (2011). "Right View and the Scheme of the Four Truths in Early Buddhism". *Canadian Journal of Buddhist Studies*, *7*: 11-44.

Berlin, S.B. (2005). "The Value of Acceptance in Social Work Direct Practice: A Historical and Contemporary View". *Social Service Review, 79*(3): 482-510.

Bodhi, B. (2005). *In the Buddha's Words: An Anthology of Discourses from the Pāli Canon.* Wisdom Publications.

Bollas, C. (1987). *The Shadow of the Object: Psychoanalysis of the Unthought Known.* Columbia University Press.

Biestek, F.P. (1957). *The Casework Relationship*. Chicago, IL: Loyola University Press.

Coltart, N. (2000). *Slouching Towards Bethlehem.* Other Press, pp. 51- 80.

Chatterjee, S., Datta, D. (1980). *An Introduction to Indian Philosophy* (8th edn.). Calcutta: Calcutta University Press; the Buddha Philosophy [Google Scholar].

Epstein, M. (1995). *Thoughts without a Thinker: Psychotherapy from a Buddhist Perspective*. NY: Basic Books [Google Scholar].

Jayatunge, R.M. (2012). *Gautama Buddha the Unique Psychotherapist* [last accessed on 26 October 2012]. Available from: http://www.lankaweb.com/news/items/2010/04/21/gautama-buddha-the-unique-psychotherapist/2010

Kondrat, M.E. (1999). "Who is the 'Self' in Self-aware: Professional Self-Awareness from a Critical Theory Perspective". *Social Service Review, 73*(4): 451-77.

Norman, K.R. (1982). "The Four Noble Truths: A Problem of Pāli Syntax". In L.A. Hercus (Ed.), *Indological and Buddhist Studies: Volume in Honour of Professor J.W. de Jong on his 60th Birthday*. Canberra: Australian National University (pp. 377-91).

Rhys Davids, C.A. (2003). *Buddhist Manual of Psychological Ethics*. Whitefish, MT: Kessinger Publishing [Google Scholar].

Thera, N. (1996). *The Heart of Buddhist Meditation: A Handbook of Mental Training based on the Buddha's Way of Mindfulness*. York Beach [Google Scholar].

Tew, J. (2006). "Understanding Power and Powerlessness: Towards a Framework for Emancipatory Practice in Social Work". *Journal of Social Work, 6*(1): 33-51.

Walshe, M. (1995). *The Long Discourses of Budha: A Translation of the Digha Nikaya*. Wisdom Publication.

Weber, M. (1958). *The Religion of India: The Sociology of Hinduism and Buddhism*. The Free Press.

Wezler, A. (1984). "On the Quadruple Division of the Yogaśāstra, the Caturvyūhatva of the Cikitsāśāstra and the 'Four Noble Truths' of the Buddha". *Indologia Taurinensia, 12*: 289-337.

Winnicott, D.W. (1971). *Playing and Reality*. Routledge.

21

Contribution of Swami Vivekananda Towards Social Work

Role and Relevance in Present Context

Saumya Sisodia

Introduction

Serving the needy and helping one's fellowmen have been virtues greatly valued in the Indian culture and society. Devotion and service towards one's fellowmen love for charity, and brotherhood existed even in the feudal periods and far beyond. The community and the rulers were responsible for assisting the needy. The form of assistance that was provided to needy individuals on the grounds of religious duty is known as "charity" all over the world, including in India. The different traditional forms of charity that existed in ancient India were *artha* (money), *vidyā* (education), *abhaya* (courage) and/ or *surakṣā* (security), all of which have a solid reference for important components of modern forms of social work practice.

If we look at the history of social work in India, we can see that Hinduism and the Hindu way of life have acted as a driving force for social practice in the country. It has been seen as a source of inspiration for the providers of social service and social welfare and professional social work practitioners in the country. The term *dāna* has been used in vedic literature to describe the act of distributing wealth among the weaker members of society. The term "charity" was another popular word that was mainly used in the Vedic period; sprang from the idea that whenever one serves the needy people in society, he/she serves God and earns *puṇya* or blessing from God. This idea motivated people to undertake charitable activities for the needy and helpless people in society, and this concept exists even today.

People in distress, destitution, and deprivation have been helped in the past by individuals, joint families, caste communities, and religious institutions motivated by religious philosophy that assumed "charity" as a reward or medium for salvation, humanism, philanthropy, humanitarian feeling, democratic ideology, equality of all citizens; regard for human personality; respect for other's rights including the indigents, the handicapped, the unemployed, emotionally challenged and above all, those in need. The charitable work taken up by individuals and some voluntary organizations came to be termed "social work" in the due course of time. The most frequently seen misconception about social work is that people mistake charity, alms giving and voluntary activities as social work, but this, in reality, is not social work, as it does not provide any permanent solution to the person's problems and does not empower a person to face his problems by himself. Social work aims to make a person self-dependent and self-reliant. It explores the causal factors behind the problem and tries to solve them scientifically.

In a nutshell, social work is intended to assist individuals, families, social groups, and communities in sorting out their personal and social problems and permanently solving those problems through a scientific and systematic process.

From the contemporary point of view, it has been defined according to the idea jointly formulated by the International

Association of Schools of Social Work (IASSW) and International Federation of Social Work (IFSW) in their conference in 2001 in Copenhagen that—

> "The social work profession promotes social change, solving problems in human relationship and empowerment; and liberation of people to enhance well-being, utilizing the theories of human behaviour and social systems. Social work intervenes at the point where people interact with their environments. Principle of human rights and social justice are fundamental to social work."

An analysis of spiritual teachings in Indian tradition points to the fact that the concepts in Hinduism associated with human welfare are paramount in discussing spiritual dimensions of social work. Canda and Furman (2010) observe that the idea of *karma-yoga*, mainly based on the teachings of Swami Vivekananda and other yogic traditions, and the Gandhian approach to social work are the two forms of Hindu-oriented views that are most often addressed in the social work literature. According to them, these ideas provide social workers a sense of direction to carry out non-violent, spiritually-based social practice. While the Gandhian approach focuses more on spiritually based social actions, the *karma-yoga* approach focuses on *mokṣa* (spiritual liberation). The social work practice, according to the norms of Indian spirituality, should be guided by the three fundamental values. The Vedāntic world view accentuates a non-dualistic world where all beings are part of a unified whole called *Brahman*. Hence, social workers should respect each client and maintain a benevolent purpose towards them because all beings manifest the divine truth. The second value is an altruistic concept of selflessness, which implies a social worker's responsibility to keep a dispassionate attitude to the fruits of their action. This value helps the social worker escape from egoistic attachment to one's goals for clients. The third value is known as *ahiṁsā* (non-violence), which means that all human beings are provided with unconditional respect and compassion. It involves an active search for truth, helping others in their pursuit of truth, and resisting oppression and dehumanization in a way that doesn't oppress or dehumanize others (Canda & Furman, 2010). The whole theme of social work in Indian spirituality centres around this search for truth and salvation. By helping others or pursuing the truth, the social worker will naturally benefit and ensure his liberation.

In the late nineteenth century, Swami Vivekananda was considered a pioneering figure in India who worked towards bringing massive social reforms to society. He contributed and worked in the fields of secularism, looking upon untouchables with compassion, educational reforms, socialism, women upliftment, and many more. Social service was an essential aspect of Vivekananda's innovative ideas. Swami Vivekananda, the prophet and pathfinder, has given us remarkable guidelines for social work based on the plenary truth that *jīva* is Śiva (each individual is divinity itself). So, he stressed *Śiva jñāne jīva sevā* (to serve common people, considering them as manifestations of God). A spiritual genius of commanding intellect and power, Swami Vivekananda crammed immense labour and achievement into his short life (1863-1902). Vivekananda is regarded as the patriot saint of modern India and an inspirer of her dormant national consciousness. According to Vivekananda, man is potentially Divine, so, service to man as the visible manifestation of the godhead was the special form of worship he advocated for the Indians, devoted as they were to the rituals and myths of their ancient faith (Swami Nikhilananda, 1953). Thus, Swami Vivekanand said,

> "Service done as worship of God in man helps in two ways: it helps physically or mentally the person

who is served, and it helps spiritually the person who serves."

Swami Vivekananda is always remembered worldwide for his address at the World's Parliament of Religions held at Chicago in 1893, which made the Western intelligentsia turn around to recognize the great culture and tradition India had since time immemorial. During his travels all over India, Swami Vivekananda was deeply moved to see the appalling poverty and backwardness of the masses. He immediately understood that the real cause of India's downfall was the neglect of the masses, who had lost faith in their capacity to improve their lot as a result of centuries of oppression. First, infusing confidence and faith in themselves into their minds was necessary. For this, they needed an inspiring message that could energize them to lead a life full of activity for their betterment. Their faith in religion but not understanding the Vedānta philosophy and its practical application showed Swamiji the light amidst darkness. The masses needed two kinds of knowledge: secular knowledge to improve their economic condition and spiritual knowledge to infuse them with faith in themselves and strengthen their moral sense. Education was the answer that Swamiji found. To carry out his plans for the spread of education and for the uplift of the poor masses, as well as of women, an efficient organization of dedicated people was needed. It was for this purpose Swamiji founded the Ramakrishna Mission. Thus began the social engineering with a touch of spiritualism. Through his inspiring and profoundly significant lectures, Swamiji attempted to rouse the spiritual consciousness of the people and create in them pride in their cultural heritage; to bring about a unification of Hinduism by pointing out the common bases of its sects; to focus the attention of educated people on the plight of the downtrodden masses, and to expound his plan for their uplift by the application of the principles of practical Vedānta.

Major Social Works of Swami Vivekananda

Swami Vivekananda said there are three things needed to do social work. First, we should feel for the poor and socially deprived people for whom we are going to work. Only with feeling can great things be achieved. Second, we should have a workable plan for social work. Without a plan, nothing is going to be achieved. We should put effort and time into achieving the goals. Third and lastly, we should help like-minded people who are working towards the same goal.

Making an objective assessment of Swami Vivekananda's contributions to world culture, the eminent British historian A.L. Basham stated that "in centuries to come, he will be remembered as one of the main molders of the modern world". Some of the main contributions that Swamiji made to the modern world are mentioned below:

(i) **New Understanding of Religion:** One of the most significant contributions of Swami Vivekananda to the modern world is his interpretation of religion as a universal experience of transcendent reality common to all humanity. This universal conception frees religion from the hold of superstitions, dogmatism, and intolerance and makes religion the highest and noblest pursuit of supreme freedom, supreme knowledge, and supreme happiness that is accomplished by realizing one's *ātmā* as part of *paramātmā*.

(ii) **New View of Man:** Vivekananda's concept of the potential divinity of the soul prevents this degradation, divinizes human relationships, and makes life meaningful and worth living. Swamiji has laid the foundation for current interest in meditation/ *prāṇāyāma* all over the world.

(iii) **New Principle of Morality and Ethics:** Our morality in both individual life and social life is mostly based on fear of societal censure. But Vivekananda gave a new theory of ethics and new principle of morality based on the intrinsic purity and oneness of the *ātman*. We should be pure because purity is our real nature, our true divine Self or *ātman*. Similarly, we should love and serve our neighbours because we are all one in the supreme spirit, known as *Paramātmā* or *Brahman*.

(iv) Emphasis on Service: Swami Vivekananda believed in the concept of *daridra nārāyaṇa* (the poor as embodiments of God) and stressed the importance of serving the underprivileged and marginalized sections of society. He envisioned the Ramakrishna Mission as an organization that would engage in various forms of social service, including education, health care, relief work during natural disasters, and vocational training.

Swamiji's most unique contribution to creating a new India was to open the minds of Indians to their duty to the downtrodden masses. Before Karl Marx's ideas were known in India, Swamiji spoke about the labouring classes' role in producing the country's wealth. Swamiji was the first religious leader in India to speak for the masses, formulate a definite philosophy of service, and organize large-scale social service. A major contribution of Vivekananda to Hinduism is the rejuvenation and modernization of monasticism. In this new monastic ideal, followed in the Ramakrishna Order, the ancient principles of renunciation and God realization are combined with service to God in man (*Śiva jñāne jīva sevā*). Thus, Vivekananda elevated social service to the status of divine service and established the Ramakrishna Mission, a spiritual and philanthropic organization dedicated to the upliftment of society through education, health care, and relief work. The mission continues to operate worldwide, carrying out his vision and principles, reflecting the great relevance of his social works in the present time.

Vivekananda was deeply concerned about the social issues of his time, such as poverty, inequality, and discrimination. He believed that when properly understood, the Vedas contained principles that could address these challenges. He emphasized the concept of *daridra nārāyaṇa*, where he considered serving the poor and marginalized as serving the divine. His teachings inspired many to engage in social service and work towards the welfare of society, aligning their actions with the spiritual values found in the Vedas. Thus, one can see that Swami Vivekananda is a pioneering figure in India who has played an integral part in shaping modern India. Socialism, secularism, mass uplift and mass power, treating the untouchables with compassion, universal literacy, informal education, women's liberation, and inculcation of social service as a part of religious worship constituted the basic points for reforms by Swami Vivekananda.

Some of his major social work organization that profoundly boost Indian society and its people are described here:

(a) **Formation of the Ramakrishna Mission:** Swami Vivekananda was instrumental in conceptualizing and formalizing the Ramakrishna Mission. After the passing of his *guru*—Sri Ramakrishna Paramahamsa, Swami Vivekananda felt the need to spread the spiritual teachings of Sri Ramakrishna and bring about social reform. He saw the formation of the mission as a means to combine spiritual practice with service to humanity. The Ramakrishna Mission is a philanthropic and spiritual organization founded by Swami Vivekananda on 1 May 1897. Its primary objective is to promote the teachings of Vedānta, which emphasizes the oneness of all existence and the spiritual potential of every individual. The mission is based on the principles of selfless service (*sevā*), spiritual growth, and the pursuit of knowledge. The organization runs educational institutions, hospitals, and various humanitarian projects to serve society. It also conducts massive relief and rehabilitation work for victims of earthquakes, cyclones, and other calamities in different parts of India and other countries. The Ramakrishna Mission is also associated with the Ramakrishna Math, which is the monastic wing of the mission. The mission and *maṭha* work together to disseminate the teachings of Sri Ramakrishna and Swami Vivekananda and provide humanitarian assistance to those in need. Overall, Swami Vivekananda's teachings and the work of the Ramakrishna Mission continue to have a significant impact on both spiritual and social spheres in India and around the world. In early 1898, Swami Vivekananda acquired a big plot of land on the western bank of the Gaṅgā at a place called Belur where he established a new, universal pattern of monastic life that adapts ancient monastic ideals to the conditions of modern life, which gives equal importance to personal illumination and social service, and which is open to all men without any distinction of religion, race or caste.

(b) **Educational Initiatives:** Swami Vivekananda recognized the role of education in uplifting society and breaking the cycle of poverty. He established educational institutions under the Ramakrishna Mission to provide both spiritual and secular education. The Belur Math mission headquarters in West Bengal, India, houses the Ramakrishna Mission Residential College and the Ramakrishna Mission Vidyamandira, among other institutions. Swami Vivekananda's ideas on education are more modern than those of the educationists that prevailed in ancient India. Right from the beginning, he was instrumental in mass development and uplift.

(c) Furthermore, he conceived of what we now call informal education many decades ago. He placed special stress on technical education and industrial training, which have now become an essential part of the educational system of modern India. Vivekananda worked towards educational rights for women. He placed special stress on conventional values of family life and chastity for women, but he was totally against their subjection. He passionately pleaded for the extension of all educational facilities to women.

(d) **Social Work to Eradicate Poverty:** Although Swami Vivekananda was a man of meditation and religion, he advocated for work that would lead to a rise in productivity and the eradication of poverty. He has always said that "religion is not for empty stomachs". He has helped to shock people out of their comfort zone and inspired them into action. So, we see that Swamiji triggered the course of life in modern India by motivating the *rājasika* virtues in the Indian citizens. He also inspired them to enhance their present condition and not be content with the current life of degradation and poverty. Vivekananda's analysis of the causes of poverty of the Indian masses stemmed from his experience when he moved from one part of India to another as a *parikramā* before leaving for Chicago. He highlighted two major factors responsible for the extreme poverty of the Indians. One, the exploitation of the Indians by the British imperialist regime, resulting in the lack of income of the people, and two, the exploitation and repression of the poor farmers, labourers, and ordinary people by the feudal lords, *zamīndār*s, and priests. Vivekananda's main prescription for ameliorating the condition of low-income people was an all-out effort to educate them. Education was the essential need of the poor to resist and also to get rid of the oppression and exploitation that they had been subjected to. He thought that the solution to the problem of poverty lay in science and technology. He suggested for wide use of Western science and technology to create an industrial revolution in the country.

(d) **On India's Cultural History:** He tried to revitalize India with its ancient traditions along with modern science. One special characteristic of Vivekananda's reform is that he did not try to abolish the systems prevalent in then India. Rather he wants to make them grow in their true form. Vivekananda undoubtedly took immense pride in the India's inheritance from the past. Eradication of poverty, removal of illiteracy, restitution of human dignity, liberty from fear, availability of spiritual and secular knowledge to all, irrespective of their class, caste, and ending of all the monopolies, all these together made up a part of what he got from his Vedāntic socialism. With his reinterpretation of Vedānta, and its deep-rooted concern for the masses and their issues, Swami Vivekananda gave India a new way of life. He raised his voice against the feudal and colonial oppression. At the same time, Vivekananda looked for answers regarding India's historical destinies, and ways to transform it into a strong, wealthy, and independent state. He always reiterated the fact that India could only be built with the help of masses, small groups of energetic patriots, brave and strong with "muscles of iron and nerves of steel and gigantic wills".

(e) **Women's Upliftment:** Swami Vivekananda was never in active politics, yet he had a political sense of modern India which was far superior and much ahead of his time. He expressed immense outrage over the exploitation of rights and showed genuine concern for uplift of women mass and other socially backward people. He wanted a distinct social reform with the help of Western ideas and technology, yet not entrapped us with slavish imitation of the Western ways of life. In his book, *On India and Her Problems*, he wrote:

> "Remember that the nation lives in the cottages. But, alas, nobody ever did anything for them. Our modern reformers are very busy about widow remarriage. Of course, I am a sympathizer in every reform, but the fate of a nation does not depend upon the

> number of husbands the widows get, but upon the condition of the masses".

Vivekananda went a step further and said, "So long as millions live in hunger and ignorance, I hold every man a traitor."

(f) **Spiritual Rejuvenation:** Swami Vivekananda's thoughts on religion were unique. According to Vivekananda, religion had to be the primary and steering force in executing the social changes in the country. He gave India its secularist ideas, which now form an integral part of India's constitution. His views on religion were based on a common objective. He propounded all religions were but different paths that led to the same goal. His ideas were an extension of what is present in India. His thoughts were based not only on mutual respect and tolerance but also on the mutual realization of basic truth that underscores all individual religions. He was completely against the practice of untouchability. His learning from Vedānta made him a staunch critic of the concept of untouchables. He found neither religious sanction nor secular logic behind the terrible practice of untouchability, and he went out to condemn it. His social reform ideas reflected greatly on his efforts to give India its traditional religions a new orientation of social service. According to Swamiji, the rejuvenation of India is primarily a process of spiritual rejuvenation. This spiritual rejuvenation is to be supported by massive economic development programmes. To solve these twin purposes he propagated the idea of practical Vedānta which helps the masses' material and spiritual development. The major implications of practical Vedānta are: (i) Development of spirituality or the potential of divinity present in the human being, (ii) Work ethic as an approach to the realization of this divinity, (iii) Education as a means for the integrated development of man, and (iv) Positive secularism.

Role and Relevance of Swami Vivekananda's Social Works in Present Times

Swami Vivekananda's teachings continue to inspire millions of people around the world. His legacy lives on through his writings, speeches, and the institutions he founded. He remains a symbol of the potential of individuals to bring about positive change in society through spiritual understanding, compassion, and selfless service. His famous words: "Awake, arise, and stop not till the goal is reached"—still resonated among the youth of the nation, rousing their social consciousness and kindling their damp spirits.

As Vivekananda was a great observer of the human mind and society, he understood that undertaking any social change needed enormous energy and willpower. Hence, he called upon the youth to build up not only their mental energies but their physical ones as well. He wanted "muscles of iron" as well as "nerves of steel". He wanted the youth to possess the indomitable will and the strength to drink up the ocean. What he wanted was to prepare the youth both physically and mentally to face the challenges that would lie ahead of social workers. He was also practical enough to warn the young of the pitfalls ahead and the way society reacts to such endeavours. He said, "All good work has to go through three stages. First comes ridicule, then the stage of opposition and finally comes acceptance." The young need the purity, patience and perseverance to go through these stages in whatever they do. Society, though slow and sometimes treacherous in its reactions, finally comes around and accepts the good work that goes on for its own sake.

The young today are extremely result-oriented and need to understand the reasons for what they need to do as well as the benefits of what they do. To them Swamiji had a simple formula. He laid down in clear and simple terms the three levels of service that one can do. The first is that of the physical —taking care of the human body and undertaking activities to ameliorate human physical suffering. Running hospitals, orphanages, old-age homes, and various income-generation programmes would qualify for this level. The next higher level was intellectual service. Running schools and colleges and awareness and empowerment programmes would operate at this level. And finally, he prescribed the highest level of spiritual service for the evolution. He did not forget to warn us of the pitfalls of undertaking such service activities. He understood the human ego and its extraordinary potential for creating problems. He repeatedly warns us against placing ourselves higher than we should. His famous quote of not standing on the pedestal and offering the poor man five cents is legendary. He clearly wanted the young to undertake these activities, not merely for the betterment of society but for the evolution and growth of the person undertaking the same. This to me is clearly the end of what he extolled the young towards. He saw the "means" of serving society leading on to the "end" of spiritual growth of the person doing it. And he so beautifully advised us to "Serve God in man". All his philosophy is so elegantly and simplistically packed into one statement, in such simple and lucid language that makes it achievable and attractive to the youth. This ideal not only looks within the reach of each one of us but makes it so emotionally appealing and motivating to undertake.

When he started Ramakrishna Mission, Swamiji practised servant leadership more than a hundred years back. Sri Ramakrishna gave the following message to humankind *Śiva jñāne, jīva sevā* which means that the Lord is present everywhere but the greatest manifestation is present in each and every human being. Swami Vivekananda explained the message, wrote to his *guru-bhāī*s in a beautiful letter. He wrote, "so far you had heard the *mantra*s. What are the *mantra*s you had heard? *mātṛ devo bhava, pitṛ devo bhava, ācārya devo bhava, atithi devo bhava*. I am giving you some additional *mantra*s, which are more important for the modern age. *Daridra devo bhava, rogī devo bhava.* Worship the Lord who is present in the poor people; worship the Lord who is present in the sick people. It is an act of serving the God in human form. We are not doing social service. We are trying to worship the God who is present in the temple, church, and mosque; the same God is present in the poor and sick people. So Swamiji gave that new mandate, "Work is Worship".

Instead of looking upon a needy person as an object of pity, he is looked upon as an object of worship. Such an attitude elevates both the giver and the recipient. Swami Vivekananda was the first religious leader in India to speak for the poor and the downtrodden and to state boldly,

> "He who sees Śiva in the poor, in the weak and the diseased, really worships Śiva; and ... with him, Śiva is more pleased than with the man who sees Him only in temples."

It was Swamiji who coined the word *daridra-nārāyaṇa* to refer to the poor. Swamiji's love and concern for the poor continue to be directive principles in Ramakrishna Mission's service programmes. When work is done fulfilling the above conditions, it becomes a spiritual discipline: the mind gets purified and the potential divinity of the soul manifests itself more and more. Thus, work done as worshipful service benefits the doer himself spiritually: it becomes a spiritual discipline or *yoga*. With this understanding of work as a spiritual discipline (*karma-yoga*), all the service activities of the Ramakrishna Mission, such as giving food and clothing to the poor, nursing the sick, etc., are undertaken. Thus, service done as worship of God in man helps in two ways: it helps physically or mentally the person who is served, and it helps spiritually the person who serves. The need to integrate spirituality in social practice is explained by Bullis (1996) in the book *Spirituality in Social Work Practice* where the author says,

> "Spirituality offers social work experiences and insights on personal and community levels that

> promote social and personal transformations." (p. 8)

Again, it is imperative to assess the "spiritual sensitivity" and spiritual levels of the client or community as well as the social practitioner while engaging in a healing process.

Today we talk about globalization, but Swamiji spoke of globalization more than a century ago. He said,

> "Even in politics and sociology, problems that were only national twenty years ago can no more be solved on national grounds only. They assume huge proportions and gigantic shapes. They can only be solved when looked at, in the broader light of international grounds. International organizations, international combinations, international laws are the cry of the day."

That shows the solidarity. Globalization needs a globally acceptable icon like Swamiji, who not only travelled across the world extensively but also understood the nations—their people, history, culture, ideals, and hence their wants. Swamiji was certainly pre-eminently qualified for this, for he did not just looked at things from the surface but from within and sometimes from deep within. Only such personalities who can think of themselves as human beings and part of a human civilization can inspire people to think in such terms. This is the fulcrum of building a global citizen who can only think of globalization and can work for global peace, prosperity, and progress. Swamiji's vision of globalization and global civilization was always spiritual and could permanently benefit and change humans.

Belief in the divine self, philosophy of practical Vedānta, interpretation of religion, breaking of caste and class divisions, harmony with all, the message of tolerance and selfless service, inclusiveness, and equality alone will lead humanity to solve the emerging problems in the twenty-first century. Ideas of Swami Vivekananda will inspire people across the globe and will remain relevant forever. His powerful ideas will illuminate our path in the new millennium. His spiritual humanism will serve as a beacon light to communities and nations.

Religious bigotry breeds terrorism. Everything in life today, whether dress, food, or even games, is seen from a narrow religious angle. Countries are being ruled based on age-old religious doctrines. Religious bigots are killing hundreds of people. In such a polarized world Vivekananda's teachings bring a ray of hope. He advocated diversity of paths to realize God and strongly emphasized the principle of unity in diversity. Vivekananda categorically declares,

> "Religion has no business to formulate social laws and insist on the difference between beings because its aim and end is to obliterate all such fictions and monstrosities."

His messages are capable of giving a strong foundation to the modern world and modern Indian nation. Emphasizing the imperative of Women's education Swamiji said, "The welfare of the world is not possible until the condition of women improves." Today, women's education, empowerment, and equal rights are being discussed globally. It is worth noticing that a Working Framework for 2030: Sustainable Development Goals (SDGs) of the UN proposes to "attain gender equality, empower women and girls everywhere". It is crucial for elevating their status and also for accelerating economic development and social transformation. The National Education Policy 2020 too "recognizes the special and critical role that women play in society and in shaping social mores".

Indeed, a country's future depends upon its people's intelligence, creativity, and capability. He wanted education to provide "life-building, man-making and character-making assimilation of ideas" by combining India's idealism and spiritualism with Western efficiency and reason. But the present-day utilitarian education has led to complete materialism with total disregard for life—values. This has resulted in a culture of violence. Devoid of faith and spiritual satisfaction social tensions are giving an impetus to suicidal tendencies. Purely intellectual or heavily material culture bears the seed of death. While delivering a lecture on "practical Vedānta" in London in November 1896, Swami Vivekananda emphasized that we can overcome various hurdles by developing faith in ourselves. He delivered in his lecture:

> "the ideal of faith in ourselves is of the greatest help to us. If faith in ourselves had been more extensively taught and practised, I am sure a large portion of our evils and miseries would have vanished."

Swami Vivekananda's vision of economics was concerned with the wholesome development of all categories of people in the country and came within the purview of that branch of modern economics known as welfare economics. He strongly advocated what the economists in recent times called "inclusive economics". His economic views emphasize developed methods of agriculture, village industries, adoption of science and technology, and material prosperity with spirituality, which seems very relevant even today.

Conclusion

Swami Vivekananda proclaimed,

> "That society is the greatest, where the highest truths become practical. That is my opinion, and if society is not fit for the highest truths, make it so, and the sooner, the better."

According to him, society is the acme of perfection where it is practical to practice the highest ideals. He fervently believed that society could be changed and needed to be changed for the better. However, contrary to intuition, it may seem so to current traditionalist theological thinkers. Additionally, Swami

Vivekananda firmly believed that the only way to do good to ourselves is to do good to the world. That is why he prepared the doctrine of *karma-yoga* as a path of salvation and preached the importance of unselfishness.

Swami Vivekananda's philosophy is a timeless and universal beacon of wisdom that continues to illuminate the path of individuals, societies, and nations on a global scale. His teachings resonate with people from all walks of life, transcending cultural, religious, and geographical boundaries. By advocating holistic development, character building, self-realization, practical knowledge, and education for social transformation, Vivekananda's philosophy offers a comprehensive framework for personal growth and societal progress. His inclusive and tolerant outlook, promoting a universal perspective and interfaith harmony, is paramount in a world grappling with diversity and divisions. His emphasis on active learning, critical thinking, and individual freedom aligns with the demands of a rapidly changing global landscape.

Furthermore, his vision of the role of teachers as mentors and guides in nurturing intellect, character, and spirituality offers guidance for educators everywhere. The establishment of the Ramakrishna Mission and his global outreach efforts highlighted the practical application of his teachings, demonstrating the power of selfless service and the fusion of spirituality with social responsibility. Vivekananda's philosophy remains relevant in addressing contemporary challenges, as it encourages individuals to find their purpose, contribute to the betterment of society, and strive for a harmonious world. Ultimately, Swami Vivekananda's philosophy represents a holistic approach to human existence that resonates across cultures and inspires millions to live a life of purpose, compassion, and spiritual fulfilment. His legacy remains a beacon of hope and guidance, reminding us of the potential within each individual to create positive change on a global scale. The world still needs his guidance in establishing a Global village of peace and prosperity.

REFERENCES

Biswas, B. (2020). "A Study of Swami Vivekananda's Social Reforms and Its Relevance in Present Context". *International Journal of Creative Research Thoughts, 8*(11): 3653-59.

Canda, E.R. & Furman, L.D. (2010). *Spiritual Diversity in Social Work Practice: The Heart of Helping* (2nd edn.). Oxford University Press, USA.

Chakraborty, R. (2013). "Rediscovering Swami Vivekananda through the Lens of Social Justice". *The Vedānta Kesari*, pp. 379-83.

Chandrakantha, K.M. (2015). "A Role of Swami Vivekananda in Social Reforms: A Study". *International Journal of Research and Analytical Reviews, 2*(4): 107-16.

Gupta, M. Sen. (2023). *Relevance of Swami Vivekananda's Ideas in the 21st Century*. Retrieved from https://www.youthisthanfoundation.org/post/relevance-of-swami-vivekananda-s-ideas-in-the-21-st-century

Jana, S.K. (2017). "Economic Thoughts of Swami Vivekananda". *Scholars Journal of Arts, Humanities and Social Sciences, 5*(3): 241-47.

Keshavamurthy, H.R. (2015). *Swami Vivekananda: The Spiritual Scientist, Special Service and Features*. Government of India, Press Information Bureau.

Mandal, D. (2014). "Swami Vivekananda: the Great Social Reformer". *Multidisciplinary Journal of Humanities & Social Sciences, 1*(1): 1-8.

Mishra, A.K. (2016). "Economic Thought of Swami Vivekananda and Its Relevance". *Dev Sanskriti Interdisciplinary International Journal, 8*: 21-29.

Nayak, D. (2014). *History, Philosophy and Fields of Social Work*, Directorate of Distance & Continuing Education, Utkal University, Vanivihar, Bhubaneswar, Odisha.

Nikhileswarananda, S. (2013). "Swami Vivekananda: The Innovator of Management Values". In address delivered in the 5th edition of National Youth Conference of Indian Institute of Management, Indore at IIM Indore campus in January (Vol. 10, p. 2013).

Patel, I. (1987). *Vivekananda's Approach to Social Work*. Sri Ramakrishna Math.

Patel, V.R. (2012). "Engaging in the World: Seva in Hindu Bhakti Traditions" (Doctoral dissertation, University of Florida).

Pramanik, B., Maity, N. & Bera, A. (2017). "Swami Vivekananda: Today and Tomorrow". *International Journal of Research and Analytical Reviews, 4*(4): 349-52.

Saha, A.K. (2020). "Economic Thoughts of Swami Vivekananda". *Teachers' Journal*, *4*(1): 7-14.

Sharma, A.R.K. (2018). *The Vivekananda Way*. Jaico Publishing House, Delhi.

Sirswal, D.R. (2014). "Swami Vivekananda, Indian Youth and Value Education". In Atanu Mohapatra (ed.), *Vivekananda and Contemporary Education in India: Recent Perspectives*. Surendra Publications, pp. 167-80.

Swami Nikhilananda (1953). *Swami Vivekanand*. Ramakrishna-Vivekananda Center, New York. Retrieved from https://ramakrishna.org/vivekananda.html

Vincent, S.M. (2019). "The Approach of Indian Spirituality Towards Social Work: Integrating Swami Vivekananda's Teachings in Social Practice". *International Journal of Research in Engineering, IT and Social Sciences, 9*(2): 62-66.

Zai, A.F. & Wani, G. (2023). "Swami Vivekananda's Enduring Legacy: Inspiring Education, Global Unity, and Social Transformation". *International Journal for Multidisciplinary Research*, *5*(4): 1-11.

22

Community-centred Indigenous Rural Development Models

Gaurav Kumar

Introduction: Understanding Indigenous Rural Development

India's rural landscape faces numerous development challenges, particularly in indigenous communities. These challenges include socio-economic disparities, inadequate infrastructure, and environmental vulnerabilities. Indigenous groups often reside in remote rural areas and have limited access to education, health care, and livelihood opportunities. Furthermore, traditional knowledge systems and cultural practices are deteriorating due to modernization and urban migration, further exacerbating their challenges. To address these issues, community-centred development is crucial. This approach prioritizes the active involvement of local communities in decision-making processes and ensures culturally sensitive and inclusive development initiatives. Integrating traditional knowledge, spirituality, and modern methods is vital to achieving sustainable development in indigenous communities. Traditional knowledge systems often provide environmentally sustainable agricultural, health, and resource management solutions. Combined with current technology and methods, they can enhance productivity while maintaining ecological balance. Spirituality, which is a cornerstone of indigenous cultures, also plays a significant role in shaping ethical and sustainable lifestyles. Therefore, a development model harmonizing these elements can lead to a more holistic and sustainable outcome.

Philosophy and Ideology of Deendayal Research Institute, Kaneri Math

Deendayal Research Institute: Under the visionary leadership of Bharat Ratna Nanaji Deshmukh, the Deendayal Research Institute was established on 8 March 1968, to validate the ideology of Integral Humanism. Integral Humanism emphasizes the importance of balancing material and spiritual values in society. The institute has since been dedicated to research, training, and implementing projects promoting sustainable development and upliftment of marginalized communities. Through its various initiatives, the Deendayal Research Institute continues to uphold the principles of Integral Humanism and work towards creating a more inclusive and harmonious society. Various development models, including the provision of services for health, cleanliness, basic education, and self-employment training, have been devised to attain comprehensive socio-economic development and transformation of Indian society. The developmental initiatives have been implemented in six different locations: Delhi, Gonda, Balrampur (Uttar Pradesh), Chitrakoot (Uttar Pradesh & Madhya Pradesh), Beed, Nagpur (Maharashtra). The institute's objective is to develop a social structure that can effectively facilitate change in our long-standing Indian society, aligning it with the contemporary scientific age and grounded in timeless principles of comprehensive humanism. Through these initiatives, individuals are equipped with the necessary skills and knowledge to become self-reliant and contribute to the country's overall growth. The institute aims to create a supportive environment where individuals can thrive and achieve their full potential. By focusing on both personal and professional development, the institute is paving the way for a brighter future for all members of Indian society (Deendayal Research Institute, n.d.).

Vivekananda Kendra: Vivekananda Kendra, a service organization with a spiritual focus, was established by Eknathji Ranade in 1972. Eknathji Ranade, the founder of the Vivekananda Rock Memorial, established Vivekananda Kendra in 1972 as a welfare service organization with a spiritual focus. A group of committed full-time *swayamsevak*[1] and thousands of local *kāryakartā*s and lakhs of supporters, well-wishers, and subscribers to their publications comprise the living legacy of Swami Vivekananda. Vivekananda Kendra continues to uphold the values and teachings of Swami Vivekananda through various service projects, educational programmes, and cultural initiatives. The organization aims to promote a holistic approach to personal and societal development, blending spiritual growth with social responsibility. With the support of dedicated individuals and the larger community, Vivekananda Kendra strives to positively impact society and inspire others to lead a life of purpose and service. Established with the dual goals of "Man-Making" and "Nation Building", Vivekananda Kendra focuses on activities such as *yoga varga,*[2] *svādhyāya varga,*[3] *saṁskāra varga,*[4] and more to fulfil these objectives. To realize Swami Vivekananda's vision, the Vivekananda Kendra operates more than 1,332 branch centres throughout twenty-six states in India. These centres strive to assist all segments of society in the process of reconstructing the nation. To achieve this, full-time *kāryakartā*s and local *kāryakartā*s of the Kendra carry out various service activities through *yoga varga, svādhyāya varga, saṁskāra varga, kendra varga,*[5] and more, positively impacting communities through initiatives like rural development, education, and youth empowerment. For example, in the rural development initiative, the Vivekananda Kendra establishes vocational training centres and self-help groups to empower women and improve livelihoods in remote villages. *Svādhyāya varga* and *saṁskāra varga* programmes educate youth on moral values and character building, fostering a sense of responsibility towards society and nation-building. The Kendra strongly encourages all individuals to participate in this endeavour of national revitalization, offering a chance to contribute meaningfully to the betterment of society and the nation. Through these initiatives, Kendra aims to foster a sense of social responsibility and unity among individuals, creating a network of dedicated volunteers working towards a common goal. By engaging in these activities, participants contribute to the betterment of society and experience personal growth and fulfilment in the process (Vivekananda Kendra n.d.).

Kaneri Math: The highest sacred site of the Kadsiddheshwar tradition is Siddhagiri Kaneri Math, located in Kaneri, taluka Karvir, district Kolhapur. According to historical records, the first Kadsiddheshwar Swami, Shri Niramay Kadsiddheshwar, arrived and established his residence in the seventh century CE. From then on, the Math has been providing spiritual and community guidance to its followers. The Math is known for its peaceful and serene atmosphere, attracting devotees from all over the country. The teachings of Kadsiddheshwar Swami have been passed down through generations, continuing to inspire and uplift those who seek spiritual enlightenment. Math also plays an active role in various charitable activities, contributing to the betterment of society as a whole. For example, during times of natural disasters, the Math has organized relief efforts to provide food, shelter, and medical aid to those in need. Additionally, Math regularly hosts educational programmes, organic farming activities, animal husbandry activities, health-care facilities, and workshops to promote personal growth and well-being among its followers. The Siddhagiri Math is the sacred focal point of the Kadsiddheshwar Tradition. It was formerly referred to as Kaneri Math. Throughout generations, Siddhagiri Math has been diligently striving to improve society, primarily focusing on enhancing village development. Competent communities contribute to the development of a competent nation. This tradition plays a crucial role in shaping the future of India. By providing resources and opportunities for personal growth and community development, the Siddhagiri Math is helping to build a stronger and more prosperous society. Through its various initiatives and programmes, Math is preserving tradition and actively shaping India's future. Math's dedication and commitment to improving society inspire others to follow suit and contribute towards the overall progress and development of the nation (Matham, n.d.).

Three organizations that exemplify effective community-centred indigenous rural development are Deendayal Research Institute (DRI) in Chitrakoot (Madhya Pradesh), Kaneri Math in Kolhapur (Maharashtra), and Vivekananda Kendra in Kanyakumari (Tamil Nadu). DRI operates on the principle of Integral Humanism, focusing on self-reliance and holistic development in rural communities. Kaneri Math promotes eco-friendly, self-sustaining village models based on traditional farming and spiritual values. Inspired by Swami Vivekananda's teachings, Vivekananda Kendra engages in educational, cultural, and rural development activities to empower indigenous and rural communities. Understanding the philosophy and ideology behind rural development models is crucial for grasping their long-term impact, ensuring alignment with community values, and fostering sustainable outcomes. These organizations base their development initiatives on deep-rooted philosophical principles, blending traditional wisdom with modern approaches to uplift indigenous communities. Community-centred indigenous rural development models, such as those by DRI, Kaneri Math, and Vivekananda Kendra, demonstrate how blending deep philosophical principles with practical implementation creates sustainable and culturally relevant rural development models that prioritize the well-being of individuals and communities.

Frameworks for Community Participation and Empowerment

Community participation is crucial for the success of rural development initiatives, especially in indigenous communities where traditional knowledge, cultural values, and unique local practices play a crucial role. By integrating indigenous knowledge systems with modern practices, these organizations can create innovative and sustainable development solutions tailored to the unique needs of rural areas. Three organizations—Deendayal Research Institute (DRI), Kaneri Math, and Vivekananda Kendra—have implemented community-centred frameworks for participation and empowerment in rural development. DRI's development model in Chitrakoot is centred around self-reliance, with community participation being the backbone of its success. Key aspects of DRI's framework include village committees known as Samaj Shilpi Dampatti and self-help groups (SHGs) that allow local communities to participate in decision-making processes. Health, education, and organic farming programmes are co-designed and managed by the communities, empowering locals to take charge of their well-being. Kaneri Math's *nisargadhāma* model is deeply intertwined with spiritual values and ecological sustainability.

The model showcases community participation in managing natural resources, sustainable farming, and energy conservation. Key elements of Kaneri Math's community-centred development framework include the active involvement of community members in decision-making processes, promoting sustainable agricultural practices, and implementing eco-friendly initiatives such as waste management and renewable energy projects. Vivekananda Kendra's framework emphasizes training and empowering Indigenous youth and women through programmes such as skill development workshops, leadership training sessions, and entrepreneurship initiatives. Vivekananda Kendra's framework includes skill development and leadership training, rural entrepreneurship, cooperative societies, and community engagement in education, health, and cultural revival projects. These models highlight the critical role that community participation plays in achieving sustainable and inclusive rural development. By involving local communities in decision making, planning, and implementation, these organizations have created frameworks that empower individuals to control their development. Integrating indigenous knowledge systems with modern practices ensures that development is culturally relevant, ecologically sustainable, and economically viable. This approach improves the quality of life in rural areas and preserves Indigenous communities' unique cultural and ecological heritage, ensuring that development is sustainable and respectful of local traditions.

Sustainable Agricultural Practices

Sustainable agriculture is a crucial aspect of indigenous rural development, focusing on the use of local resources, biodiversity preservation, and ecological balance. These practices ensure indigenous communities' food security, environmental protection, and economic resilience. Deendayal Research Institute (DRI), Kaneri Math, and Vivekananda Kendra have integrated sustainable agriculture into their rural development models. With Krishi Vigyan Kendra's help, DRI emphasizes organic and natural farming, combining traditional farming knowledge with innovative technology to enhance crop yields, improve soil health, and ensure long-term agricultural sustainability. Kaneri Math's sustainable agriculture *lakhapati* model is deeply rooted in cow-based farming and the preservation of traditional seed varieties. This approach is both environmentally friendly and cost-effective, allowing farmers to achieve higher productivity without harming the ecosystem. The Kendra encourages farmers to cultivate indigenous seed varieties that are well-suited to the local climate and soil conditions, ensuring biodiversity is maintained and farmers are less reliant on external seed suppliers. They are using azola, fish amino for better production. Vivekananda Kendra focuses on agro-based livelihood programmes and training centres that promote sustainable agricultural practices, particularly in indigenous communities. Key elements of these initiatives include agro-based livelihood programmes that teach indigenous communities sustainable farming techniques, promote local resources, reduce external dependency, and improve food security and nutrition in rural areas. Sustainable agriculture is essential for the long-term well-being of indigenous communities. By empowering farmers to adopt sustainable practices and promoting community-driven agricultural initiatives, these organizations ensure that rural communities can thrive while protecting their natural environment and preserving their cultural heritage. By integrating traditional agricultural practices with modern innovations, these organizations demonstrate the value of sustainable agriculture in rural development.

Education and Capacity Building

Education is crucial in empowering indigenous communities and fostering sustainable rural development. By providing knowledge and skills, education builds the capacity of individuals and communities to improve their livelihoods, preserve their cultural heritage, and actively participate in development initiatives. Education must be culturally relevant, practical, and integrated with local traditions and knowledge systems for rural and indigenous populations. Deendayal Research Institute (DRI), Kaneri Math, and Vivekananda Kendra are three organizations that tailor education and training to the unique needs of indigenous communities. DRI's education model includes schools and vocational training centres that offer education tailored to the specific needs of rural and indigenous communities, life-skill education, health-care awareness, and women's empowerment through literacy programmes with the help of Gurukul Sankul, Surendrapaul Gramodaya Vidyalaya, Ramnath Ashram Shala, Kṛṣṇa Devi Vanvasi Balika Vidyalaya. Kaneri Math takes a holistic approach to education, combining traditional values with modern sciences to create a balanced and culturally relevant education system for rural communities in Gurukul and one English medium school. Key aspects of Kaneri Math's contribution include informal and formal education programmes and practical training in sustainable practices. These programmes equip individuals with the skills needed to lead self-sufficient lives while contributing to the preservation of the environment and local traditions. Every Poornima Parents-Guru Meet is organized in Gurukul to discuss and share students' growth and problems. Vivekananda Kendra is deeply committed to promoting holistic education in rural and tribal areas, emphasizing character development, leadership, self-reliance, and academic learning with Vivekananda Kendra Vidyalaya. Kendra's education model is inspired by Swami Vivekananda's vision of man-making and nation-building, which prioritizes the development of the individual as a whole—physically, mentally, and spiritually. Vivekananda Kendra established rural and tribal schools that focus on holistic education, integrating academic subjects with leadership, ethics, and self-discipline lessons. Youth are trained in leadership, self-reliance, and cultural pride through camps, workshops, and youth programmes. Collaboration with local communities is also crucial to integrating indigenous knowledge into formal education systems. Education and capacity building are essential for developing indigenous and rural communities sustainably. By providing culturally relevant education, practical training, and leadership development, these organizations empower individuals to improve their livelihoods, preserve their cultural heritage, and contribute to the broader development of their communities.

Spirituality as a Pillar of Development

Spirituality is a crucial aspect of holistic development in indigenous communities, as it fosters community resilience, self-reliance, and moral development. Organizations like Deendayal Research Institute (DRI), Kaneri Math, and Vivekananda Kendra integrate spiritual values into their development frameworks to promote ethical practices, mental well-being, and community empowerment. DRI emphasizes integrating spiritual values in the development process, viewing spirituality as essential for the holistic well-being of individuals and communities. DRI's spiritual approach integrates spiritual principles such as selflessness, service to others, and ethical living into its rural development initiatives. This approach encourages individuals to act for their personal benefit and the greater good of their communities. Programmes that promote *yoga*, meditation, and mental health awareness are integral to DRI's approach, helping individuals maintain mental clarity, emotional stability, and resilience in the face of challenges. Kaneri Math, founded on a deep spiritual ethos, views spirituality as critical in encouraging ethical practices and promoting harmony between humans and nature. Their spiritual philosophy informs their agricultural, environmental, and social initiatives, creating an ecologically sound and morally grounded development model. Vital elements of Kaneri Math's spiritual model include spiritual teachings and practices such as simplicity, non-violence, and reverence for nature, which encourage individuals to lead sustainable lives in harmony with the environment. Inspired by Swami Vivekananda's teachings, Vivekananda Kendra advocates for a development model centred on the spiritual awakening of individuals, which in turn leads to societal transformation. Vivekananda Kendra's spiritual perspective includes Swami Vivekananda's teachings on self-realization, which drives Kendra's initiatives in areas such as education, health care, and cultural revival. Spirituality is central to the way development is understood and practised in indigenous and rural communities. By incorporating spirituality into their development frameworks, these organizations have created models that promote economic growth, mental well-being, moral development, and social cohesion. This ensures that development is not just about material progress but also about fostering a deep sense of connection to the environment, the community, and the inner self.

Health and Well-being Initiatives

Health and well-being are crucial for successful rural development, and organizations like Deendayal Research Institute (DRI), Kaneri Math, and Vivekananda Kendra focus on integrating traditional health-care practices with modern medical services. These initiatives aim to provide comprehensive health coverage for underserved communities while promoting preventive care and wellness. DRI's health programmes include mobile health services known as *Dadi Maa Ka Batua*, Medical Camps that reach remote villages with limited access to health care, providing essential medical care, education programmes, and health education about hygiene, nutrition, and disease prevention. The institute values the role of traditional medicine, such as Ayurveda and herbal remedies, which have long been part of indigenous healthcare systems. DRI's Arogyadham promotes using locally available herbs and treatments that align with cultural beliefs while integrating modern medical practices for a more holistic health-care approach. Kaneri Math's health initiatives are rooted in the principles of Ayurveda and traditional healing practices, focusing on natural health-care systems that are easily accessible and culturally resonant for rural populations. They actively promote Ayurvedic medicine, encouraging the use of natural remedies, dietary adjustments, and lifestyle changes that align with Ayurvedic principles to promote long-term health. They also provide the best health-care facilities for allopathy treatment, operations and diagnosis. Vivekananda

Kendra emphasizes the importance of holistic health in its rural and tribal development work, combining modern health-care services with traditional practices to address the comprehensive well-being of communities. Their health programmes focus on prevention, education, and sanitation, aiming to uplift health standards in rural and indigenous areas through awareness campaigns and practical interventions. Vivekananda Kendra runs health and sanitation campaigns to improve hygiene practices and prevent common diseases in rural areas. They integrate holistic health practices such as *yoga*, meditation, and natural therapies alongside modern medical treatments to maintain physical health, reduce stress, and foster mental clarity. Health awareness campaigns empower rural populations with the knowledge needed to make informed health choices and adopt healthier lifestyles. Health and well-being are foundational to the success of any rural development initiative, as they create more resilient and self-sufficient communities. These organizations create more resilient and self-sufficient communities by addressing physical and mental health needs.

Conclusion

Community-centred indigenous rural development models, exemplified by organizations like Deendayal Research Institute (DRI), Kaneri Math, and Vivekananda Kendra, demonstrate the transformative power of integrating traditional knowledge, spirituality, and modern practices. These organizations emphasize self-reliance, ecological sustainability, and cultural preservation, creating development frameworks that are both locally relevant and sustainable. By involving communities in decision-making processes, promoting sustainable agriculture, and integrating health, education, and spirituality into their development approaches, they empower indigenous populations to address socio-economic challenges while preserving their cultural identity.

The success of these models lies in their holistic approach, which combines modern techniques with deep-rooted traditional values. Whether through sustainable farming, culturally sensitive education, or the integration of spiritual and health practices, these models showcase how development can uplift rural communities while maintaining ecological balance and cultural integrity. The active participation of local communities ensures that development is sustainable, inclusive, and tailored to their unique needs, setting a strong foundation for long-term growth and resilience. This approach allows indigenous communities to thrive harmoniously with their cultural heritage and natural environment.

NOTES

1. *Swayamsevak* (Full-time Volunteer).
2. *Yoga varga* (*Yoga* Session).
3. *Svādhyāya varga* (Welfare Services Discussion and Seminar).
4. *Saṁskāra varga* (Moral, Culture, Tradition Session).
5. *Kendra varga* (Monthly, Weekly, Occasionaly Session).

REFERENCES

DRI (n.d.). *DRI.* Retrieved 9 September 2024, from DRI: https://dri.org.in/

DRI (n.d.). *DRI.* Retrieved 9 September 2024, from Self Reliance Campaign: https://www.dri.org.in/self-reliance-campaign-home/

Deendayal Research Institute (n.d.). *Deendayal Research Institute.* Retrieved 9 September 2024, from Deendayal Research Institute: http://chitrakoot.org/driindia/home.html

Vivekananda Kendra (n.d.). *Vivekananda Kendra.* Retrieved 9 September 2024, from Activities: https://www.vrmvk.org/regular-activity

Vivekananda Kendra (n.d.). *Vivekananda Kendra.* Retrieved 9 September 2024, from Vivekananda Kendra: A Spiritually Oriented Service Mission: https://www.vrmvk.org/vivekananda-kendra-spiritually-oriented-service-mission

Math, S.K. (n.d.). *Siddhagiri Education.* Retrieved 9 September 2024, from Siddhagiri Education: https://www.siddhagirimatham.org/education

Math, S.K. (n.d.). *Siddhagiri Hospital and Research Center*. Retrieved 9 September 2024, from Siddhagiri Hospital and Research Center: https://www.siddhagirimatham.org/healthcare

Math, S.K. (n.d.). *Sidhhagiri Kaneri Math*. Retrieved 9 September 2024, from Organic Krishi Vigyan Kendra, Kaneri, Kolhapur: https://www.siddhagirimatham.org/agriculture

Matham, S. (n.d.). *Siddhagiri Matham*. Retrieved 9 September 2024, from Siddhagiri Matham: https://www.siddhagirimatham.org/about-matham

Index